CORNWALL'S FALLEN

THE ROAD TO THE SOMME

CORNWALL'S FALLEN

THE ROAD TO THE SOMME

Nick Thornicroft

First published 2008

The History Press Ltd
The Mill, Brimscombe Port
Stroud, Gloucestershire, GL5 2QG
www.thehistorypress.co.uk

British Library Cataloguing in Publication Data.
A catalogue record for this book is available from the British Library.

ISBN 978 0 7524 4528 1

Typesetting and origination by The History Press Ltd.
Printed and bound by TJ International Ltd, Padstow, Cornwall

Contents

Maps

Western Front, Northern France and Belgium, 1916

1 July 1916: The Attack

List of Plates

26. Memorial to the 7th Yorkshires, Fricourt (private collection)
27. West of Fricourt, 2007 (Barry Thornicroft); 2nd Lt A. Colmer (*Cornish Guardian*)
28. German front line, Fricourt, 2007 (Barry Thornicroft); L/Cpl H. Bennett[s] (*Cornish Guardian*)
29. Aeriel view/Lochnagar Crater (reproduced by permission of Richard Dunning and The Friends of Lochnagar)
30. Grenville Hotel, Bude, post-First World War (private collection)
31. Men of the 2nd Devons, pre-First World War (private collection)
32. Thiepval Memorial/German trenches, 2007 (Barry Thornicroft); Lt E. Hampson (*Salford Reporter* – now *Salford Advertiser*)
33. Drawing of Capt. E.N.F. Bell gaining the VC (from *Deeds That Thrill The Empire* – reprinted by The Naval & Military Press)
34. Public Schools Battalion, 1 July 1916 (Q755 – reproduced by permission of the Imperial War Museum, London)
35. The Quadrilateral, 2007 (Barry Thornicroft); 2nd Lt C. Watson (Rondebosch High School, Cape Town)
36. Original First World War graves and Ovillers Military Cemetery (private collection)
37. British dead on the Somme (Jane Jones – WW1 Photos); Capt. R. Michell (*Cornish Guardian*)
38. Queen Mary visits wounded soldiers, 1916 (private collection)
39. Pte Oscar Zimber (*Cornish Guardian*)
40. Hawthorn Crater, 2007 (Susan Thornicroft); Ronald Vibart (Cornwall County Cricket Club)
41. Somme landscape (private collection); four Cornish soldiers (*Cornish Guardian*)
42. Lt F. Thomas (Wycliffe College, Glos.) & Sgt H. Curtis, VC (*Cornish Guardian*)
43. PO E. Pitcher, VC (The Victoria Cross Society) & Pte J. Fynn, VC (Bodmin Town Museum)
44. Trenches around Ypres, 1920 (private collection); Sgt-Maj. C.R. Watson, DCM, MC, MM (DCLI Museum, Bodmin)
45. The Thiepval Memorial, 2006 (private collection)
46. Lochnagar Crater, 2006 (private collection)
47. Gwennap Pit, pre-First World War (private collection)
48. Launceston war memorial, 1920s (private collection)
49. Rough seas at Polzeath, 1930s (private collection)
50. Launceston recruit, DCLI, *c.* 1915 (private collection)

Abbreviations

FM/Fd Marsh.	Field Marshal
Gen.	General
Lt-Gen.	Lieutenant-General
Maj.-Gen.	Major-General
Brig.-Gen.	Brigadier-General
Col	Colonel
Lt-Col	Lieutenant-Colonel
Maj.	Major
Sgt-Maj.	Sergeant-Major
Capt.	Captain
Lt	Lieutenant
2nd Lt	Second Lieutenant
T/… or Temp/…	Temporary rank
CO	Commanding Officer
NCO	Non Commissioned Officer
RSM	Regimental Sergeant Major
CSM	Company Sergeant Major
RQMS	Regimental Quarter Master Sergeant
Sgt	Sergeant
L/Sgt	Lance Sergeant
Cpl	Corporal
L/Cpl	Lance Corporal
A/…	Acting rank
Pte	Private
Gnr	Gunner (Artillery)
Spr	Sapper (Engineers)
Tpr	Trooper (Cavalry)
RFA	Royal Field Artillery
RHA	Royal Horse Artillery
RGA	Royal Garrison Artillery
RE	Royal Engineers
RAMC	Royal Army Medical Corps
RFC	Royal Flying Corps
DCLI	Duke of Cornwall's Light Infantry
OR	Other rank (i.e. not an officer)
DCM	Distinguished Conduct Medal
DSO	Distinguished Service Order
MC	Military Cross

MM	Military Medal
VC	Victoria Cross
CMG	Commander of the Order of St Michael & St George
KBE	Knight Commander of the Order of the British Empire
SDGW	*Soldiers Died in the Great War* CD-Rom (Naval & Military Press)
ODGW	*Officers Died in the Great War* CD-Rom (Naval & Military Press)
CWCG	Commonwealth War Graves Commission
POW	Prisoner of War
VAD	Voluntary Aid Detachment

Acknowledgements

I have no hesitation in placing one name above all others – that of Bob Richards, Cornwall Family Finders, whose knowledge of Cornish history and culture, plus his cheerful enthusiasm and constant support have enabled this book to be published in its present form. He was regularly bombarded with several queries at once, always replying diligently and with good humour, taking the time to find the answers to some often challenging questions. Thank you, Bob. The following individuals and organisations have all played their part, and I am extremely grateful for their assistance (in no particular order): Richard Dunning and 'The Friends of Lochnagar'; Rondebosch High School, Cape Town; the Great War Forum; National Archives; Andrew Hesketh; Jack Sheldon; Wycliffe College, Stonehouse, Gloucestershire; Customised Mapping, Barnstaple; Cornwall Record Office, Truro; Cornish Studies Library, Redruth; Cornwall Cricket Club; Somerset Record Office, Taunton; Martin Williams, MA, Archivist at Hurstpierpoint College, W. Sussex; Alan Smith (Preston); Soren Hawkes, Passchendaele Prints; Frances Daniels (Somerset); Liz Carter (Cambridge); the Imperial War Museum; Bodmin Museum; the Devonshire & Dorset Regimental Museum; The Naval & Military Press – www.naval-military-press.com; Truro College Archives; the Duke of Cornwall Light Infantry Museum, Bodmin, Jane Jones, WW1 Photos; and Stuart Mann, Sunesis Imaging. To the editors of the following newspapers for granting their permission to use archive text and photographs from their publications: *Royal Cornwall Gazette, Cornish Times, West Briton, Cornish Guardian, Falmouth Packet, Cambridgeshire Chronicle, Salford Reporter, Burnley Express, Taunton Courier, Somerset Guardian.* Finally, to Lindsay for compiling the index, and to my family, whose support has been unceasing.

Introduction

On 1 July 1916, an Allied offensive began on either side of the River Somme in France, designed to smash the German defensive systems once and for all. The date was almost exactly halfway through the most devastating war the world had ever seen, and is now remembered as, without parallel, the worst day in the long history of the British army; when almost 20,000 men had lost their lives by nightfall, with twice that total wounded or missing. Some historians baulk at the process of simply quoting figures, claiming: '… no set of numbers, no matter how well collected or collated, can tell the whole story'[1], and stress the personal tales of valour, suffering and devotion to duty are much more conducive to expressing the wider picture of a particular conflict or battle. 'In my opinion,' claims one such historian, 'dates, times and statistics should be used as a means to an end, not an end in themselves; if statistics alone are used to draw conclusions then much of what actually happened in the past is lost, and, much more importantly, history's lessons for today become even more obscure.'[2]

I have sympathy for this point of view, but I think the two methods of conveying the horrendous losses on the battlefields to the modern world are worthy of a careful union. To imagine 57,000 individuals as collective 'casualties' within twenty-four hours is difficult in the extreme, yet to picture that same number of people in terms of the masses of spectators crammed together at a large sporting event is much more straightforward. In 1991, Cornwall took on Yorkshire at Twickenham for the honour of being crowned County Champions of Rugby Union, and, after a thrilling game, the Duchy came back from 16–3 down to take the match into extra time, eventually sealing a famous victory by 29 points to 20. It was their first such triumph since 1908, and the game was watched by an estimated 54,000 people – most of them supporting Cornwall under the banner of 'Trelawney's Army' (after the famous Pelynt-born Bishop of Bristol who defied the religious edicts of King James II in 1688 and was imprisoned in the Tower of London). The numbers in attendance at this one rugby match equates roughly to the amount of human beings who were killed, wounded or taken prisoner during a single twenty-four hour period seventy-five years previously.

The first day of the Somme offensive is remembered for many reasons – most notably the dreadful loss of life, as well as the expected breakthrough which never happened, the decimation of whole battalions, and the crushing of Britain's youth in a matter of minutes. Yet it has also been put forward that without the tragedy of 1 July 1916 the Allied cause – and more specifically the British contribution – could not have gone on to win the war. This date was a watershed in history, a moment of carnage in four years of horrific slaughter which ultimately marked the passing of the old ways and finally ushered in the modern era. Lessons were learned and eventually acted upon, yet those who lay dead or dying on the Somme battlefields on one sun-drenched summer's morning could not possibly have known the full extent of their sacrifice.

A Soldier of the King. After the War every man who served will command his Country's gratitude. He will be looked up to and *respected* because he answered his country's call … Field Marshal Sir John French wrote in an Order of the day,

Drawing of 'The Somme, 7.30 a.m. 1 July 1916'.

'It is an Honour to belong to such an Army'. Every fit man from 19 to 38 is eligible for this great honour. Friends can join in a body, and serve together in the same regiment

Cornish newspapers printed the above call to arms in the autumn of 1914, in line with a nationwide recruiting drive, and the often-quoted legacy of 1 July 1916 is the fate of the Pals battalions which mainly originated from the industrial north of England. Men who had grown up together, attended the same school, worked in the same factories or played sports together were encouraged to join up with their mates, thus creating a strong bond of camaraderie and togetherness even before the individuals had been issued with uniforms. When these units marched through their home-towns prior to training or deployment to the war zone, thousands of citizens proudly cheered their men folk, and eagerly charted their subsequent progress via the columns of local newspapers. These were largely made up of so-called 'Kitchener's Men' – fresh recruits who had patriotically joined up at the outbreak of hostilities when the Minister for War, Lord Kitchener, had made a national appeal for support in creating a 'New Army' to eventually assist the professional pre-war Regulars who were already fighting on the Western Front. Conscription would not begin in earnest until after 1 July 1916, so each and every man who lined up on the 16 miles of British Front at 7.30 a.m. on the morning of this infamous date had volunteered to do so. Many county regiments were represented, and with only one Empire battalion – the 1st Newfoundlanders from North America – bucking the trend, the regional lottery of Army Orders and fate pitted soldiers from every county and region of England, Ireland, Scotland and Wales against the might of the German war machine.

For the purposes of this book, I decided to gather together the information relating to individuals from the county of Cornwall who fell on 1 July 1916. I knew it would not be a case of listing hundreds of names, as the Duchy's own regiment – the Duke of Cornwall's Light Infantry – was not required to send any of its battalions to the front lines or reserve positions on this date, yet I was also aware that Cornishmen would *undoubtedly* be present in other units, most notably the three battalions from the neighbouring county of Devon – the 2nd, 8th and 9th. Further research revealed that men born in Cornwall who then moved away often joined up with their new local regiment, or alternatively some individuals who migrated to the South West from their home towns preferred to enlist under the cap badge of the area which bore them. For soldiers in the ranks, this is, perhaps, a simplified version of the reasons why – it may logically have been a case of enlisting into a battalion which happened to be recruiting in the area at the time. The Artillery and Engineers also claimed a proportion of the individuals mentioned in this text, although for officers, the eventual destination of a newly commissioned man sometimes rested solely on the 'availability' of a certain regiment. With only a limited number of places for second lieutenants in any one unit, a sudden 'vacancy' may determine an eventual allegiance. There was also the consideration of family connections, with generations of military men sometimes opting for the same cap badge as their predecessors. So, when all of these criteria were taken into account, the search for men with a verifiable link to the county of Cornwall could begin.

It is also prudent to establish the events leading up to the Somme offensive; how the professional British soldiers, well-versed in military ways across the pre-war Empire, dealt with the opening months of the conflict, and the manner in which the army evolved between the outbreak of fighting and July 1916. Therefore, the recruitment campaign in Cornwall between August and December 1914, as well as the fate of some of the Duchy's servicemen on the Western Front over the same period receive a close scrutiny; leading as they did to the deployment of many new recruits during 1915, replacing the Regulars who suffered terribly within weeks of arriving in France and Flanders.

In the early 1920s, the War Office published a gargantuan piece of research which listed all of the 703,000 officers and men of the British army who had died on active service between 4 August 1914 (the date of Britain's declaration of war on Germany) and the end of 1921. (Despite the signing of the Armistice on 11 November 1918, British servicemen were still engaged in Russia, opposing the Bolsheviks, or forming part of the Army of Occupation in the Rhineland.) These eighty-one printed volumes were catalogued alphabetically, by regiment, and although all of the information had been methodically stored, a random search for an individual whose unit was unknown became a virtual impossibility until The Naval & Military Press produced the hugely influential *Soldiers Died in the Great War* (SDGW) CD-ROM database, making use of the technical developments of the computer age to enable previously time-consuming quests for basic facts to appear on screen in a matter of seconds.

For the men in the ranks, the following detail (if available) can be obtained: surname, Christian name(s); rank, service number, regiment, battalion; place of birth, enlistment and residence at the time of joining up; date of death, nature of death (killed in action, died of wounds, etc.); Theatre of War (Egypt, Gallipoli, etc.), and the provision for supplementary notes such as previous regiment, gallantry awards, etc. It is therefore possible to key in a specific date of death – 1 July 1916 in this case, as well as the general casualties of 1914 – and view all of the individuals who lost their lives over these specific periods in the Theatre of War sub-titled 'France and Flanders' (Western Front). Those who had birth, residential or enlistment connections with Cornwall can then be collated and their details cross-referenced with units *known* to have been Somme fatalities. (Not all of the 1 July 1916 deaths took place in this region.)

The *Officers Died in the Great War* (ODGW) is available on the same CD-ROM, but contains none of the personal background references, along the lines of a place of birth or an address, which are required to link an individual to a particular area of the country. Therefore this category, by its definition, proved far more challenging, so the next step was to consult the Commonwealth War Grave Commission's (CWGC) Debt of Honour Register, which lists the site of burial or commemoration for each one of the British and Empire servicemen who lost their lives during the conflict. A proportion of these have accompanying details such as the address of their next of kin, but an important factor to be considered here is that this data was again compiled during the 1920s, and therefore often refers to locations relevant to several years *after* the war rather than at the time when an individual actually died. Some of the officers' widows had re-married by this time, whilst other family members had simply moved to another part of the country, while for a signifi-cant percentage no genealogical or geographical references were forthcoming at all. In this group, therefore, a few men whose links to Cornwall were not able to be established through research in local newspapers, schools, colleges, or the Census returns, have been regrettably omitted.

It is also prudent to mention that the first Casualty Rolls – from which the SDGW, ODGW and CWGC were compiled – were written by hand, in ink, from official military records which varied widely in legibility, and the final entries depended upon several past interpretations of informa-tion – from the Recruiting Sergeants attempting to decipher strong regional accents of the new recruits, to the staff employed post-war to transcribe often indistinct (and, to them, obscure) place names from around the country – with the result that some of the data is erroneous.

The National Archives at Kew contains millions of original documents relating to the First World War, and these proved to be an invaluable source in the overall task of research. Unfortunately, only a small percentage (estimated to be 25–30 per cent) of army papers concerning men in the ranks who served during the years of the conflict – the Attestation Forms, personal details, next of kin, military progress and ultimate fate of an individual soldier (whether he was discharged or died on active serv-ice) – survived the Blitz in 1940, when the factory which housed them received a direct hit. Officers' equivalents fared a little better, and generally contained more information than the former. Battalion War Diaries – written daily by officers 'in the field', describing the events of each twenty-four hours in their own particular sector – give a fascinating insight into what actually happened on any given day, as they are essentially eyewitness accounts of some of the most historic moments of the First World War. (These were not released to be viewed by the general public until many years after the Armistice.)

Cornish newspaper archives were also consulted, and it is interesting to discover how the press tried to put a positive 'spin' on events unfolding across the Channel, even when the reality of the gruesome events of 1 July 1916 finally began to seep through into British society. Along with reference books and the almost infinite amount of data available electronically on the Internet, I was finally able to begin writing the true story of men from one county in the south-west of England who were involved in the catastrophic events of one day, in one month, in one year of a conflict which took millions of lives, changed the course of the twentieth century and ultimately shaped the entire modern age.

The reader may, by this stage, be wondering why the soldiers of Cornwall were chosen as the focus for an entire book, and there are several reasons for this. Firstly, the Pals battalions of England's industrial north have been the subject of many articles, television programmes and large volumes of text, rightly reflecting the huge sacrifices made by whole communities which ripped the heart and soul out of those left behind. (As we shall see, some Cornishmen were in fact attached to these famous regiments on 1 July 1916.) Secondly, the impact of observing three names on a tiny village war memorial is just as moving as feeling almost overwhelmed by the endless entries on their counterparts in major towns and cities across the country. The grief and loss ran equally as deep however many individuals were lost from a particular community. Thirdly, it is hoped that this venture will not only appeal to military enthusiasts, but also to those who have an interest in Cornish social history. Finally, and on a personal note, Cornwall has always had a special place in my affections, and it is a place I keep returning to again and again; it has a character all of its own, a special identity and heritage. So, the old adage 'write about what you know' came to the fore when I first formulated the idea for this book. The numbers involved are not huge. 1 July 1916 is not – to my knowledge – spoken of in Cornwall with revered tones as it is in Ulster, or Tyneside, or the Lancashire town of Accrington, or Manchester, or Bradford, Leeds and Sheffield. Closer to home, Devon suffered many more casualties, as did Somerset and Dorset, yet it was to Cornwall that I turned.

It has been said that 1 July 1916 overshadows all other dates during the First World War, and that the significance of other crucial moments of the conflict – the battles at Mons, on the Marne, Ypres, Loos, Gallipoli, Arras, 'Passchendaele', the 'Advance to Victory', and even the later 1916 fighting on the Somme – has been diminished by the apparent fixation on this one day. But I believe that the tragedy of 1 July encapsulates the suffering of the entire war – the pride felt by the men involved, their belief that this was *right*, their patriotism, their comradeship, their often genuine love for King and Country. These character traits may almost seem naïve with hindsight, and even as early as 1914, when Kitchener's Men were enlisting in their thousands, the German newspapers chillingly referred to them as *kannonenfutter* – the since much-used phrase 'cannon fodder'. For anyone wishing to begin to understand the legacies of the First World War, the build-up to the slaughter on 1 July 1916 is a sobering place to start.

During the Somme campaign, the *West Briton* newspaper put forward a proposal that every church in the county should follow the lead of others by initiating – and perpetuating – a Roll of Honour, adding that

> … it is just that Roll, with its record of familiar names, now united with heroic deeds and noble deaths, which links up the remotest rural parish with the tremendous struggle out of which a new world will emerge … The doing of this throughout the war has in many places brought within its walls those who were formerly strangers to their parish church. In one Cornish village, from which many men have gone into His Majesty's ships, the daily service of intercession has been maintained each evening since August 1914 … The names of those who are serving from that village are always read. This is of the utmost importance.

I

War is Declared: Cornwall Prepares, August–October 1914

The shadow of potential war had been looming over Europe for many years when a seemingly localised assassination in Sarajevo lit the fuse for all of the major countries to plunge headlong into conflict during the long, hot summer of 1914. Rivalries, border disputes, treaties and aggressive military expansion all contributed to the slide into combat, with firstly Austria-Hungary presenting Serbia with an ultimatum (which was flatly rejected), followed by Austria-Hungary declaring war on the latter, leading to the mobilisation of Russian troops in support of the small Balkan state. Germany, which had designs on building an empire to rival and even out-shine that of Great Britain, warned Russia of her actions, but now no-one was backing down. On 1 August, Kaiser Wilhelm – grandson of Queen Victoria – ordered his own troops to prepare for action on Germany's eastern and western frontiers. The allies of Russia and France collectively received the wrath of the German nation, which swiftly by-passed the strong French defences by invading neutral Belgium in a bold plan to capture Paris before the Russians could muster enough soldiers to effect a decisive counter-strike. Having promised the Belgian monarch that Britain would intervene if such an act took place, King George V was true to his word, and by midnight on 4 August, the most powerful European nations were at war.

The *Royal Cornwall Gazette* summed up the feelings of dire foreboding with the headline: 'A Continent in Arms. Great Britain Accepts Germany's Challenge. A Fight for Honour, Truth and Justice.' Speaking at Bodmin Congregational Church as the news came through, the Revd J.P. Southwell shrewdly observed:

> … there was a complete absence of trust and goodwill in international politics in the relation of one people to another. The evidence of that was the huge number of men drawn away from the reasonable and productive pursuits of life, and trained to destroy life … The cause of this feeling was that the men who were responsible for the governments of the various countries would not deal squarely and above board, not speak the truth one with the other. Diplomacy was the art of double dealing. Clever politicians believed that if they spoke openly, and the truth, other nations would take advantage, and so they stooped to intrigue and secret dealings … The secret history of Europe would never be written, but if it were, what a tale it would unfold – war, plunder and oppression!

Canon Westmacott informed the worried gathering at Truro Cathedral that, '… England seemed to have gone back 100 years', and added: 'From the information to hand … it would seem as if England before very long would be called upon to give forth all her courage and her energy and force.' Revd S.F. Marsh, of St Ives, told his parishioners that they met '… under the shadow of a dark cloud', and at Redruth Baptist Church, Revd Edgar Whitton remarked that:

> … events had sprung upon them so suddenly and so tragically during the past few days that the nation was excited from one end to the other. They seemed to be on the verge of international strife. In fact, already there had been the roar of the cannon, the destruction of property and loss of life. The war dogs were let loose …

Newquay, August 1914. Inset: Capt. Clutterbuck.

Major-General Sir Reginald Pole-Carew, KCB, a retired army officer whose home was at Antony House near Torpoint, was recalled to London immediately, informing a reporter on the way he felt that war was '… bound to come, and … we could not possibly avoid being drawn into it'. In the Major-General's opinion, the Navy was in a '… high state of efficiency', and ventured: 'Germany could not have chosen a worse time for waging war, but she was making a bold bid, which … might bring disaster'.

Writing from his residence known as the 'Haven', in Fowey, Sir Arthur Quiller-Couch noted that as '… a nation of honest men, we must stand by our engagements…', yet insisted: 'It is madness … which commits England to this foolish balance of power, and may call out Englishmen to die, fighting Germans (with whom they have no quarrel), for a set of Serbs in whom they have not the smallest interest. The whole business, in short, is monstrous …'

MOBILISATION AND RECRUITING

With the declaration of war came the urgent need for the Army and Navy to mobilise as quickly as time would allow. At Truro Cathedral, a message was read from the Mayor stating that he had received a communication from the Admiral at Devonport asking him to inform all Naval Reservists to report themselves to their respective depots as soon as possible. Between forty and fifty men left the city at 6 p.m. on 4 August, boarding a special train which had begun its journey in West Cornwall. 'They were given an enthusiastic send-off by a large number of people,' recorded the *Royal Cornwall Gazette*, which also revealed:

> Great excitement prevailed in Looe when it became known that the Naval Reservists had been called for duty. They left by the 6.45 p.m. train, and long before that hour Churchend was packed, practically the whole inhabitants of Looe turning out to give the men a good send-off …

Similar scenes were witnessed at St Austell, where coastguard men joined His Majesty's sailors from the surrounding districts of Mevagissey and Gorran, whereas those called up from Polperro '… asked their mates to either look after their boat, or to keep an eye on their fishing nets'. (On 6 August, Petty Officer Stoker Charles Olver, from Landrake, St Germans, lost his life when HMS *Amphion* hit an enemy mine and sunk in the English Channel. Aged tewnty-nine, he was one of the first British casualties of the war.)

German liners which had been expected in the South West swiftly changed course when hostilities broke out (one had a large quantity of gold on board), whilst others were ordered by the authorities to remain in key places such as Falmouth. Regattas planned for Wadebridge and the Royal Fowey Yacht Club were postponed indefinitely, whereas French fishermen in Cornish waters were recalled to their own ports.

For the army, speed was also of the essence. Britain was the only major European country which did not enforce conscription and, as a result, its own volunteer soldiers – highly-trained professionals known as the Regulars – were vastly smaller in numbers than the millions on the move across the English Channel. (In the strict class society of Victorian and Edwardian Britain, it was a general rule that officers came from the privileged backgrounds of well-to-do families and public school education, whilst the ranks were filled with former labourers, fishermen, miners and the like. There were, of course, exceptions, and the distinctions became less rigid as the First World War progressed.)

Many of the county regiments consisted of two battalions, with one usually stationed within the shores of the UK or Ireland, whilst the other was garrisoned overseas, guarding the outposts of the Empire. The 1st Battalion of the Duke of Cornwall's Light Infantry, for example, was in southern Ireland on 4 August 1914, whilst the 2nd Battalion was undergoing a tour of duty in Hong Kong. Both were required for service in France and Flanders, with the former – not surprisingly – arriving there first (on 15 August). These men formed the vanguard of the British Expeditionary Force (BEF), and were welcomed with great jubilation by the French, who saw the troops arriving from across the sea as the saviours of Europe. [The role of the DCLI in the fighting across the Channel, along with other units containing Cornishmen, is focused upon in the next chapter.]

The 1st DCLI was, however, under-strength when it was dispatched from the Curragh – where it had been deployed to monitor the delicate situation in Ireland – to the Western Front, and this was where the Reservists played their part. Like their contemporaries in the Navy, these were individuals who had already received their training and served in the ranks before their allotted time had expired, although they were required to make themselves available to rejoin the Colours at short notice should a national crisis occur. The events unfolding on the continent warranted such an order, and former soldiers were summoned straight away. In a sparsely populated county as Cornwall, the local regiment could not entice large numbers of its male citizens to enlist in the Regulars during the years prior to the First World War, and as a consequence, the places were filled by individuals mainly from London or the Midlands, as well as further afield. (A famous old recruiting song in the county went along the lines of: 'Then let the bells of Bodmin ring, the Cornish boys are come to sing, with Irish lads – God Save The King – sing "one and all"'.)

The 2nd Devonshire Regiment – which would later take part in the first day of the Somme offensive – was many miles away in Egypt, and it, too, soon began the hurried journey back to Europe. Meanwhile, another branch of the army – the Territorials – was being put to good use. In 1908, the military had received a large-scale overhaul, absorbing the local militia into a new outfit which became known as the 'Terriers', made up of part-time troops who trained on a regular basis but were not initially required for service overseas. This approach was far more appealing to many than the rigours of professional soldiering, and by its very nature attracted an almost exclusively 'home town' cross-section from the surrounding area. Therefore, at the outbreak of war, the DCLI comprised five battalions; the 1st and 2nd (Regulars), the 3rd (Royal Cornwall Rangers Militia, a Reserve unit based at

Cornishmen gather for a group photograph, *c.*1914.

Bodmin which later took up duties on the south coast for the rest of the conflict), plus the 4th and 5th Territorials (stationed at Truro and Bodmin respectively). A proportion of troops from these latter two battalions were deployed to defend the Marconi Station at Poldhu, the signal station on the Lizard, and various other key instalments, whilst the rest were billeted at Pendennis Castle or in sheds at Falmouth Docks. 'When later in the evening the men were allowed into town,' recorded the *Royal Cornwall Gazette,* 'those who were not too tired made quite a raid on some of the refreshment houses'.

The initial progress of local artillerymen was also charted:

> The war has been brought home very closely to the citizens of Truro. The R.G.A. [Royal Garrison Artillery] Territorials have been placed on a war footing, and the Truro [Company], together with Hayle and Marazion Cos, have received orders to take charge of the St Anthony batteries, and the St Ives and Looe Cos have been told … to guard Falmouth.

With home defence being the Terriers' priority in peacetime, the 'war footing' abroad now produced the possibility of eventually sending these part-time soldiers – who at least had some military experience – across the Channel to assist the Regulars, and the former were given the opportunity to volunteer for active service, to which the vast majority agreed. This increase in potential manpower was a welcome boost, but Lord Kitchener – who had never been entirely approving of the Territorial reforms – envisaged the conflict would not be 'over by Christmas' (the popular rallying cry of the press), so he set about creating a 'New Army' comprising entirely of volunteers who would enlist for the duration of hostilities and agree to fight in any Theatre of War. On 6 August Parliament sanctioned the recruitment of 500,000 men, and within two weeks, the 'First Hundred Thousand' had joined up nationwide.

The reasons behind this mass call to arms can perhaps be broken down into two distinct categories. Across Great Britain, there was widespread – if not universal – support for the war, and although some had harboured their doubts as to the circumstances which had brought the country into conflict, it was the minority who believed going to the support of France and Belgium against the German aggressors was a mistake. Patriotism for King and Empire was rife, and all sectors of society urged its young men to 'do the right thing' by enlisting. Those of school age during the recent Boer War (1899–1902) had been told tales of gallantry and heroism on the battlefields, and now here was a chance to emulate their feats of adventure and glory. Local dignitaries, well-known politicians, school masters and the gentry all stood up to make impassioned pleas which were widely reported in the newspapers. The *Royal Cornwall Gazette* revealed in September: 'Lady Warmington stated at Falmouth yesterday week that enthusiasm in Cornwall had been awakened, and when 400 men were wanted for the Foreign Service Battalion they got them in five days.' At St Merryn, '… four recruits for Kitchener's Army came forward at a meeting … on Monday evening', whilst some of their counterparts in St Austell were '… undergoing daily drills under Col W.T. Lovering, Capt. M.F. Hitchins, Sgt-Maj. Dickinson, and Sgt Broom'. In Lostwithiel, a number of speakers invoked the old spirit which '… is still in evidence amongst Cornish people', and their words '… sank deeply into the hearts of the audience'. The Oddfellows' Hall in Perranporth was the setting for one such gathering, presided over by Mr William Thomas, the Commandant of the Perranporth Co., National Reserves. Addresses were given by Lady Warmington, Capt. Gush, DCLI, the Revd T. Wearne, and Mr F. Marshall, whilst 'patriotic songs' were sung by Mrs Mauritsi and Mr Healey, accompanied by Miss Polly Mitchell:

> The hall was crowded, and seven men enlisted in the room, and three others the next day. A striking feature was a short address by Mr H.V. Westcott, of the Post Office, Perranporth, who was the first to come forward in the room. He said he was the fifth brother to volunteer for service during this war. Including the ten referred to above, the total number enlisted from Perranporth since war was declared is thirty-five. Of these no less than eleven were members of the original Boys' Brigade Company formed in Perranporth ten years ago by the Revd Hy. Edwardes and Revd A. Hume-Smith. They are distributed amongst the Yeomanry, the R.F.A. [Royal Field Artillery], the R.A.M.C. [Royal Army Medical Corps], the Public Schools' Battalion, the Motor Cycle Service and the 4th D.C.L.I.

The other contributing factor causing the multitudes to join the army lay in the working conditions of the average man in Britain. There had been industrial unrest across the country in the preceding years, leading to de-valued wages and inevitable strikes for better pay, while for some, there were simply no jobs at all. In a time before the Welfare State, those who did not work were in dire trouble, and many families at this time were large. Even for those who *were* employed, hours were long, the tasks arduous (and in many cases dangerous), whilst the recompense at the end of the week barely allowed even the most basic standards of living to be enjoyed. In Cornwall, where the rigours of the tin and copper mines (which were already in decline), clay-pits, fishing and agriculture provided the majority of employment, the tantalising alternatives of a life in uniform with regular pay, food, accommodation and a chance to 'see the world' were widely advertised by the military. Yet the fighting in Europe was already having worrying consequences for Cornish products:

> The war will have a serious effect on the china clay industry. On Saturday [early August] the West of England and Great Beam China Clay Co., the largest individual employers in Mid-Cornwall, issued a week's notice to all their employees, and upwards of 1,000 men in the West of England pits alone will down tools at the end of the week. This unemployment, coming so soon after the serious labour troubles, from which the district has only barely recovered, is regarded with apprehension, not only by the labourers, but by local tradespeople, who were hard hit by the previous stoppage. Two-thirds of the

Sergeants of the 2nd Devons.

exports of china clay goes to the Continent, and not only will that trade be ruined for the time, but drafts for the payments due for china clay already exported will be indefinitely suspended.[1]

In addition, the London Metal Exchange – vital to the Cornish ore trade – was closed for the first three months of the war, bringing several mines to the edge of bankruptcy. (The crisis was alleviated by Thomas Bolitho, a former West Cornwall MP, who stood a proportion of personal loans against stocks of black tin.) However, the prospects for many workers in these precarious occupations were bleak, and so, seizing the initiative, Sir. A.T. Quiller-Couch presided at a recruiting meeting in St Austell shortly afterwards, the proceedings of which were reported by the *Royal Cornwall Gazette* under the headline: 'Rousing Appeal to Clay-workers. Hundreds in the Streets':

Men of the DCLI at camp, 1908.

The Chairman appealed to the men of St Austell and district to come in and help the gallant soldiers who were … defending the name, the glory, the Empire of England, as well as the liberties, homes, and the very existence of England on the bloody battle-fields of north-east France. He was as sure as he stood there that we should win in the end, but we should win only if we went into it one and all, men and women, with their hearts for England. He had never asked a Cornishman to do a thing without giving him a reason or a cause … When the first of our brave fellows went out to the front the corn was coming to harvest. There would be another harvest, and proud would be the young men who went out to gather it, and proud would be the women who had encouraged them to go out. The sheaves they would bring in with them would have in them a far nobler England than we had ever yet known …

(Quiller-Couch's own son – who died in 1919 – served throughout the conflict.)

Mr J.C. Williams added that the roll of those from Fowey and District numbered some 200, out of a population of approximately 2,000. The *Royal Cornwall Gazette* reported that:

One of his ambitions was to see that admirable example imitated in every town and village. In his tiny parish they had made a pretty clean sweep of eligible men between the ages of 20 and 35 [applause]. When people of the West really understood the need and meaning of it all, it was certain that districts would provide their full number, and Cornishmen would stand where they all wished them to stand – among the best of the counties and of the people over whom the king now ruled.

But the war was not going well on the Western Front, and not every prospective new recruit was putting himself forward to enlist, to which the *Royal Cornwall Gazette* scorned: '… the eligible man who now sings "Rule Britannia" and carries the Union Jack in his button-hole … can only be taught by some method of compulsion that in these times there is no place in civil life for pseudo patriots.' (Even football was slated by the *West Briton*: 'It is disgusting to find in this national crisis thousands of men paying money week after week to watch professionals play a game. Hundreds of such men ought to be at the front'. It noted with some disdain that a concerted recruiting drive at football matches across London on a recent Saturday produced just one new soldier out of potentially thousands, but at the same time championed Cornwall's approach of abandoning amateur soccer and rugby matches with a view to emphasising the need for athletic young males to sign up instead. 'Men who refrain from joining the Army or Navy when they have no adequate reason for remaining at home throw an unfair burden upon others and bring compulsory service nearer.'.) However, the numbers *were* swelling, as these following figures for the week ending 12 September indicate:

	Regular recruits	**Territorial recruits**
Penzance	12	25
St Just	0	2
Hayle	7	4
Helston	12	1
Camborne	17	76
Redruth	12	13
Perranporth	0	8
St Austell	60	0
Bodmin	10	14
Newquay	6	4
Padstow	1	11
Liskeard	4	9
Launceston	37	12
Fowey	7	10
Bude (since 1 September)	10	67[2]

There were some quarters who would later favour a change from the patriotic speeches and fervent tub-thumping to adopt a more practical line, where possible additions to Kitchener's Army could ask questions and obtain relevant information about becoming a soldier before enlisting.

The St Columb Workhouse had interned seventy-one German 'aliens' by the end of September, whilst a further forty of the Kaiser's 'reservists' were detained at Falmouth from the Dutch liner *Gelria* and placed under arrest in a store on the Docks by a 'strong military escort'. Stephen Wernhard, a German national, was the joint proprietor of Falmouth's Albion Hotel, and he was charged with possession of firearms and ammunition six weeks after the outbreak of war. Any individuals of Germanic persuasion were treated with great suspicion, and one man – who turned out to be a Dane – was taken into custody for apparently signalling to a German vessel from Budock Downs as it sailed close to the coast. He was later released. Military matters were now part of everyday Cornish life.

THE REGIMENTS EXPAND

To accommodate the influx of 'Kitchener's Men', each regiment grew accordingly, with the 'New Army' units becoming known as 'Service Battalions'. The 8th and 9th Devons, for example, were formed in Exeter a month apart, between August and September 1914. Both would take a glorious but costly part in the fighting on 1 July 1916. For the DCLI, the 6th, 7th, 8th and 10th Service Battalions (the first three were raised in Bodmin, the last in Truro) had come into existence by March 1915, with the 6th being part of 'K1' (the first Divisions of 'Kitchener's Army') the 7th, 'K2', and so on, leading to the next step in their army careers – training. Preliminary instruction for these Service Battalions often took place in the locality of its origin before moving on to more rigid military establishments set up across the country.

The conduct of the men has been exemplary, and their keen-ness in drill and deportment on parade are the outward manifestations of that spirit of loyalty which now animates every true Englishman.

Dolcoath Mine, Camborne. Inset: Lt J. Holman.

> They de-trained [in Truro] on Monday raw recruits, and are already smart and disciplined men, eagerly
> awaiting their uniforms.[3]

In September, some of the Kitchener recruits stationed at Redruth were faced with a frightening scenario – Germans had been reported massing on the summit of Carn Brea Hill. This was, in fact, an exercise, but it was treated as if the unthinkable had happened and Cornwall was facing the threat of invasion. Commanded by Major F.D. Bain and Lieutenant W. Andrew, the Company proceeded to the base of the Carn, where scouts were dispatched to ascertain the strength of the 'enemy', and, after encountering no resistance, the men were requested to advance up the hill in 'extended order'. Halfway up the incline, their targets were 'spotted' hiding in trenches by the advance groups, and the entire complement was ordered to attack, resulting in the dislodging of the defenders who were said to be '… utterly dismayed at the irresistible charge of the company'. The *Royal Cornwall Gazette* spoke to one of the combatants, who remarked: 'Nothing would have given us more delight than to have found real Germans in the trenches. We all thoroughly enjoyed the skirmish, but I can tell you it was hard work running up that hill.' Another added: 'Why, we are having the time of our lives!'. The officers also commented upon how they had never seen a company of soldiers '… drill with such precision', adding: '… the men are quick with perception, and do the movements almost with the precision and correctness of [the] Regulars. The men are keen, and do not require half the instruction as the ordinary recruits – even of the Regular Army.'

The 4th DCLI (Territorials), meanwhile, had been sent to Perham Downs in Wiltshire for further exercises. The thoughts of Sir George Smith, who spoke at Truro's St Mary's Wesleyan Sunday School towards the end of September 1914, were also published in the *Royal Cornwall Gazette* following his review of his old battalion on Salisbury Plain:

> He was pleased with all he saw, not only with the military personnel, moral, cleanliness and material
> surroundings, but the quietness, order, discipline, cheerfulness and soberness of the men … Whilst they
> were strengthening the country in those strenuous days and dark times they were at the same time

preparing for brighter days and laying the foundation for a binding peace. If the war cloud was to pass, and they were to have peace, it must be striven for …

Peace was, however, still four long years away, and the men tasked with confronting the advancing aggression overseas were soon to be sent into war. Lord Kitchener, who also addressed the assembled Brigades on Salisbury Plain during September, informed them that the German army was '… getting short of food', as well as adding he did not think that the war '… would last a long time'[4]. (Privately, he had a more realistic time-scale in mind.) He did concede that it was prudent 'not to take risks', so he required all of the new recruits to be in a state of readiness as soon as possible.

The Cornish newspapers kept up to date with the fortunes of its local men, revealing in September that 'E' Company of the 4th DCLI, which had strong links to Truro, had promoted several of its men to the rank of Sergeant – notably G. Oakes, A. Sweet and B. Noble – whilst Bert Coles, formerly of N. Gill's & Son[5] in Plymouth, had received his first 'stripe' to become a lance corporal. 'It is the wish of his fellow Tommies that he will reap further reward,' noted one of his comrades to the *Royal Cornwall Gazette*. (The slang 'Tommy' referred to the average British soldier in the line, a nickname accredited to an actual servicemen called Thomas Atkins from a previous military era.) G.H. Bell, of 'E' Company, wrote and thanked the *Royal Cornwall Gazette* for sending copies of its editions which were distributed amongst the troops each week. 'They are eagerly sought after by the men for the news from Truro, and also the doings in the county', the officer added.

Many column inches were inevitably set aside for the progress of the conflict, both at home with the new recruits, as well as those already fighting. Under the heading of 'WAR ITEMS', it was announced that Mr R.F. Bolitho, of Penzance, had declared: 'So much do I sympathise with Tommy Atkins in his desire for cigarettes that I am sending you a second donation of £25 towards assisting such funds'. The same publication of the *Royal Cornwall Gazette* also noted how wives of recently enlisted troops were astonished at the much-changed appearance of their husbands after a few short weeks of training. One exclaimed: "Why, you look as if you'd been abroad for your health! I'm not sorry if this is what soldiering does for a man"'.

Yet further down the page, the first of the DCLI's Territorial units had received orders to sail for India: 'Some [emotional] scenes were witnessed at Truro Railway Station on Sunday morning when about 25 young men of the Foreign Service Battalion, E Co., 4th D.C.L.I., left after being home on three days' leave prior to going [abroad]. The station was crowded, and many were moved to tears at the parting of sons and parents, wives and husbands, but the recruits were in good heart and had a rousing send-off'.

Embarking from Southampton on 9 October, 1914, the 'Terriers' who had volunteered for such a campaign were now heading off into the unknown. They would soon be joined by thousands more, most of whom would make the much shorter journey over to the Western Front, where heavy fighting had reduced many British regiments to mere handfuls of soldiers. Bodmin's Pte Jane had noted back in September: 'The men of the Middlesex Regiment refused to budge, and out of 1,130, only 110 came back'[6]. Cornish farmers who demanded their sons were exempted from military service were reminded that French and Belgian farmers had lost everything in the past few months, including members of their families. Lt Gage Williams, 19th Hussars, of Scorrier House, wrote he had passed numerous burnt farms, and heard how a British soldier had been crucified on a tree. Propaganda was now just one part of this brutal war. Writing in the *Royal Cornwall Gazette*, Col C.B.Vivian implored: 'We want all the men and the best men we can get, and the sooner they start training the better. Germany … is far from being at the end of her resources'

Cornishmen at War: Western Front, August–December 1914

At approximately 5.30 p.m. on 13 August 1914, the 1st Battalion of the Duke of Cornwall's Light Infantry set sail from Dublin bound for an 'unknown destination', and the following afternoon, the SS *Lanfranc* passed round the tip of Land's End before entering the English Channel. For a number on board, this would be their last glimpse of the county whose cap badge they proudly wore, whether natives of Cornwall or affiliated to the South West by fate.

On the 15th, the French coastal port of Havre was sighted, and the 1st DCLI duly disembarked just after midday, although the weather soon turned wet and unpleasant, rendering the operation a subdued one. By the 18th, the battalion had arrived at Le Cateau, and soon marched to Landrecies, all the while getting closer to the massive German war machine which was now sweeping through Flanders and Northern France. The Kaiser's ultimate goal was Paris, and he had bypassed the heavy French fortifications on the border between the countries by invading neutral Belgium – the act which finally brought Great Britain into the conflict.

Reconnaissance confirmed that the German First and Second Armies were making rapid and destructive progress towards the advanced units of the British Expeditionary Force, now forming a significant line around the Belgian town of Mons, with the Cornwalls holding a position to the east along the banks of the Conde Canal. At 6 a.m. on the morning of the 23rd, the DCLI received its first taste of action during a skirmish with an enemy cavalry patrol, but it was not until late afternoon that the Germans arrived in significant numbers upon this sector, providing easy targets for the concealed defenders. Thronging the road, shoulder to shoulder, the invaders' apparent lack of military acumen appears astonishing, especially when their later methodical approaches to entrenchment and shrewd defensive policies on the Somme are brought into consideration. Men of the BEF were proud of their ability to level a heavy and concentrated rate of rifle-fire upon the enemy, and German survivors reported later that they believed the British had numerous machine-guns at their disposal, such were the casualties inflicted.

Sapper W. McKenney, from Redruth, wrote to his brother: 'I tell you the Germans are devils. They come up in large numbers; not like us. We extend, but they don't. As soon as you shoot down twenty, a hundred come up in their place …'[1]

The *Royal Cornwall Gazette* also revealed the impressions of Bodmin resident Pte Gordon Jane, who was serving with the Army Service Corps at Mons: 'We were just going to have some breakfast when the Germans started … As the poor fellows rushed to their own trenches so they were shot down. There was more slaughter caused in that first half hour than for the rest of the day.' As darkness fell, the combatants were dug in on either side of the Conde Canal, and enfilade fire ensued almost constantly. By now, it was clear the enemy possessed a far superior quantity of troops, and before the 1st DCLI was withdrawn according to orders at 11 p.m., it was revealed that one man had died and five more were wounded. *The History Of The Duke Of Cornwall's Light Infantry 1914–1919* (hereafter referred to as the Official History) notes that this individual was London-born Pte Gow, and the SDGW CD-ROM agrees, although the latter also records the death of another soldier on the 23rd (which is corroborated in the Official History's Roll

Kitchener Recruits of the DCLI.

of Honour) – Pte John Leggo – whose place of birth is given as 'St Just, Cornwall', the coastal town near Land's End which the DCLI had sailed past just a few short weeks before. However, the location of the soldier's final resting place – Cement House Cemetery, to the north of Ypres (now Ieper) – some distance away, suggests this date is possibly an error. For obvious reasons of logistics, soldiers were buried as close to where they fell as was feasible, yet on the occasion of a swift withdrawal by their surviving comrades, bodies were inevitably left behind. (The area around Mons remained in German hands virtually until the Armistice of November, 1918.) Hailing from a tin mining family which had links to the New World, Pte Leggo is, relying upon the official data (including the CWGC), the first Cornishman to fall on the Western Front.

The following day, a general Allied retreat began southwards, and on the 25th (according to the SDGW and CWGC), Lance Sergeant Frank Lovell, a resident of Penryn, lost his life whilst serving with the 1st Royal Berkshire Regiment at Maroilles, near Landrecies. The War Diary indicates it was more likely he died the following day, when the Berkshires formed part of the rearguard action in and around Le Cateau, thus enabling the bulk of the BEF to continue their march unmolested. Sixty-one men in the ranks were reported to be dead, wounded or missing by the end of the day, including the twenty-four-year-old lance sergeant, whose parents lived at Mylor Bridge. The deceased's brother, Jesse, a corporal, broke the news to their family via a postcard, and the latter himself was injured just weeks later, receiving three bullet wounds to his leg.

To the east of Le Cateau, men of the 1st King's Own (Royal Lancaster Regiment) were also in the firing line, and at 8.30 p.m. they came under attack from 150 Germans. At this point, Capt. Clutterbuck took fifteen of his own troops and led a bayonet charge in order to drive a group of the enemy away from a church where British wounded were being treated. Called upon to surrender, the captain refused and was killed instantly. Born in Chacewater, near Redruth, during 1874, he had served in the ranks of the Coldstream Guards before receiving an officer's commission into the King's Own, serving with distinction throughout the Boer War (1899-1902). A highly experienced soldier, he was mentioned in Field Marshal Sir John French's Despatch of 8 October 1914, and it was later said of Capt. Clutterbuck: 'No one could have died a more noble death.'[2]

The desperate fighting at Le Cateau was a bitter triumph for the BEF; the relentless German tide had been checked, but only briefly, despite the heavy casualties inflicted upon them. As the end of August neared, hunger, exhaustion and desperation set in, with adequate rest and recuperation an impossibility as the Kaiser's men kept up their own breathless pursuit. The *Royal Cornwall Gazette* soon printed a letter written by Lt Edgcumbe, 1st DCLI, to his Newquay-based father, Sir Robert Edgcumbe, revealing that the officer had been attached to the General Staff and was therefore unable to obtain accurate information as to the fate of his former comrades:

> My regiment has had a bad time, and I am dreadfully afraid they have been badly cut up, although I cannot as yet get any details. They were caught in a village by Germans in the houses, who had managed to get there by wearing our uniforms. Never again shall I respect the Germans …

At the small village of Nery on 1 September, German scouts happened upon a small British force of cavalry and artillerymen bivouacked in and around the hamlet, prompting the unseen aggressors to return to the main force and suggest a detour. Field guns were swiftly brought up and began bombarding the unsuspecting encampment, causing casualties amongst the men and horses, but the defenders soon retaliated with shells of their own, manned by gallant soldiers who were nearly all killed or wounded during the fight. Such was the dedication to duty of the small band of the BEF, the Germans withdrew their much larger force in the evening, stunned by the reverse of an apparently straightforward victory. Three VCs were awarded to 'L' Battery of the Royal Field Artillery, whilst one of the forty-two overall fatalities is recorded as Saltash-born Pte Charles Miller, of the 5th Dragoon Guards. (In 1901, he was a seventeen-year-old grocer's apprentice, living in Fore Street.) Despite the inexorable push towards Paris, Le Cateau and Nery provided the Kaiser's staff with timely reminders that the invasion of France was not the foregone conclusion many amongst them had predicted.

By 5 September, the Germans finally succumbed to their own problems of supplying the forward-most troops, who were within striking distance of the French capital before being checked and pushed back over the River Marne. The 1st DCLI, which experienced its own traumas during the withdrawal, now had the opportunity to go on the offensive, and took part in an attack on the 9th, advancing through woodland, vineyards and open fields. The mortally wounded were seen calmly handing ammunition to their comrades, and the commanding officer – Lt-Col Turner – along with his second-in-command, were amongst the injured, whilst Pte William Trevena, a native of Tuckingmill, and Pte Arthur Small, who lived at Scorrier, numbered amongst the twenty-eight men in the ranks who lost their lives.

Now it was the Allies' turn to try and press home their advantage, crossing the River Aisne on the 13th, only to encounter an intransigent German army which had decided to hold its lines and fight. Pte Badcock, of Illogan, serving with the 1st Coldstream Guards, would later recall:

> We crossed the river by pontoon bridges on Sunday, 13 September, and soon we discovered the Germans were entrenched on top of the hill, being well prepared with artillery. As it was impossible to get our artillery in position, we had to advance without being covered by artillery. … We suffered tremendous losses … Out of 1,000 in our regiment, only eighty of us are left. A lot of my pals lost their lives[3]

Among the missing was Second Lieutenant the Hon. Gerard Freeman-Thomas, who had been severely wounded in the thigh before being bound up by a captain, and left by a haystack. A corporal later stated he had witnessed the junior officer being taken prisoner by the Germans, who soon took the position, and for many months it was assumed the also had also been interned. However, it was later established that his name was not on any of the POW lists, and it was assumed for

Pre-war regulars on manoeuvres. Inset: Capt. J. Savage and 2nd Lt the Hon. G. Freeman-Thomas (top right), Bandsman T. Rendle, VC (bottom left).

official purposes that he had died on or after 14 September. His father, Lord Willingdon, was the MP for South East Cornwall between 1906 and 1910. (On the same day, Pte Leslie Fuller, nineteen, of the 1st Queen's, also fell. Shortly afterwards, his mother received a letter from him at her home in St Thomas' Street, Penryn, revealing he was in good health, but just an hour later, she was handed a telegram from the War Office, stating that her son was dead. He is now commemorated at St Gluvias Church, Penryn, although his body was never found. The Cornwalls were also in action on this day, attacking uphill across open ground swept by machine-gun fire, suffering nearly 150 casualties in the process, including Pte William Vincent, from Duloe, near Looe, who was killed.)

The Battle of the Aisne proved to be a turning point in the fledgling war, changing it from a conflict of mobility, horses and skirmishing – indicative of the recent Victorian campaigns – to one of stalemate, digging in, and consolidation. Fatigue undoubtedly played its part, but with so many hundreds of thousands of combatants on the battlefields, the 'cat and mouse' chase inevitably came to an end once Paris had been saved. Instead, the two armies tried to 'out-flank' each other, notably northwards towards the Channel ports, whilst also snaking south-eastwards in the direction of the Swiss border. Acknowledging the onset of autumn and eventually winter, the troops started to create defences for themselves out of the natural terrain, and so the Western Front was born. From rudimentary holes in the ground, hastily dug to provide scant cover from snipers' bullets, the trench systems would become ever more elaborate, but initially, this different type of warfare provided the opportunities for some distinctly treacherous behaviour.

On Wednesday, 17 September, Capt. John Savage, of the 1st Northamptonshire Regiment, took command of 'B' Company in the forward trenches near the Aisne, following a number of officer casualties. During the afternoon, he was informed that a white flag – the signal for surrender – had been seen raised above the enemy positions opposite, upon which he laid down his revolver and sword before walking across the intervening stretch of ground which soon became known as 'No Man's Land'. Met halfway by his adversary, a short conversation ensued, and both men then returned to their own lines, but just as the British captain – whose father was the one-time vicar of Flushing near Falmouth – reached his trench, the Germans fired upon him, killing him instantly. The War Diary indicates that two officers and many men were slain, including forty-two-year-old Sgt Vivian Harris, from Camborne. 'It was a trap'[4], the official account records, bluntly.

Several days later, Lt William Eliot, of the 1st West Yorkshire Regiment, was killed in the trenches near Troyon. Aged twenty-four, his parents lived at Mullion, and he was a former pupil at Falmouth Grammar School. Reports of local men losing their lives prompted the following letter to appear in the *Royal Cornwall Gazette*, penned by a St Austell 'Tommy' in the firing line:

> I myself am a married man, and I found it a hard thing to do when I left home, and I long to return again. But if I am less fortunate and find a soldier's grave, my wife would think more of me as a soldier who died fighting for my country than she would if I had been a coward and hid behind her.

Other messages implored: 'If only we had more men now!', 'Every able-bodied man is wanted to defend his country against these devils of Germans who are fighting without any sense of chivalry or mercy' and 'This war is a terrible thing … is there any man worthy of the name of a Briton who can read these messages and appeals from the Front without emotion?'

Bolstered by their years of pre-war training and efficient communication lines, the Germans switched from their initially aggressive offensive to a short period of waiting, confident in the belief that their superior manpower, equipment and military hardware were more than adequate for the time being to cope with the armies which opposed them. Crucially, the Kaiser's men held the higher ground almost everywhere, and the simple tactical advantages of drainage and observation soon became abundantly clear.

The beginning of October saw the BEF start to take over the lines around the Belgian town of Ypres, surrounded as it was by gentle, flat plains and almost indiscernible ridges, which would soon become synonymous with the First World War's most appalling carnage. Determined to wrest this prize from the Allies, the Germans also infused the region with a significant quantity of men, and the war of attrition began in earnest on the 17th, when the invaders launched a concerted assault against the salient. One man to lose his life during a night attack was Capt. Arthur Magor, of the 2nd Wiltshires, whose late father, a JP, hailed from St Tudy. (The captain himself had been born in the Bodmin area during 1879.)

The following day (18 October), the newly arrived cavalrymen of the Royal Horse Guards (Blues) encountered a large number of enemy cyclists, although the surrounding terrain was deemed impractical to effect the use of horses, so the troopers fought skirmishes on foot. The War Diary states: 'Capt. BRASSEY brought to notice the conduct of Cpl BROWNING & Trp. SANHAM who stayed with Cpl CLAYBYN when wounded and surrounded by the enemy.'[5] Cpl William Claybyn (aged thirty-six), a native of Fowey who had served in the army since 1899, later died of his injuries. His grandfather, Sgt-Major Denison, was a former soldier with the Royal Artillery.

The 2nd Sherwood Foresters, meanwhile, had also been in the thick of the fighting. During October, Pte Henry Styring was severely wounded by shrapnel, whereupon his great friend (and brother-in-law) L/Cpl Sam Elliott, promised him he would get help. Styring lay out in the open for three days, hiding amongst the corpses of his dead comrades to evade German patrols, but, true

DCLI group.

to his word, Elliott sent help and Styring was rescued, eventually returning to a hospital in the UK. He never had the chance to thank his pal for saving his life, as L/Cpl Elliott was killed in action on the 20th. Both men had enlisted in 1908, and whilst stationed at barracks in Plymouth, they met up with two Cornish girls, Elsie and Jane Riddle, whom the new recruits married several years later. L/Cpl Elliott and his wife, Jane, were living in Liskeard at the outbreak of war, and the soldier's body was never recovered to be identified.

The intensity of the conflict was now increasing again, with the Germans hammering away on a wide front, grimly repelled by the Allies. During the night of the 25th into the 26th, the 1st South Staffordshires had been under attack, but Lt Frederick Tomlinson – a native of St Michael Penkevil near Truro – had succeeded in capturing six enemy snipers, only for the British officer to be wounded shortly afterwards. As he was being evacuated to receive medical treatment, a shell burst over the cottage he was passing, killing him just days after his twenty-fourth birthday. His comrades placed a blanket over his body as the Germans advanced, and, several days later, Cpl Thomas Hamley, a St Mabyn man in the same regiment, also lost his life. The Staffordshires were just one of many regiments now facing a fierce enemy onslaught at Ypres.

With the line under huge duress on the 29th, four companies of the Coldstream Guards became completely surrounded, but '… in the best traditions of the regiment', 2nd Lt the Hon. Vere Boscawen, the third son of Viscount Falmouth, '… refusing to surrender, met his death nobly fighting against overwhelming odds'[6]. The owners of the Tregothnan Estate near Truro for generations, the Boscawen family have provided a number of Lord Lieutenants of Cornwall as well as Mayors of Truro over the years. A Memorial Service for the deceased – who was buried where he fell by the Germans – was held at St Michael Penkevil Church a short while later.

'We have orders to hold our positions at all costs', wrote Sgt E. Tabb to his brother at the Swan Hotel, Truro, 'so you can judge that there will be no retirement. You will never be able to realise what nerve-racking work it is here for the troops, shells dropping and exploding day and night, and comrades dropping wounded and killed, never knowing whose turn [is] next.'[7]

Lord Roberts VC, inspecting the troops, 1914. Inset: Capt. W. Moore (top, right) and 2nd
Lt the Hon. V. Boscawen.

Lt John Holman, serving with the 4th Dragoon Guards, penned these words to his mother at
the family home 'Tregenna', Camborne:

> We are holding our own well and hope to 'scupper' the Germans in front of us. We are taking tons of
> prisoners every day … I have often been under rifle and shell fire, and do not like it one bit … Hope
> to be with you again soon …[8]

Lt Holman was assisting an injured officer near Armentières on the 29th when he too was struck
down by a bullet which went through his spine, taking his life in Boulogne shortly afterwards.
Born at Basset Villas in Camborne and educated at Rhindell's School, he was part of the family
which ran the engineering firm Holman Bros in the town, as confirmed in the 1901 Census,
where his father is described as an 'iron founder'. Widespread expressions of grief were sent to the
lieutenant's mother when news of the death filtered through to Cornwall, and comrades spoke of
his constant care for others.

Back at Ypres, on 31 October, one of the most critical days of the entire conflict dawned. The
Germans launched an all-out assault in the vicinity of Gheluvelt, on the Ypres–Menin Road,
and the BEF fell back, with the line creaking like never before. Battalions fought to a standstill
until they were overrun, but a remarkable stand by the 2nd Worcesters saved the day, along with
incredible untold bravery and desperation by the soldiers involved. (The SDGW reveals that over

Ceremonial duties for the Royal Horse Guards. Inset: Capt. A. Magor.

1,000 men in the ranks lost their lives on the Western Front during this one day, with significantly more wounded or missing.)

> On Saturday morning, 31 October, I was in Mr St Aubyn's Platoon [No. 3, A. Coy]. We went up to reinforce The Queen's in the trenches. Just before we got to the trenches I saw Mr St Aubyn fall, he did not move, he was hit in the head and leg. We retired from the position and the Germans took it.[9]

Another eyewitness in the 2nd King's Royal Rifle Corps added: 'This officer was seen to be riddled by bullets and in a dying condition. The Germans gained the ground so that it was impossible for our men to bring him in.'[10] 2nd Lt the Hon. Piers Stewart St Aubyn was the fifth son of the 1st Baron St Levan, and the family home was at St Michael's Mount near Penzance. A JP for the County of Cornwall, and a Boer War veteran, the Old Etonian was reported 'missing' until the High Court decreed he must have succumbed to his injuries, as no further report of his whereabouts was forthcoming.

Partially concealed by woodland, the British riflemen kept up a ferocious rate of fire upon the enemy throughout the day, but the sheer weight of numbers advancing towards them led to the grim reality that a break-through appeared imminent. Launceston-born Capt. Waldo Moore, of the 2nd Welsh Regiment, was one of the many officers to fall, killed after a message sent ordering him to withdraw was never received. Encircled and under heavy artillery fire, he was part of a desperate counter-attack which also led to the death of his commanding officer, Colonel Morland. (Over 500 men of the battalion had become casualties in a matter of days.) The captain was the son of Gwennap and Mary, who lived at Garlenick, Grampound, and he was another experienced soldier, having seen action in South Africa fifteen years before.

By the end of the day, the Allied defences had held, but only just. 1 November saw no let up, with the London Scottish ordered forward through Wytschaete towards Messines, all the while subjected to heavy shrapnel and shell bursts from the enemy. Under almost constant fire, the Scots – credited as the first Territorials to see action during the First World War – repulsed several

German counter attacks with bayonet charges, yet their losses had been high. Advancing up a slope in broad daylight with no cover, they had become easy targets, and this grim scenario would be repeated on 1 July, two years later. Penzance-born Pte Eldred Banfield, aged nineteen, was amongst the dead. (His parents later lived at St Mary's on the Isles of Scilly.) The survivors of 1 November – including future Hollywood actor Ronald Colman – struggled back as best they could, a shadow of the proud force which had set off in the morning with bagpipes playing and kilts swirling.

On the 2nd – the official date of the end the battle for Messines – twenty-six-year-old Lt Richard Graves-Sawle was killed by a sniper in Polygon Wood after having taken part in every major action since the outbreak of war. Married just days before leaving for Flanders, the officer of the 2nd Coldstream Guards was the son of Rear Admiral Sir Charles Graves-Sawle, Bart., and Lady Graves-Sawle, of Penrice House near St Austell, hailing from a family which had been connected with Cornwall since the days of William the Conqueror. As with the fate of many servicemen at this time, there was confusion as to whether the lieutenant was, in fact, dead, or wounded and a prisoner. His name is now inscribed on the Menin Gate at Ypres – one of nearly 55,000 British troops who have no known grave – and when the memorial was officially inaugurated in 1927, Lord Plumer stated: '… now it can be said of each one in whose honour we are assembled here today: he is not missing, he is here.'

In early November, the *Royal Cornwall Gazette* remarked: 'The German attempts to break through to the coast in Belgium are slackening and weakening, and there are confident predictions of a retreat. For three weeks desperate attacks have been launched against the Allies at a stupendous loss to the enemy without any tangible advantages …'. First Class Stoker Albert Hill wrote to his parents in Boscawen Row, Truro: 'I think it [the war] will last a long time, but I think that England will come out on top … We all hear the latest news up here; the last we heard was that Germany lost 100,000 men in a thirty-six hour fight with England …'[11]. The Kaiser and his Generals had undoubtedly suffered grievous losses (perhaps not on the scale of the above, which has obvious propaganda leanings), but had, in return, inflicted crippling casualty figures upon the Allies (the BEF is estimated to have recorded a staggering number of 89,000 dead, wounded or missing by this stage). Far from contemplating a retreat, the Germans resolved to dig deeper and establish themselves even more, taking stock of the brutal methods of warfare which both sides had witnessed and employed since August.

The desperately needed overseas battalions which had been guarding the Empire now began to arrive on the Western Front, forsaking the hot, dusty climes of India or Africa for a bleak Flanders winter. (The 2nd Devons, for example, had sailed from Cairo in mid-September and finally marched into the trenches on 11 November – precisely four years to the day before the Armistice. At exactly the same time, Lord Roberts, VC – Field Marshall of the British Army and a soldier for over sixty years – disembarked at St Omer in order to review the Indian troops. Aged eighty-two, he caught a chill and soon succumbed to pneumonia, prompting a period of national mourning at a time when the Allies could ill afford any more setbacks. The BEF in particular felt his loss most keenly.)

The environment which the newcomers found themselves in was chilling. Both combatants possessed more or less the same pattern – three lines of trench systems was the norm, consisting of the reserve (often situated several miles behind the fighting), the support (designed to act as a potential second line of defence if the forward positions were overrun), and the front lines themselves, guarded by sandbags and almost impenetrable masses of barbed wire. Between these two monstrous constructions sat No Man's Land – a phrase which would strike a chord with some from mid-Cornwall who were aware of the tiny hamlet of the same name, yet the comparisons began and ended here. This ghastly strip of land was invariably fought over many times, and the unfortunate dead who fell upon its shredded soil often lay out in the open for weeks, months, or even years, suffering from the effects of bomb blasts and the extremes of nature. These became the

St Michael's Mount, Marazion, *c.* 1914. Inset: Lt W. Eliot.

countless numbers of soldiers who were never afforded a marked grave – the 'Missing' of the First World War.

Back in the trenches, it was soon realised that a zigzag pattern would lessen the effects of an exploding shell blasting outwards along a confined space, so the contours were deliberately jagged. Planks of wood raised the inhabitants above the base of the hollow in an attempt to negate the hazards of flooding, yet for the Allies – generally having to 'make do' with the lower ground in comparison with the Germans – the water table was sometimes barely beneath the surface, so for those spending endless hours stood in liquid mud, the long-term effect on the health of the sentries does not require much imagination. Dug-outs were created for officers and NCOs, but these offered scant protection from the cold, rain and hostile bombs. Latrines, first-aid posts, stores, field kitchens and primitive sleeping arrangements all had to be squeezed into the narrow, congested spaces, and everyone had to be out of sight of ruthless enemy snipers.

Routine became the order of the day. Dusk and dawn were considered to be ideal for trench raids, so most available men were ordered to 'stand to' at these sensitive hours. Weeks and sometimes months would pass without any significant movement across No Man's Land, and tedium set in amongst the troops of certain sectors. Chores were allotted, inspections announced, kit had to be cleaned, food prepared, but all the while the nagging threat of danger and death lurked at every hour. Because of its static position, the range of a front-line trench could soon to found by the opposing artillery, and regular reminders were sent over as to the precarious nature of soldiering. Various types of shell were launched by the Germans (as did the Allies, of course), including the so called 'Jack Johnson', and the 'Whizz Bang'. The trajectory of each made a slightly different noise in its approach, and the trained ear was often able to determine where the explosion would occur, and how close. At night, repairs to damaged parapets and barbed wire entanglements could

St Mary's, Scilly Isles, early 1900s.

take place, carried out by men with blacked-out faces and devoid of shiny metal such as their cap badges. As both sides undertook such dangerous tasks, each tried their best to harass the other by directing flares and sporadic machine-gun fire in the general direction of their foe. Bolder raids crept across No Man's Land to reconnoitre the activities of the enemy, and sometimes close-quarter fighting ensued with medieval weapons such as clubs, spikes and bludgeons. Bombs and grenades were also used by human beings who now inhabited a brutal, unforgiving world where little mercy was shown, or expected in return.

> We are men of the twentieth century, pulled backwards through the ages into ages of which history has no count. Yet out here we are not men, we are crosses between a rabbit, a tramp and a dog that has never been washed. We pop into our holes when danger threatens, and bob out again when all is safe … Neither can we call these holes our home. Here today, there tomorrow, we have all the faults of the homeless casual[12]

There were quieter sectors, however, where the two sets of soldiers sometimes adopted a 'live and let live' policy, rarely troubling each other for long periods of time. But in the early months of the war, the 'upper hand' needed to be maintained in any number of ways, and on 6 November, the Royal Horse Guards lost its commanding officer, Lt-Col G.C. Wilson, in a skirmish, despite the War Diary entry of the following day revealing: 'Information from all sides points to the fact that the German offensive in the neighbourhood is breaking down'[13]. Eight days later, just before the regiment was due to be relieved, casualties were caused in the trenches by enemy shelling, and one man who clung to life as a result was Tpr Frederick Jenkins, a native of Tresco on the Isles of Scilly. Leaving his job as a boatman, he had joined up during 1909, when he was aged eighteen. Standing over 6ft tall when he enlisted, the young soldier died forty-eight hours after he was injured, and news was sent to his wife, Edith, in Middlesex, and his father, Horatio, at Point House on Tresco.

Also in mid-November, the positions held by the 2nd Welsh Regiment were attacked by grenade throwing Germans and a field gun brought up to within 75 yards, but the line did not break. Withdrawn shortly afterwards, the War Diary of the Welsh estimated that 25 per cent of the rank and file had become casualties during recent fighting. Pte Stanley Whitty – originally from Bodmin – succumbed to his wounds on the 21st, aged twenty-two, and his body now lies buried at the Wimereux Communal Cemetery, where a major military hospital network had been set up nearby.

The Cornwalls, meanwhile, had not yet been sent to Ypres, but remained to the south between Neuve Chappelle and Laventie. In this part of the line, the low-lying ground around the River Lys made digging to any depth an impossibility, and the reliance upon the height of sandbags became ever more crucial. The Official History of the DCLI gives a grim indication of the appalling conditions its men had to endure through the first winter of the war. It notes how soldiers stood for days in water and developed the previously unknown ailment 'trench foot', where the lower limbs became so saturated that the flesh and bone literally started to rot. References are also made to sentries who had become so numb with the cold they had to be lifted from their posts by comrades, or even pulled out of the unforgiving quagmire with ropes. Corpses were dotted everywhere '… in all the contortions of a violent death … crying silently for burial'. The decaying flesh of dead animals was another dreadful sight, putrefying in the endless pock-marks of shell craters, but the most dangerous factor here was the width of No Man's Land – the two sides being a mere 45 yards apart at one stage. (This was not unusual where strategic ground would not be ceded by either army, yet more realistically, the gap could be measured in several hundred yards or more.) Marksmen, howitzers and rifle-grenades were put to their most deadly effect in this claustrophobic cauldron, and even artillery shelling was kept to a minimum in case of a fatal error of judgement.

Recruiting posters back in the UK were now trying to employ some 'reverse psychology', aimed at encouraging the 'less than eager' to enlist. One such proclamation in the *Royal Cornwall Gazette* enquired: 'Is your name on a roll of honour?', whereupon its Editorial added: 'When the war is over a more significant question to those who have not answered the call will be 'Is your name on the roll of shame?'. Elaborating upon the traditional 'Your King and Country Needs You' demands, another posed the scenario: 'You may win a Victoria Cross'. On 20 November, after being moved up to Messines Ridge near Ypres, the 1st DCLI found itself once again with a portion of their new trenches only 50 yards distant from the enemy, and an intense barrage soon caused widespread casualties plus material damage. In the afternoon, a German aeroplane hovered over the same location, thus inviting its gunners to pin-point their target once more, wounding 2nd Lt Colebrooke in an exposed portion of the damaged lines. Bristol-born Bandsman Thomas Rendle, who had attended to many injured under heavy fire, rescuing a number from being buried alive, now set to work on his stricken officer before carrying him to a place of safety. Rendle received the DCLI's only VC of the entire conflict – which he survived – and this is but one example of heroism, devotion to duty and the sheer horrors of war which confronted the men who fought it each and every day. Just under a week after this VC action, Pte Richard Jones, a nineteen-year-old from Ludgvan near Penzance, died of his injuries. His father, a 'marble and granite mason' in 1901, plus his young family, were living in Churchtown at the turn of the century.

Severe frosts now set in, and if these in themselves were virtually unbearable, the slight thaw which often followed rendered living conditions agonising in the extreme. Penetrating cold and unrelenting damp had to be endured night and day, and the psychological effects upon the men cannot be understated. Lt Spaight, of the Royal Army Medical Corps, and a resident of Porthleven, wrote this bizarre diary entry which found its way into a Cornwall newspaper:

Nov. 26th – A curious thing happened last night in the trenches. A lance corporal in one of the regiments was accused of being a coward … So in the night he got out of his trench, walked across

Winter landscape, Flanders. Inset: Lt R. Graves-Sawle and Lt F. Tomlinson.

quite slowly and calmly, as if he was out for a stroll, to the German trenches, looked into them, and strolled back. He was quite half-way back when the Germans got over their astonishment and began to fire. He never hurried, in spite of the storm of bullets, but just as he [returned] to his own trench a bullet got him through the head …[14]

Whilst obliged to print details of British casualties, the media was also eager to point out the short-comings of the enemy, most notably letters supposedly written by senior German commanders and officials which had been intercepted: 'The war is not going quite as well as we expected. The resistance of the Allied Forces is extraordinary, and we are beginning to feel very nervous as to the results. Our (German) losses are terrible, so terrible that the Emperor has forbidden their disclosure.'[15] The figures quoted are between 350,000 and 400,000 by mid-September, although these numbers are closer to the *entire* 1914 casualties published in a report by the German Army Medical Branch during the 1930s. The breakdown for August–December 1914 includes those 'sick', suffering from 'minor wounds', 'illnesses', and individuals who had 'recovered in hospital', but the total of dead, wounded and missing alone on the Western Front surpassed the 400,000 mark. September was the Kaiser's worse month, with almost 26,000 of his men losing their lives, 45,000 being unaccounted for, and over 71,000 seeking medical treatment. From this sobering statement to a puzzling one, allegedly found in the wallet of a dead German officer: 'According to this map [of a 'Future Europe'] only Devon and Cornwall will remain English, the rest of England being a German colony.'[16]

The Kaiser – also engaged on the Eastern Front – now knew his planned 'swift victory' in the west had failed, but there was never any indication he would withdraw from the partial gains he had secured on foreign soil. He had to be content with the 'waiting game', and wait he did.

For the Cornwalls, a brief respite came in late November when the battalion marched ten miles to the rear into the so-called 'rest areas' – abandoned farms or derelict village dwellings which appeared unbelievably luxurious compared to the squalid trenches – but the relief was

Soldiers of the 1st DCLI, 1915.

only temporary. In early December, they were back at the Front, deluged by heavy rain which submerged part of the defences to above knee level, with water cascading down from the German positions into the water meadow which had become the DCLI's new abode. Trying to sleep behind a parapet of sandbags, even the most sheltered 'beds' contained at least four inches of water, and if the situation could not get any worse, Pte George Deacon lost his life on the 6th. The thirty-one-year-old son of John and Eliza had been born at Altarnun, and lived at Egloskerry prior to enlisting in Launceston. The Western Front had become one of the most unforgiving locations in the world.

Meanwhile, the 2nd Devons – still acclimatising after arriving in Flanders from North Africa – were situated in and around Neuve Chappelle, a sector the Cornwalls were only too familiar with. Although major offensives had now been abandoned due to the weather, 'minor activities and operations' continued, including delicate patrols to spy on the opposition across No Man's Land, as well as more direct measures to neutralise observation posts and snipers' dens. On 18 December, all along the locality, the British and French co-operated in an attempt to keep the enemy 'fully occupied', and for the Devons, a farm known as the Moated Grange became the focus of their attentions. The Germans had recently dug an advanced trench nearby, well in front of their main line, from where enfilade fire was predicted by the West Country regiment if it was not dealt with swiftly. With the nature of this type of warfare still very much in its infancy, the 2nd Battalion was given barely two hours' notice of the plans (this practice would be thoroughly overturned by the time of the Somme offensive nineteen months later), but, after a sharp bombardment, three Companies went into the attack, receiving steady fire from the outset. Heavy casualties were caused, although one section managed to gain entry to the hostile trenches, engaging the enemy in hand-to-hand fighting before the position was taken, allowing the consolidating troops to follow up behind. Three officers had been killed, with several more wounded, whilst over 120 men in the ranks had been killed, injured, or were unaccounted for, including four Cornishmen amongst the fatalities. Pte William Hearn hailed from Launceston, the son of Emily; Pte William Highland was born in Penzance but was living at Liskeard when he joined up; Pte Albert Knight came from Truro, and Pte William Rogers, originally from Saltash, was the son of William and Emma.

The survivors of the 2nd Devons were relieved at midnight, but the newly arrived soldiers from another regiment were driven out by a strong German counter-attack shortly afterwards, and the captured trench was lost. The four men named above are all remembered on Le Touret Memorial.

> It is for us who live in security behind the shield of our Navy and Army to see that the wives and children of our brave sailors and soldiers have as happy a Christmas as we can give them … Above all the little children should not be allowed to feel the depression of these days of storm and stress … There is grief enough without adding to it unnecessarily, and the men who risk life and limb in the country's most just cause would be the last to wish that old familiar greeting should be suppressed in the dear homeland they serve so nobly and so well[17]

One of the most famous incidents of the First World War occurred over the Yuletide, when temporary truces broke out and soldiers of the warring nations met up in No Man's Land to exchange food and drink, as well as taking the opportunity to bury their dead. (The 1st and 2nd Devons, for example, are both known to have taken part in the 'fraternisation'.) The season of goodwill did not extend along the entire line, however, and snipers were still at work in some locations, Christmas Day or otherwise. Bodmin-born Pte Louis Pitt, of the 1st Devons, lost his life on 24 December, whilst Guardsman John Whitty, 2nd Grenadier Guards, from Hayle, died of his wounds on Boxing Day, having taken part in heavy fighting twenty-four hours previously. Pte John Bailey, who had probably been struck down at the Moated Grange with the 2nd Devons on the 18th, succumbed to his injuries on the 27th, having reached the hospital facilities at Boulogne. The resident of Bude was working on a Holsworthy farm in 1901, and the rural landscape of Flanders – his final 'home' – would have been more familiar to him than those who came from the industrial towns and cities of Great Britain.

By the end of the year, the 1st DCLI had already lost over 200 men dead from all ranks, plus many more wounded or missing. Whilst taking a well-earned rest, the battalion played a football match against the Royal Artillery, but ended up on the losing side. After all their endeavours and sacrifices in the firing line, this result was hardly worthy of any lament. The final War Diary entry for 1914 reads: 'At midnight the New Year was ushered in with three hearty cheers,'[18] yet there was little cause for celebration.

The 2nd DCLI had now arrived from Hong Kong, although the equipment available to them was only suitable for tropical postings, so hurried arrangements were made to properly clothe the soldiers in preparation for the trenches, where demand for fresh troops to man the Western Front had now reached a crisis point. The original BEF which had arrived on the continent during August had been virtually annihilated, and on top of the grievous loss of human life, incalculable military experience had also gone forever. Those having to learn the new form of trench warfare did so at the very great risk of their own personal safety, whilst back in the UK, the volunteers who had rushed to join up so enthusiastically also needed more practical guidance than simple theories written down in ageing army manuals. The soldier, and indeed the entire world, was changing.

Lt-Col Treffrey, the prospective Unionist candidate for the Launceston Division and officer with the Honourable Artillery Company, declared in the *Royal Cornwall Gazette*: 'We hope we are doing good work … There is no knowing how long this war will last, but I shall endeavour to do the best in my power for my country out here'.

The Western Front, January 1915–June 1916

The first full year of the conflict began with senior commanders of the opposing armies setting out their plans and strategies for the spring and summer, when the weather would improve to allow large-scale troop movements and significant offensives. The arrival of Kitchener's 'New Armies' – comprising mainly of men who had joined up the outbreak of war – was now imminent, yet the British High Command knew these untried and untested battalions could not be expected to make a major breakthrough on their own, and would need to be carefully introduced alongside the remaining 'Old Sweats' of the BEF and French infantrymen. The British sector of the Western Front encompassed Ypres in Belgium, as well as southwards to the area around Neuve Chappelle (a region well supplied from the French coastal ports and associated railway systems), and it was at Neuve Chappelle in March where the British launched their first independent attack to overrun Aubers Ridge, but to no avail. Ypres was once again the focus for some heavy fighting during April and into May, with the casualty lists running dangerously high, and it was into this destructive Theatre of War the first of the 'K1' Divisions began to deploy. (Some were also sent to Gallipoli, an ultimately disastrous campaign which did, at least, provide essential combat experience for the survivors who were later sent to the Western Front.)

Skirmishes continued throughout the summer until the largest attack of the war to date was planned for the industrial towns of Loos and Lens, in the Artois region of France. It was to be a joint Franco-British assault, and in mid-June, the BEF had extended its responsibilities for a greater length of trench systems, thus enabling French reserves to be released. The problems which beset the campaign from the beginning, however, centred around the disagreements between the Allied commanders as to how the onslaught should be launched. Sir John French, in overall charge of the BEF, did not believe his army was fully equipped and ready for the tasks ahead of it, but his opposite number, Frenchman General Joffre, disagreed, and pressed on with the preparations. Sir Douglas Haig, French's deputy, was concerned about the terrain at Loos – flat, open and exposed – which possessed obvious advantages for the German defenders armed with machine-guns and rifles, yet Joffre was adamant the location would not change. The pressure upon the Allies to produce a stunning knockout blow against the Germans was mounting, and Loos was seen as the ideal opportunity to convince the other doubting nations that Britain and France were capable of such a victory.

LOOS

On 21 September 1915, the British began their bombardment of enemy positions at Loos, designed to obliterate the defenders and destroy the wire in front of the trenches. Neither objective was achieved on the Front held by the 7th Division, which included the recently arrived battalions of the 8th and 9th Devons – both of the New Army. Advancing behind a screen of gas on the morning of the 25th, the wind suddenly changed direction, blowing back into the faces of the

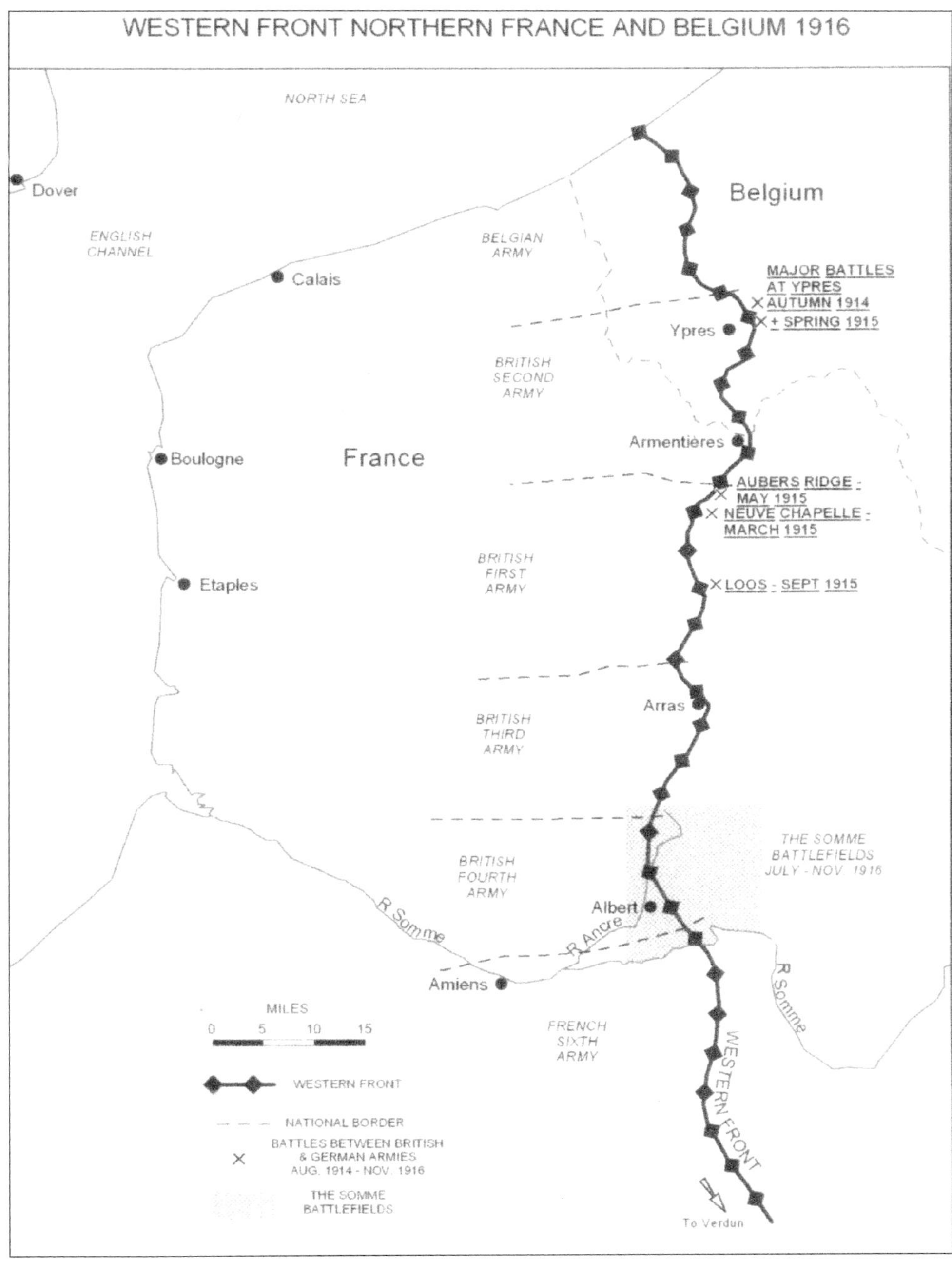

The situation on the Western Front, 1914–1916. NB: The dispositions of the British Army refers to June 1916.

attackers who were also being subjected to heavy machine-gun fire. The 8th Devons were decimated, although the 9th – sent up in reserve – was not quite so badly affected, but the entire assault was compromised by the lack of reinforcements which were not released quickly enough from the rear. (A number of these Divisions had been marching for days prior to the battle, and were in no fit state to fight anyway.) German positions which had been overrun were slowly reclaimed by the enemy, who had swiftly deployed replacements of their own in the vicinity, and Loos was an unqualified disaster. Many of Kitchener's Men were mown down before they had even gone several yards – their first and last experience of war.

J.B.S. Notley, a newly commissioned Second Lieutenant with the Devons who was waiting to be sent abroad, recalled his experiences in the immediate aftermath of Loos:

On 25 September the 8th and 9th Devons led the attack at the battle of Loos, both Battalions having very severe casualties, the 8th losing 22 officers and 753 men [dead, wounded or missing]. All these officers and men had to be replaced and so at the end of the month I, with some other officers, was ordered to leave Wareham on 1 October for France … We were told that some of us would go to the 8th and some to the 9th Devons. I was named for the 8th Devons (Buller's Own). [General Sir Redvers Buller, VC, of the 60th Rifles, was born at Crediton, Devon, and received a Victoria Cross during the Zulu War of 1879, when he rescued two comrades from the enemy on the same day but on two separate occasions. The Devons lost heavily at Spion Kop and Ladysmith whilst fighting the Boers between 1899 and 1902, where Buller was involved with both actions.]

We reported at Folkestone according to our instructions, and there were informed that we would have to stay the night … at a hotel as U-boats were in the Channel and it was unsafe to cross. The next night we did cross to Boulogne, arriving there about midnight in pitch darkness, and then went on to Etaples Bull Ring (very famous in the First World War). We arrived the same night and were led to some tents, and we had our valises and groundsheets. There were three or four of us in a tent and all we had was a smokey Hurricane Lantern. Whilst lying down and trying to sleep I felt wet and found the water had seeped in under the tent: it had been raining incessantly for hours. I got up and found my clothes were very wet (we had not undressed) and we just waited till daylight.

We spent about a week at Etaples Bull Ring, just waiting for orders … Then one afternoon we were informed we had to catch a train starting at about 11 p.m. during the night for an un-named destination. We found there were a lot of men on the train going up to the front line, like us, to replace the troops lost at Loos. This train travelled at about walking pace, no faster, 3 to 4 miles per hour, and some of the men sat on the running boards, and some ran and got their water bottles filled from cottages we passed and still caught up with the train.

It was still night time. At last as the daylight broke we could hear – a long way off – the sound of shells bursting, so we knew we must be nearing the rail head. At long last the train ran into a station (I should say crawled into it) and we were there! When we saw two officers with the Devon Regimental Badge on their caps weren't we pleased! We surrounded them and they told us to which Battalion we were posted. The town was Bethune.

I, with four or five others, was for the 8th Devons, and Capt. G.P. Tregelles was to lead us up to where the reserve trenches were at that time. [The captain was a native of Penzance.] He told us both the 8th and 9th had had a terrible pasting as they led the attack at Loos, and the gas blew back on top of them as the wind had changed; gas that they had used themselves, and was not from the enemy lines. Many of the 8th were gassed, and also the 9th Battalion.

On our walk up to the trenches, during which we could hear shells bursting in the distance, we were told we were now passing through a village – the only sign was red brick dust! Suddenly a shell screeched overhead and we all ducked. I said to Capt. Tregelles "That was close" and he replied "About half a mile above us!" Eventually we reached the reserve trenches and met the new Colonel

German machine-gunners.

and Adjutant, the previous ones were killed at Loos [the commanding officer who fell was Colonel A.G.W. Grant]. I was given command of No. 1 Platoon 'A' Company. This then consisted of a Sergeant and three men! All that were left after the original 40–60 men. The position the 8th Devons were in was the reserve trenches at Cambrin.

The 8th and 9th Devons were in the 20th Brigade with the 2nd Border Regiment and the 2nd Gordon Highlanders [remaining so through the Somme campaign of the following year], and our Brigade Commander was Brigadier Trefusis, brother (?) of the Bishop of Crediton in Devon … [The Honourable J.F. Hepburn-Stuart-Forbes-Trefusis, of the Irish Guards, took over command of the 20th Brigade in August 1915, after receiving a Distinguished Service Order earlier in the year. A Boer War veteran, and having taken part in the initial skirmishes of the present war, he lost his life in action on 24 October 1915, at the age of thirty-seven. The Bishop mentioned by 2nd Lt Notley lost two sons on the Somme. The Trefusis surname is linked to the Barons Clinton, and is also a place-name in a suburb of Flushing in Cornwall.]

There was a battery of 12 pounders about 150 yards behind us, dug-in and camouflaged, and at intervals they fired over our heads. The noise was terrific, but we got used to it. We listened to the shells – Little Lizzies – passing overhead from behind the German lines to a destination miles behind us. Whilst here recruits joined us, and eventually I had about forty to sixty men, several Cockneys, and no better soldiers ever existed; other platoons were made up to a reasonable strength and we then went back to a lovely little village called Essars, not far from our Rail Headquarters, Bethune, quite a sizeable town. Here we stayed for several days, where the newcomers and the few original 8th got to know each other and settled down in their platoons and companies. The men were billeted in barns with plenty of straw, and the officers slept on the floor in the farms on their valises which had come over with them from England[1]

This descriptive passage was typical of the tens of thousands of individuals who made the same journey from 'Blighty' to the Western Front. It gives an insight into the strange mixture of eagerness and foreboding of finally being sent to the firing line, the monotony and the primitive methods of transport, the approach to the battle zone, the sound of the bombs, the shock of the losses, and the eventual settling in to a certain way of life which was experienced by all those who had never been on active service before.

The year 1915 had been one of failures for the Allies. The trench systems had barely moved from their positions twelve months before, and both opposing armies knew that 1916 would bring the opportunities – and expectations – of fresh offensives. The men who had enlisted so enthusiastically back at the outbreak of the conflict were now, in many cases, considered veterans of the Western Front – despite their lack of prolonged fighting experience – and the much-hyped reasons for going to war in the first place had become bogged down in dreary months of inactivity followed by the odd moment of utter terror.

There was also increasing unrest about the industrial problems back home. As soldiers in the front line literally risked life and limb every day, those tasked with supplying the war effort from the factories and workshops – often manned by individuals who had failed to volunteer for the armed forces and were yet to be conscripted – had been, in some instances, striking over pay and working conditions. (It is interesting to note that approximately 10 per cent of the 1,000-strong workforce at Dolcoath Mine, Camborne, answered the call to arms during 1914, and the company's own annual report for 1915 reveals that there was a severe shortage of labour during this year, with youngsters who were not old enough to enlist providing the mainstay of the pay roll. For a trade which had been suffering for decades, as cheaper foreign tin came onto the market, the outlook was grim. The metal industry in Cornwall was, ironically, closely linked to Germany, with many British mining engineers having been educated at Freiburg's School of Mines, whilst the miners from both locations had developed a mutual pre-war respect for their joint professional abilities wherever they were in the world. As conscription loomed in Britain, 2nd Lt Roach of the 9th DCLI wrote 'An Open Letter To The Young Men Of Cornwall', published in *The Cornishman*, which noted, somewhat despairingly: 'The recruiter has had a barren thankless task in Cornwall … after all his painful attempts to awaken you to a sense of duty you have remained impervious and cold …' This sense of gloom detracted from those individuals who *had* volunteered, but the message was clear and becoming desperate – the United Kingdom and her Empire were in dire straits.)

Back in France and Flanders, the senior Staff officers who rarely paid a visit to the forward-most British positions were rapidly becoming the subject of derision and mistrust as the apparent shambles of the Allied military machine stumbled into another year. The oft-quoted label administered to this point of view likens the situation to 'Lions led by donkeys', and this was certainly symptomatic of the vast gaps which often existed between the 'rankers' and the 'brass hats' in terms of actual mileage and approach to the fighting. (There were, of course, competent Brigade Commanders who possessed a thorough grasp of military strategy, and are often overshadowed by the so-called 'butchers'.) The battalion officers, however, endured the same hardships in the cramped, dangerous trench systems as the men under their immediate command, with a significant majority becoming both revered and respected. It was an officer's duty to 'lead by example', and for many Lieutenants and Second Lieutenants – some just out of school – this was a gargantuan task indeed.

1916

A change in leadership, and a further deployment to a new sector of the Western Front, were two significant moments as the old year faded and a new one began. Sir Douglas Haig took over as Commander-in-Chief of the BEF in December, 1915, following Sir John French's failure at Loos, whilst the British extended their responsibility further south along the Western Front until it

German officers, *c.*1915.

reached a position just before the marshy banks of the River Somme. The nearby town of Albert became the new HQ of the recently formed Fourth Army, under the command of Gen. Sir Henry Rawlinson, and just as had been discussed at the beginning of 1915, plans for a major Franco-British offensive destined to take place later that summer began to take shape. Once again, Kitchener's New Armies were to play a major role, although the more battle-hardened French soldiers were to lead the way on Rawlinson's southern flank, but these theories were roundly thwarted when the Germans launched their own all-out assault on the city of Verdun, many miles to the south-east of the Somme sector. With fanatical zeal, the French troops declared that the fortress would never fall to the enemy, and poured thousands of men into its desperate defence. Realising the full extent of Gallic pride, morale and fighting spirit was at stake, the Kaiser's men fought with equal ferocity, and the casualty figures on both sides were astonishing. France was bleeding to death at Verdun, and her leaders pleaded with Haig to unleash his own armies to relieve the pressure on the beleaguered garrison.

This posed a huge dilemma for Haig, who was fully aware of the critical situation at Verdun, but was also mindful of his own troops' inexperience of battle. He eventually agreed to send his massed Divisions along the axis of the old Albert-Bapaume Roman road, across which the Germans had spent nearly two years building awesome fortifications to repel just such an assault. The British infantry was to lead the advance, backed-up by the full might of the Royal Artillery, and the Reserves were to be close enough behind so as to exploit any gains, followed by the swift deployment of the cavalry (which was rapidly becoming impotent in the modern theatre of warfare). The sheer numbers involved would dwarf those at Loos, and it was generally believed that this would be the decisive moment of the First World War.

Firing trench, Thiepval, 2007.

THE PLAN

Whilst the main assault was being delivered, a simultaneous advance would take place on either side of the Albert-Bapaume road, tying up the Germans along many miles of front line. The northern-most objective was Gommecourt, a strong, enemy-held salient which jutted out into No Man's Land, and this was to be the focus of two Divisions of the Third Army, under Gen. Sir E. Allenby. Its design had two distinct functions – to prevent the Germans from sending reinforcements to the primary attack opposite La Boisselle, and to eliminate this awkward 'bulge' in the trench systems once and for all. Officially classed as a 'diversion', the British at Gommecourt were at a distinct disadvantage from the outset, as the immediate Division to the south – the 48th of Rawlinson's Fourth Army – was not destined to move forward with the rest of the line, and likewise the men beyond the 46th (North Midland) Division were to remain static, inviting the defenders on these flanks to assist their comrades who would face the onslaught head-on. These problems would have to be addressed as Zero Hour moved closer.

Rawlinson had received intelligence from Verdun of the methods employed by the Germans, who had unleashed a devastating artillery barrage which destroyed the French forward positions before the infantry advanced to occupy these obliterated defences. The British gunners would then target the second line, and so on, until a breakthrough was achieved into the open countryside behind the ruins of the once formidable barricades. However, the success of the entire operation hinged on two crucial factors – the efficiency and accuracy of the Royal Artillery.

The date for this momentous campaign was set for 29 June, with even the exact hour specified – 7.30 a.m. This was to allow time for the dawn mists to lift in order to afford the gunnery observers a supposedly clear view of their quarry. Inevitably, this also meant that more than three hours of daylight would have passed before the troops went over, and the same clarity of vision afforded to the gun teams would also be in the possession of any Germans left alive after the devastating bombardment. The onus now rested squarely upon the shoulders of the men who were to charge the breaches several hundred times a day, and the competence of the ammunition at their disposal.

As the first months of 1916 passed by, more and more soldiers gathered in the Somme sector, accompanied by the logistical nightmares of transport, food, billeting and eventual deployment, yet the raw materials for the attack – plentiful manpower and adequate supplies – were gradually being put into place. Rawlinson would eventually have eighteen Divisions at his disposal, numbering over half a million soldiers by the end of June, although the percentage of experienced servicemen was still a niggling concern. The Regulars had been left battered by their exertions of 1914, and few of the original combat troops remained, whilst the Territorials did not benefit from the scale of early recruiting to the extent of the New Armies, which accounted for approximately 60 per cent of the strength on 1 July. Battalions were heavily regional, with Yorkshire providing no fewer than twenty-nine, Lancashire twenty-two, Ireland (predominantly Ulstermen) twenty, Tyneside seventeen, the Midlands fourteen, and London thirteen. In addition, the Scots and Welsh were represented to a lesser degree, as was the English West Country, where the 2nd, 8th and 9th Devons had arrived, along with the 1st and 8th Somersets, plus the 1st Dorsets and 2nd Wiltshires. Several units of the Glosters, Worcesters and Ox. & Bucks. would witness the advance from their positions in the 48th (South Midland) Division, which – as we have seen – would not be required to advance on the opening day. Add to this mix the singular battalions from Suffolk, Norfolk, Bedfordshire, Berkshire and Hampshire, as well as those of the Fusiliers, Engineers and Artillery, the eventual total of *volunteers* on the Somme from every corner of the United Kingdom and Ireland would out-number their German counterparts by a considerable proportion. Confidence began to grow – surely the colossal amount of soldiers in uniform would be enough to drive the enemy out of their defences once and for all? Kitchener's Men had been compelled to enlist for just such an assault, but less than a month before the campaign was due to get underway, Lord Kitchener himself became a casualty of war, when the cruiser he was aboard hit a German mine and sank close to the Orkneys as he was travelling to Russia to encourage its leaders who were flagging within the Allied cause. Suddenly, the omens were not looking so bright.

By May 1916, the 1st Somerset Light Infantry – part of the 4th Division (and one of only four Regulars amongst the eighteen in the process of assembling for the initial attack) – was in the area of Serre, to the north of Albert and the main focus of the assault. Having been on the Western Front since August 1914, its experiences of combat were far greater than the New Army battalions of the 31st Division on the left flank, although the 29th (Regular) Division on the other side had distinguished itself with honour at Gallipoli the previous year. Sgt Arthur Cook, of the 1st SLI, was a pre-war career soldier who had been in the thick of the fighting for nearly two years, and he kept a diary of events as he saw them in the lead-up to the Somme offensive. The Somersets, which contained a small number of Cornishmen in its ranks, was not a 'Pals' battalion, but the sense of camaraderie engendered by its soldiers was just as strong. On 23 May Cook wrote:

> It seems as if things are planning for a large attack here. This quiet little sector we arrived at … is now bustling with men and guns. Everybody is wanted for fatigues, digging assembly trenches, carrying R.E. [Royal Engineer] stores, ammunition, grenades, etc., into the line. The roads … are a mass of men all night, especially the Serre Road. Our casualties during these operations were very small, which is very remarkable, as Jerry must hear all the noise and preparation going on, as occasional shell and burst of machine-gun fire disturbed the night and broke the monotony of digging, causing everyone in the open to flop on their stomachs in the quickest possible manner.
>
> 11 June – Training at Beaval [Beauval] for the Somme attack … A special plan of the area … we have to attack was made on the ground, showing the objectives we were all supposed to take. [It] looks quite easy on the ground, but what a ghastly affair it was going to be[2]

The reasons for this 'ghastly affair' are best reviewed from the opposite side of No Man's Land.

THE GERMAN PERSPECTIVE

Whilst Britain's pre-war army had been numbered in tens of thousands, Germany could call upon literally millions of trained men by 1914, as conscription had been in place for a considerable time, allowing the traditional Teutonic character traits of efficiency and organisation to be honed into a slick military machine. Discipline and rigid methods of soldiering were paramount, with much emphasis placed upon the handling of weapons, whilst the regional aspect of British battalions also applied to their German counterparts, who took great pride in the origins of their regiments. Prussians, Saxons and Bavarians formed the bulk of the Kaiser's army, and each had a different reputation amongst the Allies in the opposite trenches, varying from a generally placid tolerance shown towards their foe from the Saxons and Bavarians, to ruthless aggression employed by the Prussians.

After the initial breathless months of the war, life in the trenches on the Somme had settled down to be regarded as a relatively 'quiet' sector, manned at first on the Allied side by the French. This was agricultural ground – tactically far less important to the Germans than the industrial areas further north, along with their strategic towns and proximity to the vital Channel ports. When the British began arriving in numbers during the first half of 1916, however, the Kaiser's men – many of whom had been there since the autumn of 1914 – began to sit up and take note. Here, as elsewhere, the higher ground was in the hands of the invaders, allowing the benefits of observation and less problems with drainage, yet the topography permitted a far more sinister element to be exploited. In the long months of waiting, the Germans had begun to dig – downwards into the chalk to create elaborate underground systems reinforced with concrete. They knew that the British build-up of men and hardware opposite was not a ploy to fool them into *thinking* an offensive was imminent, only for the blow to fall elsewhere along the line. The sheer scale of the preparations was simply too large for such a feint, so with the blood still flowing at Verdun, an Allied counter-strike on the Somme was virtually certain.

Not only were the methods of sheltering men underground fully exploited, the Germans also set about strengthening their capabilities of resisting the attack when it came. Villages along the front line were turned into almost impregnable fortresses, guarded by strong-points, sandbags and impassable barbed wire. The placing of machine-gun nests was carefully thought out to provide the widest achievable arc of devastation to be wrought over the furthest possible stretch of No Man's Land. In the event of a position being overrun, well-rehearsed procedures to re-locate to *another* powerful spot were established, and it was vital that if one team was knocked out, two, three or four more could unleash just as much ferocious fire-power upon the advancing infantry. These tight-knit groups of men had undergone extensive training at special schools set up in Germany, teaching them how to service, dismantle and repair a variety of weapons – including those captured from the enemy – in addition to range-finding and swift reloading. Targets as far away as 4,400 yards were just within their reach, and with a rate of fire of between 400 and 500 rounds per minute, it is little wonder that British casualties on the Somme were so appalling. There were 250 rounds to each belt of ammunition, and fresh water was added to cool the mechanics of the gun after every fourth belt had been expended.

The landscape of the Somme was also fully sympathetic to the requirements of the defenders. Between the villages which were now bristling with weapons of war, the ground was fairly open, with no hedges or walls, which had allowed agriculture to flourish over the previous centuries, and the only cover was afforded by clumps of trees or larger woods dotted here and there, fully defended around their edges if the positions were located within German territory. The chalk elements ensured that there were no jagged edges or sharp inclines – the fields rolled gently along the contours of gullies and ravines – and at the apex of these natural 'funnels', as well as along the exposed sides, the Germans inevitably positioned their strategic machine-guns. Tunnels led away from the front lines, often linking one dug-out to another, which allowed movement during a bombardment, and communication lines snaked back several kilometres to where the second and third systems were situated, fortified with just as much consideration as the forward trenches. As a further precaution, extra obstacles were dug and constructed in between, thus providing yet more problems for any prospective attacker.

In the absence of a hamlet to turn into a fortress, the Germans once again shrewdly selected a site in the open countryside which had far-reaching views across to the enemy, and these became known as redoubts. Along the entire length of the British Somme Front, there were to be eleven of the latter to storm, in addition to the nine villages which were defended in great strength. Once the campaign was underway, the British Press revealed the significance of these place-names which had never been heard of before, citing the Tommies' dry predilection for Anglicising every foreign syllable they encountered:

> It is evident that the battle of the Somme is going to give some fresh household words to our war vocabulary. 'Wipers' is veteran by this time. 'Plugstreet', 'Booloo' and 'Armintears' are old friends. We must now make room for 'Monay-ban', 'La Bustle', 'Fry Court' and 'Gum Court'[3]

Ypres, Ploegsteert, Bailleul and Armentieres had all been part of the British sectors since the early part of the war, but the emergence of other points on the map which would gain grim notoriety amongst the New Armies was largely due to the way they were defended in such depth by the Germans on the first day. Montauban, La Boisselle, Fricourt and Gommecourt claimed thousands of lives, as did the other mere specks on the landscape known as Serre, Beaumont Hamel, Thiepval, Ovillers and Mametz.

Commanding the higher ground, the German observers watched, waited and fine-tuned their defences according to the activities of their foe on the opposite side of No Man's Land. They also sent over reminders that they were not in any mood to submit to such an overwhelming force, launching all kinds of calibre of shells into the midst of the British preparations, causing inevitable casualties along the way. The psychological effect of the Germans looking 'down' on the British from their strongholds was not lost on either army, and the former adopted a stance of 'we know something which you do not'. Confident in their ability to withstand an inevitable artillery bombardment by sheltering in the concrete bunkers, the Germans were also safe in the opinion that the men who were about to attack them were almost certainly unaware of how formidable the mostly concealed defences actually were, both on the front line and behind. The total belief in the efficiency of their machine-gun teams was not ill-founded, either, and rested on tried and thoroughly tested methods.

This, then, was the state of the German presence on the Somme by June 1916. The British had several nicknames for them – 'Jerry', 'Fritz', 'the Hun', 'the Boche' – two nations linked by the bloodlines of their respective Royal families, and who many in the UK did not initially have 'any quarrel' with back in 1914 when the war was obscurely sparked off in the Balkans by ethnic disputes. But time had moved on since then. The few men of the Regulars still surviving who had been part of the original BEF had a number of scores to settle as they recalled their numerous fallen comrades. The Territorials, who had originally been exempt from service abroad but had agreed *en masse* to help out in whichever way they could, were now about to get their biggest opportunity to prove themselves, and were eager to begin. The New Armies, too, were ready to proudly announce their own sizeable presence in France, backed by the goodwill of the citizens back home who had followed their progress from the earliest days. Yet to the Kaiser's men, they were simply the enemy in khaki who had to be stopped at any cost. At Verdun, the French issued the rallying cry 'They shall not pass!'. The Germans were about to face the sternest of tests on another battlefield, but defensively they were ready.

THE COUNTDOWN BEGINS

On 18 May 1916, Pte G.W. Manners, a one-time pupil of Truro College, wrote to his former school:

> I am in France and getting my share of excitement. We left England two or three weeks ago, and are at present close behind the firing line. At night we can see where the firing line is by the star shells and searchlights. During the last three days we have seen two or three German aeroplanes shelled. We are billeted in a barn, the floor of which is covered with straw. At night the place is overrun with rats, which go for our bread and cheese. We are not working very hard, and receive good food and plenty of it. We can even get eggs and coffee at the farmhouse[4]

The Royal Flying Corps – the predecessor to the RAF – undertook many missions designed to establish the strength of the German defences on the Somme, and how many reserves were in the area. As has already been established, much of the badly needed data was deliberately hidden away underground, but the sorties continued unabated. Lt F.E. Gilpin, another former student of Truro College, informed the latter:

> There is a great difference between war flying and other types of flying outside the war zone. In ordinary flying there is very little risk at any height above 1,000ft; the most dangerous parts of a flight are when the machine is taking off from the ground and when landing is being effected. During flights over the lines our low-flying machines are in constant danger from machine-gun fire, from anti-aircraft guns, and from attacks by enemy aircraft. Our airmen in these low-flying machines do counter-battery work, photography, and contact patrol work, and are under a continual nervous strain for the duration of the flight, which lasts about three hours. Any bullet or piece of shell striking a vital part of the machine, such as a control wire or petrol tank, might mean [the] death of both airmen and the loss of the machine. It is an almost daily occurrence when flying low over the trenches to return and find several bullet holes in the wings. The dangers in the air during war are ever increasing, as anti-aircraft defences become more efficient, and the speed armament and capacity for manoeuvre of new types of aeroplanes are improved ... During active operations preceding an attack, and during the progress of the battle and afterwards, our airmen often work strenuously in the dangerous atmospheric conditions. To aid our low-flying machines to co-operate effectively with artillery and infantry, strong fighting patrols fly above them in order to protect them from attacks by hostile aircraft. Our Scout machines are splendidly managed by courageous men who have no thought for personal danger[5]

In the skies, the British enjoyed a rare superiority over the Germans, and not one observation balloon was destroyed as the day of reckoning drew ever closer. On the ground, confidence was still high, and on 22 June – despite being bivouacked in woods outside the village of Mailly-Maillet to avoid enemy shells – Sgt Cook of the 1st Somersets noted in his diary: 'Our guns are now getting active, but the German response is still feeble.'[6]

There was to be a carefully planned timetable of moving masses of troops from the reserves, to the assembly trenches, and finally into the forward positions in time for the beginning of the assault – still set for 29 June. Since Loos, the 8th and 9th Devons had undergone a period of recuperation and consolidation as the new recruits inter-acted with the old. Still part of the 7th Division, the West Country regiment was now in the south of the line, opposite Mametz, whereas their sister battalion, the 2nd (of the 8th Division), took over the front lines which faced the German-held villages of Ovillers and La Boisselle, on 5 April. Positioned slightly to the north of 'La Bustle', in 'Mash Valley', they were overlooked by one of the Germans' clever use of natural inclines. The enemy defences at La Boisselle tapered almost to a point towards the British lines, which were only 50 or so yards away, and this salient became known as the 'Glory Hole'. To the north, this trench system then suddenly turned at ninety degrees and followed the edge of the slope up to Ovillers before it levelled out once more, with the result that any infantrymen advancing up 'Mash Valley' would be subjected to fire from the front as well as one of the flanks. (This gruesome predicament was exacerbated in nearby 'Sausage Valley', where, instead of an exposed German strong-point jutting out into No Man's Land, the formidable 'Sausage Redoubt' was situated in an inverted 'V', ensuring any attack could be repelled from *three* angles, funnelling the unfortunate soldiers into a narrower and narrower zone of death.)

Raids were carried out by both sides, and on one occasion, a German prisoner revealed a night-sortie was imminent on the trenches held by the 2nd Devons, which then placed further coils of barbed wire beyond the parapets as a consequence. The insurgents never came. Successful operations under cover of darkness which *did* take place often resulted in an angry retaliation by the enemy's artillery; persuasive reminders that the upper hand was not to be gained in perpetuity.

Away from the forward positions, the menial tasks of digging, carrying and constructing went on in between training for the actual assault itself. On June 13th, the 2nd Devons held a memorial service in respect of the late Lord Kitchener, and after receiving a draft of forty-eight new soldiers three days later, moved back to the firing line on the 17th, where the battalion was soon targeted by German shells. One man was killed and a further four wounded, but all the material required for the forthcoming assault still had to transported by hand, and amidst the barrage this work continued, as it did the following day when an estimated sixty bombs came over at regular intervals. Sgt Bellingham, another Old Boy of Truro, wrote a letter which was later published in the College magazine:

'Our work consists of repairing trenches, which at times is extremely dangerous, especially when the first-line trenches have been heavily bombarded and badly torn up. Besides repairing the trenches we have to remove the dead and bury them. Our work is done mostly in the morning, starting at 2 a.m., and finishing about 10 a.m. The house I am in is fairly decent; of course, like the rest there is plenty of fresh air, as the windows and doors and parts of the roof are gone …'[7]

In the War Diary of the 1/2nd Monmouthshire Regiment – a Pioneer unit of the 29th Division at Beaumont Hamel – thirty-eight points of note were recorded across six pages in the lead-up to the assault. Number 38 is marked 'Secrecy', and points out the consequences brought about by improper discussion of information, adding this '… may endanger the success of operations and cost the lives of many comrades'[8] if ignored. With the Royal Artillery priming their big guns along many miles of the Somme Front, one secret was about to be revealed.

4

The Final Ten Days: Cornishmen Amongst the Wounded

Amongst the 'War Items' of the *West Briton* newspaper during July 1916, was a reference to: 'Lieut. J.A. Reeves, 12th London Regt., son of the late rector of Tregoney, was wounded in the recent advance in France'. The 12th Londons were also known as the 'Rangers', and were part of the 56th (London) Division at Gommecourt, in the north of the line. A territorial unit, the Rangers had been in France since December 1914, joining the 56th Division in February 1916.

The 1901 Census reveals sixty-one-year-old John Fry Reeves as a Church of England clergyman in Tregony (between St Austell and Truro, on the River Fal), along with his thirty-five-year-old wife, Edith, and their son, John Arthur, who was five. Both of the latter had been born in the village, and John junior went to attend Bristol's Clifton College (1911–1914) before he received an officer's commission two months after war broke out. By July 1915, John Arthur Ramsay Reeves was a full Lieutenant, and proceeded to France the following month, although the Somme offensive would be the battalion's first taste of heavy combat just under a year later. The officer's service record[1], held at the National Archives in Kew, reveals he was born in 1895, and he left his occupation as a 'transport carrier' to join the army. Promoted to captain (according to his records) on 1 June 1916, he stated he had carried out the duties of Battalion Transport Officer for ten months prior to receiving his injuries in action, which were indicated to have been a gunshot wound to his leg inflicted at Hebuterne on 21 June. (Hebuterne was a small village in British hands close to Gommecourt, and today contains many Commonwealth graves of those who fell in the area during 1916. At midday on the 20th, the Rangers took over a stretch of support line trenches, with several Companies employed as working parties until 10 a.m. the following day, when the men marched to Halloy. Lt Reeves' injury is not mentioned in the Battalion War Diary.) The date of Reeves' return to the UK is given as 1 July 1916 – the same day as his comrades went into battle at Gommecourt – but the stricken officer could only glean scant information from his hospital bed as to the welfare of familiar faces on the Somme. Attending a Medical Board at Priory Road, Clifton, it was noted that '… the patient gets about on crutches', and he was not passed fit to return to France until the following year.

Appointed to the King's African Rifles in July 1918, Reeves served in Africa from September 1918 until October 1919, whereupon he returned to a Western Europe now free from war. Remaining with the KAR until July 1920, he relinquished his affiliations with his original unit, the Rangers, by informing the War Office: '… my future work will not lead me anywhere near London … I shall not be able to carry out my duties as an officer in the battalion.' By this time he was living at Pensford vicarage, near Bristol, and returned to civilian life.

THE ROLE OF THE ARTILLERY

On 24 June, the British gunners finally began their heavy and concentrated bombardment of the German lines, heralding to the defenders – at long last – that the infantry attack was only a matter of days away. Each morning, an eighty minute barrage was launched, but this was to be reduced to sixty-five minutes on 'Z' day, when it was assumed the enemy would be expecting a further fifteen minute salvo before the inevitable advance. Throughout the rest of the daylight hours, a regular timing of shells would mean there was no let-up for the Germans, and even at night, the artillery and British machine-gunners interspersed their firepower for maximum disruption across No Man's Land. Whilst the forward positions were the most obvious target to destroy, communication lines and reserve sectors were also focused upon, ensuring that the entire German defensive system was under threat of relentless destruction.

For the assault to succeed, the shelling had to achieve two very distinct aims; namely, the annihilation of the defenders whose machine-guns were primed and ready, plus the dismantling of the forests of barbed wire in front of the enemy parapets. These entanglements often consisted of two belts, 40 yards broad, held together by iron stakes, and were virtually impenetrable to an attacking force – a sign, once again, of the Germans' contentedness to sit back and wait for the Allies to make the decisive moves on the Somme. The removal of the latter obstacle could only be attempted by specially made shells, as vast teams of soldiers with wire cutters would be required to hack their way through the wire – each strand was as thick as a man's finger – even before the attentions of enemy machine-gunners and snipers were taken into consideration. Such large-scale operations would inevitably lead to slaughter, and so bombs loaded with shrapnel and fixed to a timer were developed, tasked with exploding over the entanglements and ripping significant paths through the razor-sharp coils if deployed in sufficient numbers. The setting of the fuse was crucial, however, and many did not detonate at the correct point, leaving the inanimate metal guards in front of the German trenches in varying degrees of completeness. In some parts of the line, there *was* success, but not of a proportion to ease the anxiety of the observers who could see what was happening – and what was not – through their binoculars.

Dud shells were another crucial problem, which was not realised until it was too late. Although night raids were sent across No Man's Land to assess the damage all along the Front, only the state of the enemy's forward trenches could be ascertained with any great clarity. As the German communication and reserve lines could not even be seen from the British positions, the columns of black smoke which rose into the air were the only indication that targets further back might be in a state of disarray. The spotter planes of the Royal Flying Corps could not get close enough to the ground to see that thousands of unexploded shells had thudded harmlessly into the soil, but one fact *was* abundantly clear – not many Germans could be seen in any great numbers once the barrage was underway. A telegram from Berlin was obtained by the Associated Press and published widely in the British newspapers under the heading 'HAVOC OF ALLIED GUNS', giving a German officer's account of the artillery cavalcade he had to endure in the final days of June. Situated 'close to the Somme', he was actually opposite the French positions to the south of the river, but the article was intended as an example of the *joint* endeavours and successes of the Allied cause:

> The second day's bombardment … brought [a] surprise in the shape of aerial mines of unheard of calibre and thrown in incredible numbers. The explosion of the first of these air torpedoes caused such a tremendous detonation that the windows of our bomb-proofs were shattered and a massive pillar of black earth was thrown up perhaps 100 yards into the air. This showered the whole neighbourhood with turfs, bricks and earth. It was a regular eruption of Vesuvius … The entrances of two bomb-proof shelters were buried within a few minutes, and the inmates had to be dug out. A few minutes later an orderly who had been sent with a message to the left of the company returned with the report that the trench had been completely levelled. Going to verify this, I saw as far as the eye could reach, crater after crater each about 6ft. deep. The earth in between was thrown up in a wild, high-heaped chaos of trench timbers and wire entanglements. Nine months' work, day and night, had been destroyed in a few minutes[2]

This destruction was also being wrought by the British guns, but the 'heavies' which were required to collapse the deepest enemy dug-outs were in short supply amongst the Royal Artillery, and its men instead had to rely mainly upon the medium-sized shells and howitzers. These, inevitably, did not cause the type of devastation created by the French, and although the Germans were *undoubtedly* suffering at the hands of the British shells, most were hidden away in their bunkers, along with their machine-guns and rifles, waiting for the moment of retribution. Each failed attempt to bring men, supplies and food up from the reserves strengthened the resolve of those who were currently pinned down underground to unleash a fury of inhuman proportions when the time came. Their wait was soon to be over.

At Fricourt, in the south of the line, the 96th Brigade of the Royal Field Artillery was issued with its final orders for the offensive. One of its officers was Lt Arthur Colmer, who had family links with Liskeard and Newquay in Cornwall. His Battery was informed of a number of key points, including the necessity for bringing a heavy fire upon the enemy lines about to be attacked, the lesser harassment of objectives in the rear, the attention to communication trenches, the gradual lifting of a barrage when the infantry went over, plus '… woods and hollows beyond the actual line laid down should [also] be searched'.[3]

Battery Commanders (BCs) were ordered to remain in their Observation Posts on the day of the assault, and use their discretion if they considered it necessary to deviate from the targets which had already been issued to them. This might involve fire being directed upon an enemy strongpoint which was holding up the assault, or the sudden launch of a German counter-attack. The BCs were also permitted to go forward after the consolidation of a line, provided he did not lose touch with his Battery or Brigade Commander via telephones, which were carried by soldiers trailing the communication wire behind them. Three days' rations were to be issued to each Battery, which were to be harnessed up and 'ready to move at short notice' on 'Z' Day. 'Arrangements will also be made for a supply of drinking water.'[4]

Close by was the 6th Siege Battery of the Royal Garrison Artillery, which was at one time commanded by Colonel David Logan, CB, CMG, who lived at Woodlane Crescent, in Falmouth. (His son, a Second Lieutenant in the 2nd Border Regiment, was serving in the same Brigade as the 8th and 9th Devons by the end of June, a few miles away at Mametz.) The Battery's War Diary notes:

23 June. Register[ed] several strong points with aeroplanes with satisfactory results.
June 24th. Demonstration with gas.
June 25th. Fire all day at counter battery work – assisted by aeroplane observation. 650 rounds fired.
June 26th. Bombed trenches all day and fire all through night. 760 rounds fired by day and 360 by night.
June 28th. Bombardment … continues. 297 rounds fired.[5]

2nd Lt F.E. Gilpin, of the Royal Field Artillery, and former pupil at Truro College, wrote to remind his place of education that the cavalcade in war was not all one-sided:

We have had rather a rough time ourselves of late, and it is rather marvellous that I am alive today. Fritz has destroyed my splinter-proof dug-out by dropping an 8in. armour piercing shell on the roof, which was only 6in. deep and made of clay and sheet-iron. I'm pleased to say I was not there when that one fell, although I was in it when a previous shell came 5 yards away … [We] scrambled out after having been rattled like army biscuits in a biscuit tin! The blast of the explosion blew out the candle and threw it with a smack on to my face. The other poor fellow just out from England was scared terribly, and, as Tito Tregea would say, he was 'tremblin' like a leaf! I was badly frightened myself … I rescued several things which had been hurled about in all directions, but I had not much except what I was wearing at the time …[6]

The 63rd Company of the Machine Gun Corps was part of the 21st Division at Fricourt, and it too, had Cornish connections. Lt Edward Boultbee had married Gertrude Bolitho – the daughter of the late Colonel Otho Bolitho, of Kenegie near Penzance, in 1915 – although the officer was now a widower after the unfortunate death of his spouse from the effects of appendicitis just a few months earlier.

At La Neuville on 24 June, the attack was practiced in what was described as a '… very successful day', whilst 'Brigade sport' was also arranged. The 25th was punctuated '… by the timely arrival of many spare parts', whereupon the 26th saw the Company leaving for Ville at 9.30 p.m. The next two days are marked by two very significant entries – 'heavy rain'[7] is repeated for both the 27th and 28th, casting serious doubt over the plans for the general attack which was still set for 7.30 a.m. on the 29th. A review took place at 11 a.m. the day before, when it was decided to postpone the assault for forty-eight hours due to the roads and trenches becoming saturated during the recent summer storms. (It is interesting to note that some of these new roads, constructed across fields to allow the troops and horses an easier passage to the front lines, were sometimes built using stone from as far away as Cornwall, as the natural materials in the immediate or wider vicinity were simply not to hand.) This new timetable had obvious repercussions and logistical headaches, not least for the artillerymen, who had nearly expended their quota of shells according to the plan of attack, but it was also a huge burden for the infantrymen, waiting for the order to 'go' for weeks only to be told at the last moment there would be another delay. Thousands of men were pressing onwards from the reserves into the communication lines, and finally up to the forward trenches in a carefully controlled flow, yet all this would now have to be changed. Sgt Cook, of the 1st Somersets, wrote in his diary on 26 June as two of his Companies went up into position: 'The attack is summoned to commence on morning of 28th' [he was one day out], whereas on the 28th itself – the day of the actual postponement – he added:

> Owing to heavy rain the attack has been delayed until 1 July. The brigade attacks on a three company frontage; two platoons in front and two in support. My platoon to be one of the leading platoons.[8]

2nd Lt 'Charlie' Watson, of the 1st East Lancashires (serving in the same 11th Brigade as the 1st Somersets) recorded on June 28th: 'The camp is alive with excitement, and everyone is perfectly confident … The rain is coming down in torrents, which is a great drawback.' In the early hours of the 29th, he added: 'The attack put off; go into the trenches now, and show starts in about a day. Goodbye. Charlie'. A South African of Cornish descent, 2nd Lt Watson was a former pupil of Rondebosch High School, in Cape Town, which today still maintains a number of the officer's last letters home before he went into the attack on 1 July. One such reveals:

> I am in my tent with a light afforded by the means of a candle stuck in a bottle. Without, the sky is one great illuminated area caused by the firing of hundreds of guns … These trenches are crowded with rats … It is hard to realise July is nearly here, and the trenches still knee deep in mud and water. I am covered in mud; there is no such thing as changing. One sleeps and lives in the same things all the time in the trenches …

THE INFANTRY PREPARES

With the artillery now well underway in their task of obliterating the German positions, attention was turned to the men who would follow up the attack by occupying the supposedly empty trenches – or what was left of the battered defences. The stipulations for 'Dress and Equipment' give an unquestionable reminder that it was firmly believed this task would be simple – at 7.30 a.m. the infantry walks across No Man's Land unopposed and sets to work consolidating the newly captured lines before moving on to the next one:

> Each man will carry Rifle and Equipment, 120 Rounds S.A.A. [small arms ammunition], Iron Ration and Rations for 'Z' Day, two Sandbags in Belt, Steel Helmet if received, Smoke Helmets in satchel, Water Bottle and Haversack (Mess Tin inside) on the back. Field Dressing and Identity Disc, one Pick or one Shovel. Water-proof sheet to be taken. Packs and Greatcoats are not to be taken to the 'forming up area'. Bayonets will be sharpened. All men carrying Wire-cutters will have a white label fastened on their back – marked W … Battalion Grenadiers will carry Equipment less packs, Rifles slung and fifty rounds S.A.A. with ten Grenades, Carriers each carry two Buckets, holding ten Grenades in each.[9]

This cumbersome array of articles meant that a swift advance was impossible, and any evasive action required to dodge a sudden burst of machine-gun fire would be difficult in the extreme. (This became a major criticism of the first day, as unencumbered assault troops were not deployed in enough strength, thus denying the precious ally of speed in the attack.) Notes of caution *were* raised beforehand, however, but the general assumption was that crossing the exposed ground between the two front-line trenches would not pose any serious problems:

> The Bosche delivers small counter attacks with platoons or Companies immediately hostile troops gain their objectives. These small counter attacks have had far reaching results and must be specially guarded against. To meet these [eventualities] the Reserves in the hands of Platoon and [Company] Commanders will be of the greatest value.[10]

Such attacks were to be '… met with rapid rifle fire and machine-gun fire',[11] whilst any strong-points which were encountered '… must be rushed without hesitation from front and flanks under cover of rifle grenades and smoke bombs if necessary'.[12] Larger redoubts which still held out passed to the responsibility of Battalion HQ and were dealt with as the senior officers saw fit, backed up by the two Stokes Guns which had been specifically allocated for this task. In addition, it was advised: 'All Commanders must take necessary action to avoid surprise and all ranks must be on their guard against treachery by the enemy, especially mis use [sic] of the White Flag.'[13]

Capt. Savage, of the 1st Northamptons, had been a victim of this 'treachery' back in September, 1914 [see Chapter Two]. Another example of these underhand tactics of close-quarter fighting came via Capt. W.J. Gilpin, the brother of Lt F. Gilpin – both of whom attended Truro College – who wrote a letter to his old school telling his former teachers of how he had witnessed a successful French attack on German lines during 1916. He went on:

> The next pleasing spectacle was to see about 100 Huns, in batches of twenty, doubling towards us out of the smoke with their hands in the air, continually coming croppers over bits of barbed wire and shell holes. It is not an easy job to run about a mile with one's hands above one's head over the ground to which a ploughed field would be a lawn. In this type of warfare both hands *must* stay up – any indication of their coming down and the man would be shot or bayoneted without compunction, for the hand that drops may be after a hidden bomb or revolver, and one takes no chances.[14]

It was not uncommon for German defenders under severe threat of being overrun to call out in English 'Retreat!' or 'Retire!' in the hope that this false order would be spread along the line. On 1 July, this occurred on a number of verified occasions, and even before the British went into battle, the men were told that these two words would *not* be called out under any circumstances.

As it transpired, many forward-most troops *were* compelled to fall back, but only after consolidation was impossible, and generally the orders were issued quietly to the senior men in the vicinity who then gave their own instructions accordingly.

Any prisoners secured on 1 July were to be 'immediately disarmed', and taken under escort – one soldier to ten POWs – to the rear, with officers and other ranks kept apart. It was the job of the guards – possibly those 'slightly wounded' in the attack but still able to walk – to ensure that captives did not destroy vital documents in their possession. They were also to be marched across the open and not down the communication trenches which would be used to guide reserves up to the firing line.

With regard to casualties during combat, the measures which were put in place prior to the battle can be seen today, with hindsight, as astonishingly inadequate. Assault troops were told that under no circumstances were they to stop and assist an injured comrade. 'All ranks are reminded that the care of the wounded is the duty of the [regimental] Stretcher-Bearers and the Field Ambulances. Fighting [soldiers] are forbidden to accompany wounded men to the dressing Stations'[15]. This, of course, went against the strong sense of camaraderie and friendship which had been built up over the months and years amongst recruits whose associations went a long way back, but sentiment had no place in the modern army. They had a job to do, and were expected to do it without a thought for those who had fallen.

For the 6th Northamptons, situated between Mametz and Montauban in the south of the line, their 'Medical Arrangements' consisted of accommodation for 200 stretcher cases in a number of dugouts near Carnoy, plus similar provision for fifty 'walking wounded' at Bronfay Farm. Troops were told to familiarise themselves with the location of Regimental Aid Posts (RAPs), and in addition received the assurance that those who were incapacitated in enemy lines would be collected by their Regimental Medical Officers. 'Eight stretchers per Battalion'[16] were at the disposal of the authorities, as well as double that number stored near each RAP.

By the end of 1 July 1916 no fewer than thirty-two of the battalions which had gone into the attack had suffered more than 500 casualties *each* – dead, injured or missing. The provision of a mere eight battalion stretchers may seem derisory to us today, yet once again here is an indication of how confidence in the efficiency of the British artillery barrage was unremitting.

The various stages of caring for those who had been stricken on the battlefield is worth considering in a little more detail. The Regimental Aid Posts mentioned in the War Diary provided the first instance for a wounded man to seek medical assistance. Brought here by comrades in a similar state, or on his own initiative, the administering of appropriate medicine or bandaging of an incapacitated Tommy could begin, although facilities and suitable equipment were often rudimentary. An Advanced Dressing Station was situated as close to the front line as was feasible, and took in the more seriously disabled patients, whilst the Field Ambulances and Casualty Clearing Stations further back were staffed by doctors, surgeons and nurses. All worked tirelessly under extreme and gruesome conditions, often subjected to shell-fire and the ever present danger of battle. Approximately 100 female nursing staff received Military Medals for gallantry during the First World War, with one citation reading: 'For conspicuous coolness and devotion to duty when supervising the transfer of patients from a Casualty Clearing Station to an Ambulance Train while the locality of the [CCS] was being shelled. She set a splendid example of calmness and composure'[17]

There were various modes of transport in position to ferry the wounded away from the front line, and the severity of their injuries was taken into consideration when assessing how far they needed to be taken. For those who had 'only' received a bullet or shrapnel wound to a non life-threatening part of their body, a quick 'patching up' may be all that they received in the way of medical attention for some days, whilst the much more serious cases – those who had lost limbs, had their stomach ripped out by an explosion, or their face shot away by machine-gun fire – were given obvious priority. If and when an individual was deemed fit enough to travel longer distances, he was dubbed a 'Blighty Wound' and sent back across the Channel on one of the numerous hospital ships which ferried endlessly back and forth between the French and English coasts. (The plight of the wounded from a Cornish perspective during and immediately after 1 July is enlarged upon in Chapter Thirteen.)

Further edicts were passed on to the troops now assembling for the attack:

> Any stranger in uniform must be detained and sent under escort to Battalion HQ. There will probably be many cases of Germans dressed in English uniforms of private soldiers.
>
> Rum will be issued to all ranks actually engaged in the [advance] … No indiscriminate issue will be allowed, and issues must be made in presence of an officer …
>
> CASUALTY REPORTS must be rendered to Battalion HQ … estimated casualties … Officers … O.R. [other ranks] …[18]

The 9th Devons started the month of June 1916, by undergoing training, practicing bomb throwing and digging cable trenches. An inspection of arms, equipment and clothing took place on the 26th, as well as further physical exertions and drill, whilst packs were deposited at the Divisional Store. The strength comprised twenty-two officers and 753 ORs, and it was then decided who should remain behind in reserve – a common practice before a major assault to ensure that soldiers with an intimate knowledge of the battalion's activities could continue them in the event of heavy casualties to their comrades. Those detailed to attack were informed that gaps in the British wire would be cut to allow them access to No Man's Land, and they were also told that a '… very heavy bombardment of the hostile trenches by guns and mortars of all calibre will take place for one day previous to the [attack].[19] Four successive lines of four platoons each would lead the way, accompanied by bombing teams, Stokes guns and carrying parties .

> Should some parts of the assaulting line be held up, the remainder will render them the best assistance by advancing to their objective. The flanks so exposed must however be specially guarded until these parts which have been held up have come into the line … The position of the assaulting troops will be denoted by smoke candles and flares.[20]

[These would also be used to signal when the objective was reached. Mirrors glinting in the sunlight were another form of communication, although in the confusion of combat, these could be mistaken for any form of flashing metal.]

In one Reserve Dump sat 94,000 rounds of ammunition, 5,000 for the Lewis guns, 2,000 Mills grenades, plus 100 petrol tins full of water and 2,300 tins of preserved meat. During the march to the assembly trenches, the '… water in water bottles will not be drunk under any circumstances'[21], although liquid refreshment and mugs would be provided at various halts along the way. Finally, 'mopping up sections' were sorted out to inspect each captured enemy trench after it had been passed over by the infantry, the concern being reiterated that hidden Germans could emerge from dug-outs and fire into the backs of the advancing troops.

NIGHT PATROLS

On 5 June, men of the 1/4th Battalion of the London Regiment practiced an attack on trenches which had been constructed to represent the systems opposite the sector held by the 56th. (London) Division at Gommecourt. Two days later, the troops were inspected by the Third Army Commander, Gen. Sir Edmund Allenby, KCB, and other senior officers, with the rest of the month spent preparing for the attack. By the 27th, the 1/4th was in the front line near Hebuterne, and when the British bombardment had eased for the day from 7.45 p.m., two patrols were sent out to reconnoitre and report back on the state of the German forward positions and associated wire. Just after midnight, the men returned with samples of the entanglement, but added they had been unable to penetrate beyond the parapets. Shortly afterwards, an enemy barrage opened up, accompanied by regular bursts of machine-gun fire, and the battalion's Trench Mortar batteries came in for some uncomfortable attention.

The same process was repeated the following evening, and one of the British patrols peered over the lip of the German lines, expecting to see it deserted, but instead discovered a party of soldiers engaged in digging duties. After a short fire-fight, the enemy sent up flares which exposed the attackers in the darkness, compelling the latter to swiftly retire, and an exchange of shells ensued. At 6 p.m. on the 29th, yet another sortie arranged by the 1/4th Londons brought back some disturbing news: 'For over 100 yards north of [the Bucquoy] Road the wire was insufficiently damaged to allow free passage of infantry.'[22] Rockets were then sent up, as well as '... more than the usual number of Very lights', and the British were even treated to a demonstration involving a searchlight which was reckoned to be '... some distance behind the enemy line'.[23]

The final entry for June notes:

> ... generally the enemy artillery became very active as the day progressed – machine-guns were also more active than of late. After holding the line for the three preceding nights and suffering many casualties, the Battalion was formed up tonight in its allotted assembly areas in readiness for the advance ordered tomorrow.[24]

This sequence of events proved many points of fact. Firstly, the German presence in their own trenches had not been decimated, as had been expected, and in between the British barrage there were still enough men to carry out repairs on the damaged parapets. Secondly, the scope for swift and accurate retaliation using flares, bombs and machine-guns was still wide, as proved by the 1/4th Londons' casualty figures for this period – at least three dead and over fifty wounded. Thirdly, the wire had been confirmed to be 'insufficiently cut' along a significant length of the system about to be attacked, and with only one more full day before the assault, this situation was unlikely to change. (It must also be remembered that the Royal Artillery had not reckoned on an extra forty-eight hours of shelling due to the last minute postponement, and had to 'ration' their dwindling supplies accordingly.) Finally, and defiantly, the Germans were actually *increasing* their fire-power in the last few days, predicting that the British infantry would not be held back much longer. It was a worrying state of affairs.

(Along the entire stretch of the Front, similar raids were being carried out, with varying degrees of success. Some did, indeed, find the enemy trenches obliterated, wire destroyed and defenders absent, but other Tommies were attacked with great ferocity before they had even reached anywhere near their objective, whilst those who did were alarmed to find the entanglements still as grotesquely impassable as before. All reports were directed to their respective Battalion Headquarters before being collated for the higher command. Even senior officers are known to have expressed their doubts about the efficiency of the British artillery *before* the general advance; notably Lt-Col E.T.F. Sandys, the CO of the 2nd Middlesex (in the same Brigade as the 2nd Devons), opposite the 750-yard-long 'Mash Valley' at La Boisselle, and Lt-Col E.K. Cordeaux, in command of the 10th Lincolns (the 'Grimsby Chums') at the nearby 'Sausage Valley'. Both men carefully observed where the British shells were landing in their respective sectors, and both came to the same conclusion – the wire was not being cut, and the Germans were sheltering underground, mainly out of harm's way. This was on the very axis of the British attack – the Albert-Bapaume road – but any negative intelligence at this late stage was not welcomed by the General Staff. Sandys and Cordeaux feared a slaughter. They were to be proved right.)

In early July 1916, the *West Briton* revealed in its references to the conflict:

> Mrs E. Williams, St Clement's Cottages, Truro, received [notification] from the War Office yesterday that her second son, Pte A.G. Williams (23), 4th London Regt, was wounded in action on the 29th of June. Pte Williams left a good situation as manager of a cotton plantation in America to enlist about seven months ago. He had been in America about three years.

Both Tregony-born Lt Reeves, of the 12th London Regiment, and Pte Williams would miss the attack on Gommecourt due to injuries received in the build-up. By nightfall on 1 July, more than 200 of their comrades in both battalions – which by coincidence were in the same 168th Brigade – would be dead. The Germans, generally still holding the higher ground, and hiding in deep bunkers well out of sight, were grimly waiting. No Man's Land lay open and exposed (a consequence of the gently rolling chalk landscape and the incalculable bomb blasts), soon to be trodden down by lines of British infantry who had been told to expect no opposition.

To the south of Gommecourt, near Serre, 2nd Lt Watson, 1st East Lancashires, and Sgt Cook, 1st Somersets, added their own personal thoughts to the final hours of June: 'Another day has dawned, and with a bit of luck it may keep fine', the officer informed his parents. (On their way up to the trenches, the Lancashire men had been subjected to an enemy cannonade which blew several men 'to atoms'. Prior to this, 'Charlie' Watson had sat in a dug-out, with a tablecloth made out of newspaper, waiting for his supper which consisted of 'ham, bread, butter, biscuits and tea', and told his family: 'Outside, bullets, etc., are flying all over the place; fancy, this din has being going on for almost two years. However, I do not expect it will last much longer.')

'The [British] bombardment was very intense all last night and throughout the day [29/30 June]', noted the NCO, who was ordered to leave his non-essential kit behind, along with his cap badge and numerals. 'The men are in excellent spirits and full of hope for the morrow, it is such a change from lying in a trench and taking everything without being able to hit back.' The forward positions were reached at midnight, whereupon ladders and bridges were put into position in readiness for the attack at 7.30 a.m. Just after dawn on 1 July, breakfast was taken, and the Sergeant noticed:

> It is a lovely morning and the birds are singing.[25]

5

1 July 1916: Newspaper Reports and Personal Thoughts

Before moving on to reveal the men from Cornwall who lost their lives on 1 July 1916, the manner in which the attack was reported back home is worthy of mention alongside Sgt Cook's horrific narrative of the same events as they unfolded before his eyes, as well as a private letter of 2nd Lt 'Charlie' Watson. As has been established, the media maintained a positive angle on the Somme campaign even when it was clear that the expected breakthrough had not occurred, carefully concealing the anguish and suffering beneath tales of gallantry, pride and devotion to duty. The *Falmouth Packet* announced in early July:

> The British and French commenced a combined offensive north and south of the River Somme on Saturday, and a desperate battle is still raging. The enemy have been for nearly two years in possession of the ground, and have made every village a fortress and every 100 yards a redoubt.

The report noted that the British, who were withstanding violent counter-attacks, were making slower progress than the French on their right flank, but overall, the results were encouraging.

Other headlines adopted a much less cautious approach. 'GERMANY IN A VICE', 'VIGOROUS ATTACKS ON THE SOMME', and 'FUTILE GERMAN COUNTER ATTACKS' all seemed to herald the imminence of a stunning Allied victory. The French reports suggested that by 9 a.m. on the 1st, the advanced defences of the German lines had fallen, and that nightfall had seen a two kilometre thrust into enemy territory consolidated along a forty kilometre front. Thousands of German prisoners had been taken, according to information released by the War Office, and the general feeling was: '… the first day of the offensive is therefore very satisfactory.'[1] Even though the huge number of casualties was not known until later, it was clearly not in the interests of those in the know to reveal that a monumental loss of life may have taken place in such a short space of time, and the newspapers could only print the information they had been given by official sources. More sober facts *were* communicated to the general public, although these were often tucked away behind the more brash statements written in bolder letters. Officers admitted that the Germans had not been taken by surprise, as was suggested in some quarters, and statements from enemy prisoners indicated the exact date *and time* of the assault was known beforehand. 'The men in the [German] Front trenches were everywhere ordered to hold out to the death,'[2] revealed one source, which added that ammunition supplied from their rear was 'plentiful'.

This view contained the subtle clues that the assault had met with heavy resistance, and when the daily casualty rates began to take up more and more column inches, the dreadful truth gradually dawned. A human disaster had taken place across the Channel.

South African 2nd Lt Watson, whose grandmother still lived in Newquay, wrote to his parents in the final days of June:

> I am finding it extremely difficult to start this letter; it is beyond my power to express on paper my inward feelings at this present moment … At last the day is drawing nigh for the 'Great Advance' which

Drawing of Drummer Ritchie sounding the 'charge'.

everybody has patiently awaited. The Hun is now to realise what the Might of the British Nation is – the greatest in the world … We go into the trenches tomorrow night, and open the attack the following morning. Never has the world witnessed such a battle as is now to commence. I cannot express how happy I am at having the privilege of being in the front line, thus starting the attack along with seven other officers of the battalion [1st East Lancashires]. I feel perfectly content to die, because I know I have performed my duty; a man cannot do more than his duty. My mind is now drifting back to the days at home, and I now realise what the love of parents is. I can picture you now praying for your two sons who are fighting to keep their parents and home safe … In after years, when you read the history of the 'Great Advance', remember that your eldest son laid down his life in perfect happiness, so as to enable his beloved parents to live in freedom.

Your loving son, Charlie

Sgt Cook's observations of the final minutes before the advance were full of optimism:

The bombardment is now terrific, the German lines are one cloud of smoke that it seems impossible for anyone to live in such a hell, it's a wonderful sight. We were able to stand on the parapet to get a better view, there is not a sign of life in front and no response from the German artillery.

Reference is then made to the exploding of a mine at 7.20 a.m. This was the infamous Hawthorn Mine near Beaumont Hamel, which blew a German redoubt into the sky ten minutes prior to the main assault, sending shock-waves across the surrounding area which literally knocked British soldiers off their feet. (The impact of the timing of the explosion is focused upon in a little more detail in Chapter Eleven.) At 7.30 a.m., whistles were blown along the entire line, and Cook continued:

Troops could be seen advancing in perfect skirmishing order as far as the eye could see, left and right. What a sight it was to watch, everything going smoothly with no resistance, the first line had nearly reached the German front line when all at once, machine-guns opened up with terrific murderous fire. Our men were timed to advance ten minutes after the R.B.s [Rifle Brigade], but so eager were they to get on, that they left soon after the R.B.s and consequently were caught in the open by their guns …

Subjected to fire from both flanks, Sgt Cook recalled: '… men are falling just like skittles', soon losing his officer, 2nd Lt Tilley, and platoon Sergeant, leaving the writer of the account as the senior soldier of his unit within just five minutes of the 'off'. The devastating cavalcade forced the survivors to veer to the left, as the advance was unable to continue frontally to its objective, and with the exposed ground swept by bullets, it was declared to be 'absolutely impassable'. This change of direction did enable the leading troops to enter the German front lines and towards the second, but Cook grimaced: 'The ground is littered with our dead.' Sudden enfilade fire from the right was '… playing havoc with us all, it is terrible', yet a small consolation to the sergeant was the obvious destruction wrought by the British guns in the previous week. He soon realised, however, that most of the defenders had been sheltering in the deep underground bunkers which were now being searched by the Somersets. 'There is scarcely a square foot of ground that has not been churned up by shells', and although large gaps had been blasted through the wire entanglements, '… the dug-outs are practically safe. These were a revelation to us, being most elaborately made and down about 30ft'. Clearing parties were sent into each one, and grenade-throwing Germans were often encountered. 'Some surrendered,' Sgt Cook recorded, 'others went under from their own guns'.

The Somersets were now held up, deep in enemy territory. 'It is impossible to get any further, it is said some reached their objective and are now cut off from us.' Col Hopkins of the Seaforth Highlanders was the only officer in the vicinity, and he gave words of encouragement to the men, but an order to 'retire' was apparently issued (origin unknown), causing a number of soldiers from all battalions to begin drifting back to their own lines. Realising the serious nature of the situation, Drummer Ritchie, of the Seaforths, stood on the parapet of an enemy trench under heavy machine-gun fire and repeatedly sounded the 'Charge', rallying the troops at a critical moment. This courageous act, witnessed by Cook, resulted in Ritchie receiving a VC.

Returning to matters in his immediate area, the Somersets' NCO observed:

I have never seen so many dead in such a small area before. In places where enfilade fire caught them they are three or four on top of each other. The shell holes are full of wounded and no hopes of getting them back. It is extraordinary the positions several men died in. I slipped into a shell hole and in getting out saw a man sitting up apparently doing his puttees up. I entered into conversation with him and was getting annoyed at no reply, he was dead. Shortly afterwards I was walking on the edge of a shell hole and saw a man sitting on the edge … I told him to get up and come along, again no reply … he was dead.

As the advance faltered, German counter-attacks began, forcing the British to collect bombs from the dead and wounded which enabled them to hold out where they were for the next two to three hours until the supply ran out. 'The sight of some of the dead is ghastly. Men are being knocked down one minute with a bullet and the next minute blown to pieces by a shell. We all seem to see a similar fate in store for us … Life more fit for devils than human beings'. A 'terrible thirst' was caused by the shell fumes and battle stress, with the wounded 'crying out' for water. 'The sight is terrible … I can see very few of the battalion here, only one here or there'. Retiring to the German front line, the remainder of the Somersets tried to consolidate their precarious position by building a barricade at either end, but the enemy soon surrounded them in a 'grim duel' until darkness fell, when shells began to fall amongst the exhausted soldiers. Finally relieved at 11 p.m., the dwindling band began their retirement back across No Man's Land, still subjected to the attentions of a German barrage, with Sgt Cook jumping from shell hole to shell hole and falling '… headlong over dead bodies and barbed wire, my clothes were being torn to ribbons. I thought I should never reach our trenches, and when I did I fell sprawling into it'

Challenged by a British sentry, Sgt Cook convinced the guard he was one of the returning Somersets. The NCO could only locate about a dozen of his comrades, and the exhausted group was withdrawn to Mailly at 3.30 p.m. on the 2nd '… absolutely beat to the world'. Cook would later realise: 'No officers have returned [and] only seven Sergeants have survived'. With casualty figures amongst his pals topping 450, the Sergeant's final diary for 1 July read: 'We had had our belly-full of war for one day.'[3]

6

30th and 18th Divisions

On 5 September 1916, Pte J.P. King, of the 18th King's Liverpool Regiment (and an Old Boy of Truro College), wrote:

> It is almost a year now since we landed in France, and I can assure you we have had some exciting times. We were in the thick of it on 1 July. It was a great day, and we fairly made a name for ourselves, but I am sorry to say we lost a good many of our lads …[1]

Starting in the south of the line, close to the banks of the River Somme, the fortunes of Cornishmen can now be charted Division by Division on 1 July 1916 (see map, overleaf). The 30th comprised mainly of Pals battalions from Liverpool and Manchester, and their objectives were, initially, the Glatz Redoubt, followed by the fortified village of Montauban. With the artillery bombardment successfully cutting the German wire, the leading units – including Pte King and his 18th King's – advanced at 7.30 a.m., reaching the enemy lines within fifteen minutes. Most of the defenders were still in their dug-outs, and little resistance was encountered, but enfilading machine-gun fire began to harass the supports which were now crossing No Man's Land, whilst German bombers were about to cause problems in the maze of trenches.

At 8.30 a.m., the 2nd Royal Scots Fusiliers set off to march the 1,000 yards between its position to the rear and the British forward system before following in the footsteps of the Liverpool and Manchester men. The Fusiliers' left flank received hostile attentions, causing a few casualties, although the bulk of the battalion pressed on towards Montauban as the units around them dealt with the immediate vicinity. With the British barrage on the village not due to be lifted until 9.55 a.m., the 2nd RSF had to halt to avoid the complications of 'friendly fire', and the War Diary notes at this juncture that the ground was '… a mass of shell craters'[2] which restricted the mobility of the advance. Still 400 yards short of Montauban, momentum was resumed at 10 a.m., and the Fusiliers entered Southern Trench on the outskirts soon afterwards, leading to the capture of the fortress itself a short while later. When Montauban Alley was taken, to the north, large numbers of Germans were seen retreating across the fields beyond, and Lt-Col R.K. Walsh, the commanding officer of the Scots Fusiliers, was appointed the senior officer of the newly taken positions. Twenty-eight prisoners of war were secured, including an Artillery Brigadier and his staff, along with field guns and equipment. Consolidation took place all afternoon, and by evening every target allotted to the 30th Division had been achieved. (In June, the 2nd RSF had practiced storming nearby Briquesmesnil in preparation for the 1 July 1916 assault, and had been inspected by Maj.-Gen. J.S.M. Shea on the 30th.)

At dusk, casualty figures were assessed. Eleven officers of the 2nd Royal Scots Fusiliers had been killed or wounded, whilst thirty-eight men in the ranks were known to be dead, 198 had been injured, and a further fifty were unaccounted for. One of the fallen was St Austell-born Pte Richard H. Harvey, who had enlisted in Burnley. He was the nineteen-year-old son of Richard and Rebecca, who were still living in the Lancashire town when the Commonwealth War Graves

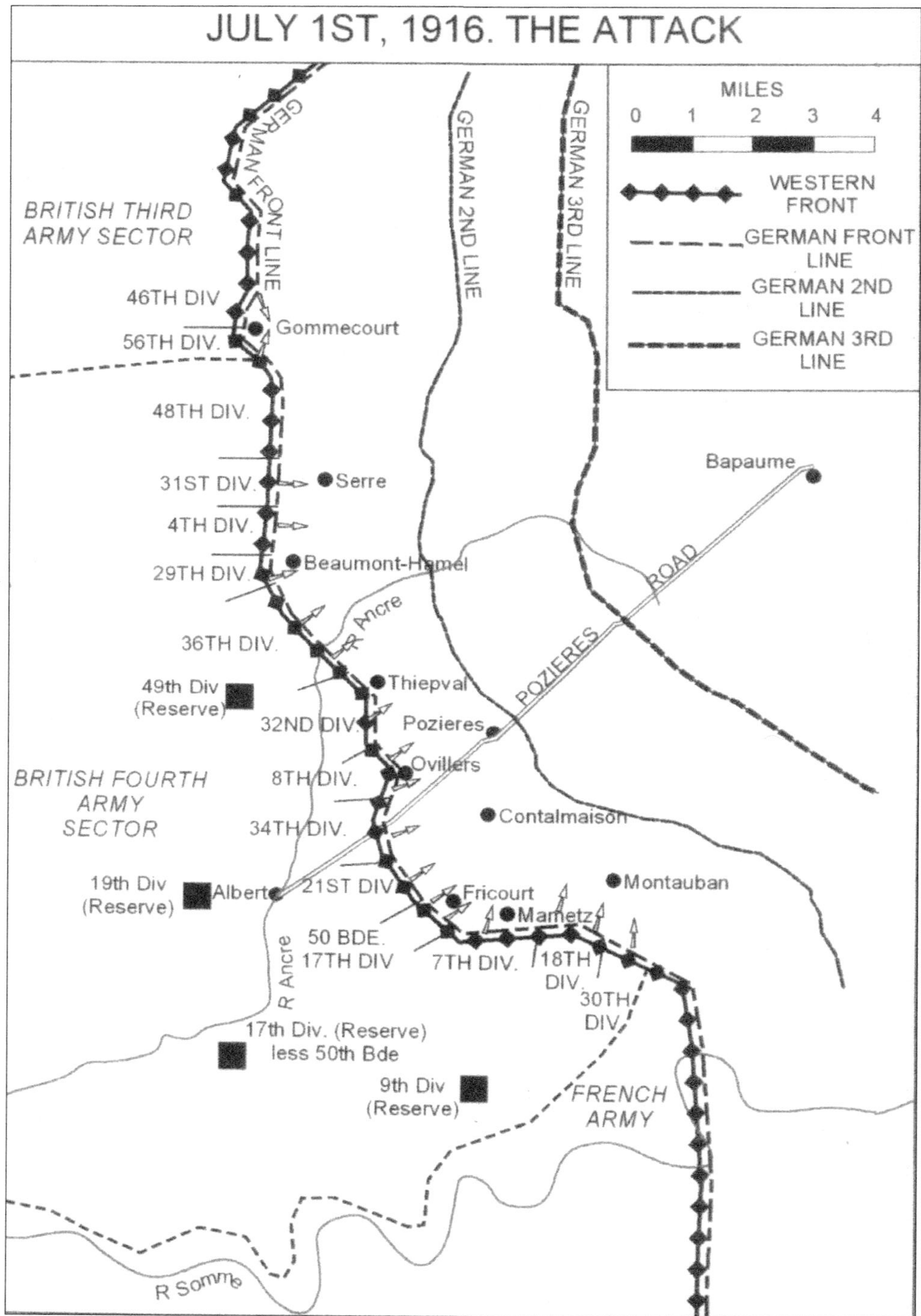

The Somme battlefield, showing the dispositions of British Divisions on 1 July 1916 and the German defences.

British troops advancing in the distance at 7.30 a.m. on 1 July, 1916. (Imperial War Museum)

Commission compiled its Debt of Honour Register during the 1920s. By 1901, the family had only recently relocated to the north of England – possibly due to the lack of employment in Cornwall – with thirty-seven-year-old Richard senior working as a 'general labourer', whereas the occupations of his two eldest children, William (sixteen) and Beatrice (fourteen), are listed as 'cotton doffers', which creates an image of the 'dark Satanic mills' so prevalent in Victorian industrial Britain.

Richard Harvey junior, who was aged four in this year, also had three other siblings, all of whom – along with their parents – were natives of St Austell, including two-year-old Arthur. The Regulars of the 2nd Royal Scots Fusiliers had been on the Western Front since autumn, 1914, even though the 30th Division as a whole was classed as one of the so-called 'New Armies'. Enlisting in early 1915 from his job as a 'weaver' at Burnley's Temple and Sutcliffe's Mill, Pte Harvey was home on leave during May, 1916, and the circumstances of his death were passed on to his parents by a comrade: 'It is with the deepest regret that I write to inform you that your son was killed in action on 1 July. His battalion join in sending their sincere sympathy with you. It may perhaps comfort you a little to know that he died without pain'. The *Burnley Express & Advertiser* added that the deceased was 'well-known' in the Gannow Lane district of the town, and a memorial service had been arranged to take place at the local St Mark's Church.

Pte Harvey – whose details were included in his local newspaper's 'Roll of Honour' by his family – has no known grave, and so he is commemorated on the Thiepval Memorial to the Missing of the Somme (Pier and Face 3C). Each Regiment which lost men during the offensive is represented at Thiepval, and the individual names are carved alphabetically, by seniority of rank, on special panels called 'Piers', which combine to remember over 72,000 soldiers who fell in the area and have no recognised final resting place.

Camaraderie in the trenches. Inset: Pte R.H. Harvey.

As the ground upon which Pte Harvey fell was taken by the British, it is, perhaps, surprising that his body could not be identified afterwards, but it should be borne in mind that he could have been blown up by a shell, or stumbled into a crater where his body was buried by the debris from subsequent explosions. (The report that he died 'without pain' lends weight to one of these scenarios.) It has been argued by some that these men are not 'missing', just 'waiting to be found'. Skeletal remains of the unfortunate victims are still being unearthed by farmers or by new construction to this day. Each is given a proper burial within one of the numerous military cemeteries nearby.

The grim work of 'mopping up' in the trenches was explained to the press by a second lieutenant who returned wounded to Southampton soon after the attack:

It was as we climbed out over their parados, making for their second line, that I got my leg punctured. And then, only a few yards further, came that confounded shrap[nel] that messed up my thigh, killed my second sergeant, and wounded two or three more ... I was in a bit of a small shell hole [so] I wriggled back to that Boche front line and crossed it into a shallow sap that had been pretty well pulverised by our heavies. I was resting there when ... I saw a Boche officer come climbing cautiously up out of a big dug-out we'd put six bombs in. He was a captain. He had a bomb in one hand and a rifle and bayonet in the other; and he was peering first one way and then the other, like a burglar. 'Oh, you beauty!' I thought. And just then he snuggled down against a gap in their parados near the dug-out and bedded his rifle comfortably for firing at our chaps in his second line. You can bet I was glad I had my rifle and plenty of ammunition. So I got a beautiful bead on this chap, and a second later he was [dead] ... I charged my breech again, and no sooner done than my next target bobs up – a lieutenant. I got him while he was looking at his captain; I aimed for his shoulder blades, but the old gun kicked a bit and I got him through the head ... Well, to cut it short, two more lieutenants came up from that same dug-out, making in all three lieutenants and one captain, and I got 'em all ...[3]

The capture of Montauban was described as a '… brilliantly successful exploit' by the British media, which added:

> In scarcely more time than it takes to describe it, the smoke which obscured the foreground was palpitating with khaki figures. On the right centre the first serious difficulties were encountered. Two battalions entered the tract of ground known as the Warren, and most fittingly named – a perfect honeycomb of mine craters, shell burrows, mashed-in trenches and torn wire entanglements. Whilst floundering through these obstructions hostile machine-guns began to rattle, and things looked ugly … On their right, the Manchesters and a Fusilier Battalion [2nd Royal Scots] were plodding forward with irresistible determination …[4]

One of the most widely publicised events of the opening day of the Somme offensive occurred within the sector of the 18th (Eastern) Division, more specifically the actions of the 8th East Surrey Regiment. Capt. 'Billy' Nevill distributed four footballs amongst his platoons and declared a prize would be given to the first unit which could kick its ball into the German trenches – a stroke of subtle psychology to encourage his men into their first battle of the war. Nevill and many others fell in No Man's Land, but two of the footballs did, indeed, find their way into the enemy lines, leading to widespread praise in Britain but sarcastic derision in Germany.

The 7th Queen's (Royal West Surrey) Regiment advanced to the immediate left of the East Surrey men, but it was noted in the War Diary that the soldiers were 'somewhat exhausted' after spending the previous two days witnessing the ferocious British barrage and receiving retaliatory enemy shelling in return. At 7.30 a.m. on 1 July, the entire battalion attacked and immediately came under heavy fire, losing many men within the first thirty minutes, although the German Front trenches were soon overrun. An hour after the assault began, the Battalion Report Centre had lost contact with all of the Companies, and Capt. Scott attempted to re-establish communication, only to be killed on the way up. Just before midday, the Queen's CO moved forward to see for himself the state of affairs, finding approximately 100 of his troops pinned down by Germans who had retired to a defensive system known as 'Back Trench', where they had dug in. With no supports or reinforcements, the Queen's consolidated until launching a concerted bombing raid at 1 p.m., driving out the most determined defenders and capturing the rest. This enabled the remnants of the battalion to push on towards its final objective of Montauban Alley, situated to the north-west of the village. Small pockets of resistance remained throughout the afternoon, but once the reserves had been sent up, touch was regained (at 6.45 p.m.) with the 8th Norfolks on the left and a mixture of Kent soldiers on the right.

In September 1914, the Public Schools and University Mens' Force had formed four PS battalions of the Royal Fusiliers – 18th, 19th, 20th and 21st – known as the 1st, 2nd, 3rd and 4th Public Schools. Proceeding to France towards the end of 1915, three of these units were disbanded during April the following year, with a number of men receiving officers' commissions with other regiments. The 20th RF – 3rd Public Schools – remained intact, but a detachment of its soldiers in the ranks were sent to join up with the 7th Queen's in the 18th Division, and went forward with them on 1 July. Ten men of the 20th RF are listed in the SDGW as losing their lives on 1 July 1916; seven of whom fell on the Somme, whilst the remaining trio were with the bulk of the battalion at Givenchy, further up the line. One of the former was Pte William Griffin, a thirty-eight-year-old native of Callington in Cornwall (according to the SDGW). The Roll of Honour also notes he enlisted in Plymouth from his home in the city, and the CWGC adds that he was the brother of John, who resided at Hill Park Crescent in the same locality. In 1881, Richard Griffin (twenty-six), a miner, was living at Hingston, Stoke Climsland, a short distance to the north of Callington, with his twenty-two-year-old wife, Elizabeth, plus their two sons

Taking supplies up to the front line.

– William (three) and John (eighteen months). All are listed as being born in Stoke Climsland. Twenty years later, William and John had moved to Plymouth, where they were employed by their uncle, Alfred, in the grocery trade.

With the battlefield of 1 July now in British hands, attention could be turned to the retrieval of the dead and wounded. Today, Pte Griffin's body lies in the Combles Communal Cemetery Extension (grave number III.E.16), which contains over 1,500 interments – the majority of which are unidentified. As had been established early on in the war, with so many fatalities soldiers were buried close to the spot where they fell, a logistical and practical necessity with the fighting still raging close by. These interments were often grouped together here and there, marked by wooden crosses, and as the front line edged further away, larger cemeteries could be constructed with less danger of being struck by enemy shells. After the conflict, a high percentage of these smaller burial grounds which were difficult to access or maintain were 'amalgamated' to form the enclosed, regimented graves we see today – the so-called 'silent cities'. Pte Griffin is one of twelve from his battalion to rest at Combles, whilst 153 men in the ranks of the 7th Queen's lost their lives on 1 July.

The 54th Brigade of the 18th Division had been assigned the task of storming the German strong-point known as Pommiers Redoubt, and the attack was led by the 11th Royal Fusiliers and 7th Bedfords, with the 6th Northamptonshires following behind. The War Diary of the latter recorded: 'The Brigade had undergone a week's previous training over ground laid out on the plan of the German trenches to be attacked and were in fine fettle when the day arrived. The German trenches and wire entanglements had been battered for seven days by our intense artillery bombardment'[5]

The 6th Northants had been split in reserve, with Battalion HQ situated in Caftet Wood, and problems were caused by the intervening terrain between here and the British forward lines, although 'bridges' across support trenches and gaps in the wire had been reconnoitred beforehand. Moving off at 8 a.m., they '… advanced as steadily as if they were on the parade ground, their instructions being that it was not to halt until the enemy second trench … was reached. All companies came under a heavy artillery barrage … but they continued to move forward with admirable coolness …'[6]

Following a short delay, bombing parties made their way along 'Black Alley', which led to Pommiers Trench and ultimately the Redoubt itself. Meanwhile, other Northants men had been detailed as 'moppers up', clearing out the enemy dug-outs in the first three lines of German trenches. Fighting continued into the afternoon, but Pommiers Redoubt had already fallen, and a number of units pressed on towards Caterpillar Wood, several hundred yards beyond the intended target. The 6th Northants had lost twenty-nine men dead from the ranks, 123 wounded, and four missing by the end of the day.

At the end of July, the *West Briton* revealed that news had been received in south-west Cornwall '… of the death in the great offensive of … Pte F. Keep, Northants Regt., of Leskinnick Place. The battalion to which [he] belonged did a good deal of training at Penzance last summer'. (Leskinnick Place is close to Penzance Railway Station.) Pte Keep was a married man, but there is no mention of any children.

A brief piece of information like this starts the chain of research, and the SDGW reveals a 1 July 1916 casualty, Pte Frederick Keep, of the 6th Northants, who was born at Woburn Sands, Bedfordshire, and enlisted in Kettering, Northamptonshire, although his place of residence is left blank. The CWGC does not elaborate on any further personal data, other than the soldier's grave is now at the Dantzig Alley British Cemetery, Mametz (V.S.7), which is situated on a strategic German trench known as Dantzig Alley. (Many 1 July casualties are buried or remembered here.) Sometimes, in the cases of little or no accompanying details for an individual casualty, it is necessary to make a few educated guesses as to his particular identity. In the final months of 1884, the birth was registered in the Bedford area of one Frederick Keep, and this same individual is to be found in the 1901 Census as a sixteen-year-old 'agricultural labourer', living in the village of Stagsden, which is several miles to the east of Bedford. His specific birthplace is given as 'Wootton, Beds', which is close by, whereas 'Woburn Sands' – the location given in the SDGW – is a short distance to the south-west. A Cpl Alfred Keep, of the 1st Bedfords, is commemorated on the village war memorial of Stagsden, killed in action on 23 April 1917, at the age of twenty-six. He was the son of Thomas and Sarah, and had been born in nearby Turvey, so it is highly likely that Pte F. Keep is the person mentioned above (aged thirty-one by July 1916), and related to Alfred in some way. When or why the former moved to Cornwall is unclear, but on the Penzance war memorial (situated on the site of the Old Battery and unveiled in 1922) is the name 'J. Keep'. I am of the opinion that this is Frederick – either known as 'Jack', 'John', etc., or the initial of his Christian name was erroneous when the information was compiled after the conflict.

More cameos of the battle came back with wounded:

We soon got into the German Front trench. I saw very few living, but in the second and third lines we found a few. At the bottom of the deep trenches were plenty of dead, and in the dug-outs, too. Prisoners we took seemed half-starved, and as soon as they saw us coming shouted out, 'Kamerad, mercy!', but they only said this when they saw the machine-guns which they had been previously working for all they were worth were about to be captured.[7]

The 18th and 30th Divisions suffered almost identical casualty figures – just over 3,000 each of dead, injured, captured or missing – yet with the first day objectives secured, the General Staff could have asked for no more from their men in this sector. Those manning the newly taken German lines would have no idea how the rest of the offensive was progressing until much later, and for now the thoughts of some were with familiar faces who had not lived to see another sunset.

7th Division

The 91st Brigade was entrusted with the attack of the Division's right flank, advancing in a similar direction to that of the 6th Northants in the 18th Division. Led by the 1st South Staffordshires (1914 veterans) and 22nd Manchesters, 700 yards of ground had been crossed under heavy fire within thirty minutes, securing the Bucket Trench-Dantzig Alley line but stalling before Fritz Trench due to large numbers of enemy bombers. Assisted by the 2nd Queen's, the dug-outs were cleared systematically, whilst the Staffordshires entered the eastern fringes of Mametz, and another consolidation took place during the afternoon.

Ten officers of the 22nd Manchesters had lost their lives by nightfall, with a further eight wounded, whereas 120 men in the ranks had been killed, 241 injured, and 111 missing. (The SDGW gives the total of fatalities amongst the latter as 195. The 22nd was a Pals battalion, raised by the city itself in 1914, and inevitably contained a high proportion of men from the immediate vicinity.) The officers, however, were from a wider background, and one of the fallen was Second Lieutenant Charles Treverbyn Gill, who had been attached to the 22nd from the 4th Manchesters, which was a Reserve unit. Aged twenty-six, he was the son of Julia and the late Thomas Gill, of Kensington in London, but also of Treverbyn in Cornwall. (There are several memorial windows dedicated to members of the Gill family in the Parish Church. A Thomas Gill was once the Lord of the Manor here, having purchased the property during the first half of the nineteenth century. Born in the early 1800s, he was a London lawyer for many years, and when the 1871 Census was taken, he was staying in a St Austell hotel. His son, also called Thomas, continued the Gill tradition of solicitors, and was living at St Quentin Avenue in Kensington by 1891. This address clearly remained within the family, as it was the residence of Julia Gill in the 1920s, when the CWGC requested information relating to her deceased son. Her husband, the third generation Thomas Gill, was yet another to practice law in the capital, where their offspring, Charles, came into the world in 1890. He was given the middle name 'Treverbyn', referring to his paternal links with the Cornish village which is situated in the heart of 'clay country' near St Austell.)

Educated at St Paul's School and Exeter College, Oxford, the young Charles was a keen rower who went on to join the law firm of Messrs Maples, Teesdale and Co. in the City of London. In September, 1914, he enlisted into the ranks of the 16th (Public Schools) Battalion of the Middlesex Regiment, giving his occupation on his service record[1] as a 'law student'. He was 5ft 11.5in in height, and listed St Quentin Avenue as his home address. Commissioned into the Manchesters the following April, he joined up with the 22nd Battalion a month prior to the Somme offensive, and his Company commander would later inform 2nd Lt Gill's mother:

> Your son was a good officer and a brave man. He was with his platoon for several days before the battle, and though it was his first experience, he behaved with great coolness under the most trying conditions. In the short time he had been with us we had all learned to like him exceedingly, and his place in the battalion will not be easy to fill … [He] fell in action … while gallantly leading his men … I lose a most promising officer, and we mourn his death.[2]

Pommiers Redoubt, 2007. Inset: 2nd Lt C.T. Gill.

Another wrote: 'He was an exceedingly nice fellow; we were all terribly sorry, officers and men alike. He was a clever officer, and, above all, was held in the highest esteem ... He died doing his duty in the fullest degree'. Gill's Platoon Sergeant added:

> [He] was my platoon officer. He took over the command about three weeks before the advance. I was with your son the whole of the time the bombardment was on, and in the best of spirits, quiet and reserved, he cheered his men, and waited patiently for the word to go. At 7.30 a.m., 1 July, over the top we went, your son, revolver in hand, calling on the men to follow, leading the way and living up to the part of a commander to the letter. We had gone about 300 yards from the German third line, when Lt Gill, who was next to me, suddenly pitched over. I dropped down beside him and found he had been hit. All that he said to me was: 'I'm beat; push on', and leaving a man to attend to him, I gathered together what few men I had left and acted on his command[3]

The body of 2nd Lt Gill was buried '... 400 yards east of Mametz', and his grave subsequently '... marked by a durable wooden cross with an inscription bearing full particulars.'[4] He is now commemorated on a special memorial within the Peronne Road Cemetery in Maricourt (III.B.30), a burial ground several miles to the south-east from where the officer actually fell. (Maricourt marks the border between the British and French Armies on 1 July.) A study of contemporary trench maps suggests that 2nd Lt Gill – whose death was reported in several Cornish newspapers – lost his life close to Dantzig Alley, which the 22nd Manchesters reached at approximately 1.30 p.m. The position corresponds with the original location of his grave, as well as the recollections of his platoon sergeant at the time the officer fell mortally wounded. (British officers were conspicuous during an advance, walking slightly ahead of their men and with distinctive differences to their uniforms. They often only carried a revolver – as in the case of 2nd Lt Gill – while some even grasped a sword or a walking stick; a reminder of the fast-disappearing style of warfare witnessed by some of the older members of Queen Victoria's army. First World War German snipers soon learned who to aim at first.)

The thoughts of captive Germans were soon passed on to the British Press, but how much of the following was true, or simply embellished propaganda, is not clear – possibly a mixture of both. Some POWs declared that the conflict had: '… reached a stage when it ceased to be war and was sheer murder. [The Allied] artillery was simply hellish. I [a British officer] told them that we were only just beginning to fight, and they answered grimly that it seemed so.' Expecting savage treatment from their captors, all expressed 'agreeable surprise' at the respect they actually received, with the German officer adding his country was now weary of war, and he himself had long since desired to be taken prisoner. He mentioned the strength of the British army was the 'despair of the Fatherland', and most Teutons possessed 'great respect' for the fighting qualities of their foe. 'Even as we talked there came a burst of … music, and a Battalion of the Manchester Regiment swung past in its brave array on its way to go in. The contrast was a striking one – the group of disheartened prisoners on the one hand, the mighty phalanx of the "contemptible little army" on the other …'[5] (Kaiser Wilhelm had coined the phrase 'contemptibly small army' – either to deride the size of the BEF, or ridicule its military spirit – when it landed in France during August 1914, to which the pre-war Regulars promptly and proudly dubbed themselves the 'Old Contemptibles'. OC Associations sprang up around the country after the war, continuing for many decades until the numbers inevitably waned with the passing of time.)

Directly opposite the village of Mametz, which was – like all other villages on the Somme Front – heavily defended by the Germans, stood the 20th Brigade. The 2nd Borders were on the left, 9th Devons in the centre, and 2nd Gordon Highlanders on the right, with the 8th Devons in support. (The two West Country battalions, it is to be remembered, suffered heavily at Loos the previous year.) Although the 9th Devons and the 2nd Gordons would advance at the same time on 1 July, there would be no contact between them, as a prominent valley, bisected with a road and railway, formed a natural barrier on their flanks. The Devons were situated on the edge of Mansel Copse, where this once peaceful clump of trees had now been blown to pieces by German shells, with only the stumps remaining, and beyond, the open ground stretched across No Man's Land towards a civilian cemetery on the edge of Mametz, which contained a devastating enemy machine-gun position known as The Shrine. Just weeks prior to the offensive, Capt. D.L. Martin, of the 9th Devons, took a few days' leave, and occupied his time by constructing a three-dimensional plasticine model of the intervening terrain between the British and German lines, as the maps at the disposal of Battalion HQ were of poor quality. To his horror, the captain realised that his men would suffer dreadful casualties due to the lack of cover as they passed the ridge next to Mansel Copse and advanced towards The Shrine. His grave concerns were passed on to his superiors upon his return, and he implored them to eliminate the machine-gun post with artillery shells prior to the assault, to which he was told that the final barrage would undoubtedly be successful.

The 8th Devons had a large percentage of officers who had barely left school, but the pending twenty-four hours would test all ranks to their very limits. During the night of 30 June/1 July, a patrol was sent out to sever the enemy wire, as it could be seen that it had not been sufficiently cut. In addition, German shelling had all but destroyed the British Front and support trenches, so new ones had to be dug some 250 yards away. At 7.27 a.m., the 9th Devons advanced, shielded briefly by the topography of the slope leading to Mansel Copse, yet once the brow had been reached, The Shrine machine-gun – which had survived the bombardment along with its crew – had a full uninterrupted view stretching for 400 yards, and set to work on the exposed figures marching

Location of the Shrine Machine Gun (farm buildings, centre, left), Mametz, 2007. Inset: 2nd Lt T.F. Adamson and 2nd Lt D. Logan.

towards positions to the west of Mametz. Dead and wounded piled up in the immediate area of the Copse, although the survivors headed grimly onwards, reaching close to the cause of the carnage but just unable to put it out of action. Reserves were sent forward only to suffer a similar fate, as did two Companies of the 8th Devons, under Capt. Tregelles, taking the same route past Mansel Copse to reinforce a gap which had appeared between the 9th Devons and the 2nd Gordons.

Two Companies of the 9th were now pinned down in Shrine Alley in desperate need of support, whilst two more had been decimated at the Copse. In the middle of the afternoon, Lt Savill took 'C' Company of the 8th Battalion on a slightly different tack, avoiding the killing ground of Mansel Copse and successfully pushed on into Hidden Wood, gathering remnants of other Devons on the way. Another Company of the 8th was detailed to clear dug-outs to the west of Mametz, whilst the village itself was stormed by separate units late in the day, and 'Bunny Trench' – to the north of the hamlet – finally fell into British hands along with hundreds of German prisoners. The cost to the Devonshires was high. The combined losses of the 8th and 9th were thirteen officers dead and fourteen wounded, plus nearly 200 killed in the ranks along with a further 400 incapacitated, and fifty-five more unaccounted for. Close on 700 – nearly an entire battalion strength – had been cut down during the hours of daylight, and men with strong links to Cornwall were amongst the fatalities.

Capt. Duncan Lenox Martin – the officer commanding 'A' Company who had predicted a catastrophe at Mansel Copse – had fallen at this exact spot. Born in 1886, he attended schools in Somerset and Sussex where he learned to speak French and German, while his leisure pursuits included painting. The Official History of the Devonshire Regiment notes that the captain was an 'artist by profession', and his passing was recorded in a Cornish newspaper which revealed he was 'late of St Ives'.[6] It may be assumed that the world-renowned artistic lure of this Cornish seaside resort was the same which brought Duncan Martin here, although the length of time he spent in Cornwall is not known. At the outbreak of war, he was living in Folkestone, and he expressed a desire to join the Devonshire Regiment, with a former colonel of that regiment assuring the War Office of Martin's 'good moral character'[7] in August 1914. Just over a year later, the twenty-nine-year-old assumed command of 'A' Company (soon after the losses at Loos), and went on leave to England during 8–15 June 1916, during which time he devised his model structure of No Man's Land at Mametz. (For many years, it was used to accompany lectures, and finally ended up on display at the Royal United Service Institution Museum. Its whereabouts was lost after the closure of the latter in 1963.)

Pte Jack Owen, of the 9th Devons (a man who witnessed the fate of many of his officers) would later recall:

> He [Capt. Martin] was CO of A Company. A Company led the attack at 5.45 a.m. [this is an error – it was 7.27 a.m.] and Capt. Martin was the first to fall. He had gone 15 yards when he was shot through the head above the right temple. He turned his head to the left, flung out his right arm and fell dead on his back. He was a Secret Service man.[8]

Pte Collins, who had been wounded, confirmed he 'crawled past' the dead body of Capt. Martin, whilst Pte Norman added that the officer was '… killed in the early morning by a machine-gun bullet'.[9] Frank Wollocombe, a friend and comrade of Martin's, wrote to the latter's sister on 17 July: '[He] was my captain for the seven months I was out there, and also in England, and it will never be the same again without him. All the men loved him and would do anything for him, as would the officers under him. He was always so cool, the best officer we ever had'[10]. Lt Smythe ventured: 'Isn't it rotten about Martin? The others also, but one feels about him so.'[11]

On 4 July, the survivors of the 8th and 9th Battalions gathered at Mansel Copse and watched as Revd E.C. Cross (Padre of the 8th) consecrated the ground which had launched the attack, before 160 of their pals were buried in the original front trench, so close to where most had fallen. A wooden cross was placed at the entrance, stating: 'The Devonshires held this trench, the Devonshires hold it still'. A permanent stone memorial was erected at a later date, but the inscription remains the same. This is now known as the Devonshire Cemetery, and Capt. Martin lies buried at grave space A.1. His sister, Mrs Jeltes, was living in Hastings by 1916, although she relocated to Hampshire after the war. She was Duncan Martin's next of kin, as he was unmarried.

When the machine-gun at The Shrine was finally silenced, by bombers who had worked their way round to out-flank it, many thousands of spent cartridges were found to be piled up around its base. A small number had also ended the life of twenty-three-year-old Capt. Geoffrey Philip Tregelles, who was in command of 'A' Company, 8th Devons. Described by the Regimental History as '… an officer of remarkable quality and devotion to duty, who had inspired the company with his spirit …', he had been born in Penzance, the only son of George – formerly of the Devon and Cornwall Bank at Truro, Falmouth, St Austell and Penzance – and Marion. By 1901, the family had moved to Barnstaple in North Devon, where George continued with his employment in the financial sector, and eight-year-old Geoffrey now had a younger sister, Olga. The elder sibling was educated at Clifton College, Bristol, before becoming an undergraduate at Caius College, Cambridge. No fewer than nine former students of the College lost their lives on 1 July alone. The captain was reported to be a '… young man of high intelligence and promise, and a direct descendant of some of the most honoured families in the Society of Friends. His grandfather was Mr N. Tregelles, formerly of Dean-terrace, Liskeard, who married a daughter of Mr John Allen, the historian of Liskeard.'[12].

Joining the Officers' Training Corps when war broke out, G.P. Tregelles subsequently obtained a commissioned with the Devons, and proceeded to the Western Front during September 1915 (an account of his meeting with newly drafted officers can be found in Chapter Three). Pte Kidd, of the 8th Devons, told an officer investigating the circumstances of the captain's death: 'He [Kidd] saw Capt. TREGELLIE [sic] who belonged to his Company lying dead on the field. At the time they were going across the open country.'[13] George Tregelles was told that his son's body had been interred at '... MANSEL COPSE, south of Mametz, 1 mile from Fricourt,'[14] in what is now the Devonshire Cemetery (the modern grave number is B.6). 'A Company 8th Devons were a very happy crowd. We had a splendid Commander, Capt. Tregelles – both the officers and men under him highly respected him, he was a good friend to ALL.'[15] (Captains Martin and Tregelles were each Mentioned in Despatches during the conflict.)

Another officer of the 9th Devons to fall was 2nd Lt Travers Farrant Adamson, who was born in London during the mid-1890s, but by the time of the 1901 Census, was living with his family at Penare Road in Penzance. His father, also called Travers (a native of Australia) and mother, Ethel (who hailed from Exeter), had the same occupation of 'landscape painter'. Travers junior was the eldest sibling to Mark and Christopher. Travers senior died a few years later and lies buried at Lelant, near Hayle. T.F. Adamson attended Hurstpierpoint College in Surrey between 1908 and 1914, where he was a Platoon Sergeant in the O.T.C., a regular contributor to the annual Shakespearian plays, and captain of the school in his last term, before receiving his commission with the Devons. His service record[16] also reveals that he had two younger sisters, Patricia and Loveday, who were residing with a Miss L.B. Michell at Bay View Terrace, Newquay. By the early part of the war their brother, Mark, was a lieutenant in the Royal Marine Light Infantry at Portsmouth, whereas eighteen-year-old Christopher was a Private in the Artists' Rifles (28th County of London Regiment), and both, it would seem, survived the war.

Pte Jack Owen, who had supplied details of the death of Capt. Martin, also did the same for 2nd Lt Adamson, noting the position was close to 'Mansel Copps': '... on the far side of it, I saw Lt Adamson killed instantly about 6 a.m. or soon after [this is once again an error]. We had just reached the German trenches.'[17] [Owen's timings here appear once again to be erroneous, as the time of death would almost certainly have been several minutes after the beginning of the attack, between 7.30 a.m. and 7.40 p.m]. Pte Ralph Jones, of X Platoon, 'C' Company, had been injured on the battlefield, but he thought the hour was about 7 a.m. – again, this is not possible: 'I was wounded and close to me was an officer. He was wounded but sitting up … He told the sergeant to carry on. I got back to the line and saw no more of him.'[18] The officer, who would have turned twenty-one the day after he lost his life, is another whose final resting place is to be found within the Devonshire Cemetery (A.7). His mother, Ethel, had moved to Wimborne in Dorset by the 1920s.

(One famous officer casualty of the 9th Devons was Lt Noel Hodgson, who had received a Military Cross at Loos the previous year when he and his men had held on to an outpost under heavy fire until they were relieved. At the end of June 1916, his poem 'Before Action' – in which he apparently foresees his own death in battle – was published, and whilst bringing more bombs up to his men in the struggle for Mametz on 1 July, he was hit in the throat and killed. Hodgson was a friend and contemporary of 2nd Lt Harold Rayner, of the same battalion, with both relishing the Greek classics as well as a few mischievous traits. The night before the battle the two men were playing pranks on their fellow officers by running up the sides of their tents. Rayner – who enjoyed listening to the skylarks which sang above the trenches – was seen on the morning of 1 July leading his men up a slope, carrying a stick, when a bullet struck him down. 2nd Lt Frank Wollocombe, who had been injured prior to the offensive and was recuperating in England when his comrades went over, stated: 'I hear the 9th Devons were made up of forty-four officers just before the "push". Twenty officers and 700 men went into action – one officer and sixty-two men reached their objective. We have the men's casualty list of 1 July here, it is awful.'[19])

The circumstances behind the individual loss of life amongst men in the ranks was not as rigorously investigated as was the case for officers, so when and where the following six soldiers of the 9th Devons fell is unclear, although 'The Shrine' machine-gun probably took its grim toll

Graves at the Devonshire Cemetery, Mametz. Inset: Capt. D.L. Martin and Capt. G.P. Tregelles.

on a proportion of them. Pte Isaac Govier was born in Tavistock and when the 1901 Census was taken he was a six-year-old 'schoolboy' living at Stoke Climsland, near Launceston. He enlisted in Redruth. His father, Frederick (thirty-two) – a native of Calstock, Cornwall – was employed as an 'arsenic mine labourer (above ground)', his wife, Jane, a Devonian, was thirty, and the couple had four children, with the other three all being born in Cornwall. The CWGC can only add that Pte Govier is commemorated at Thiepval (1C), although he may be one of the ten men of the 9th Devons who were laid to rest in an unmarked grave within the Devonshire Cemetery.

St Austell-born Pte John Richards is also remembered at Thiepval (1C). He is *probably* the same three-year-old John Richards who is recorded in the 1901 Census residing at Candledown, Treverybyn St Peters, with his clay miner father, Samuel, mother Melanie, and elder brother, Wilson. The male members of the family were all natives of St Austell – the place of Pte Richards' enlistment – whereas Melanie hailed from St Ewe. Pte Sidney Rogers came from Plymouth, although he joined up in Newquay, and was twenty-four when he fell in action at Mametz. His father, Nulcombe, was a Police Constable, and his mother, Annie, and five siblings had all been born in Devon. (Devonshire Cemetery, B.4). Pte 'Charles Thomas' (as his name appears in the SDGW) originally provided a bit of a puzzle, until it became apparent that his names had been switched, and he was actually Pte Thomas Charles, a native of Redruth who enlisted in Dartmouth (according to the SDGW). Further research did not provide any cast-iron leads, except for the birth of a Thomas Charles in Wendron Street, Helston, during 1891, the son of Thomas – a greengrocer – and Elizabeth (née Trewennack). Nine-year-old Thomas was still in Helston a decade later, part of a large family living at Wendron Street whose ancestors have long-standing connections with the town. Pte Charles proceeded to France several months prior to his death, and his grave is now situated in the Ovillers Military Cemetery (VII.E.10), at the head of 'Mash' Valley several miles away (the scene of the deaths of a number of Cornishmen in the 2nd Devons – see Chapter Nine).

His body was undoubtedly brought here after the war, unless he was actually serving with the 2nd Battalion on 1 July 1916.

Pte Aubrey Trebilcock was born in Newquay and was still living in his home town when he enlisted in Bodmin. Aged twenty when he fell, his sister, Miss E.B. Trebilcock, was residing in Newquay's Tower Road by the 1920s. (Devonshire Cemetery, A.6.) His name is also on the Newquay war memorial. Finally, Pte James Henry Trewern, a native of Penzance, was reported to have been killed in the 'great offensive' by the same edition of the newspaper which informed its readers of the death of Pte F. Keep, of the 6th Northants, although Pte *Trewren* (as it is spelt) is noted as serving with the West Yorkshire Regiment at the time. This is not corroborated by the Casualty Rolls, and the CWGC adds that he was the son of Mr W.C. Trewern, of New Street in Penzance. The *Royal Cornwall Gazette* also revealed that the soldier had spent time training with his battalion in the Penzance area during 1915, and that he was a married man. His birth was registered in 1895, and he joined up in Lynton, North Devon, only to lose his life before he had barely left his teenage years. (Devonshire Cemetery, B.7.) The soldier's name can also be found at St Mary's Church in Chapel Street, Penzance, with the spelling 'Trewern'.

The 9th Devons were soon withdrawn for recuperation, although the 8th remained at the Front for several more days, taking the opportunity to inspect the enemy dug-outs which had been concealed from their view for so long: 'We stood gaping with wonder at the long flights of steps banked up with 3in timber, and at the safe and comfortable bunks within', one revealed; 'the ordinary German soldier must have enjoyed a degree of comfort which no one short of a general tasted on our side of the line'.[20] The Devons' Regimental History concluded: 'But elaborate and formidable as the German defences were, and stubbornly as they had been defended, they had not sufficed to keep out the Seventh Division, and the 8th and 9th Devons could legitimately feel that they had contributed their full share towards starting the new offensive successfully.'[21]

On 1 July, the War Diary for the 6th Siege Battery of the Royal Garrison Artillery revealed: 'Attack launched after sixty-five [minute] artillery fire. Completely successful on a front of 2 miles of this Corps – on an average depth of one and a half miles. Moved at 8 p.m. to new position (near Waterlot Farm).'[22] The officer commanding at one stage during the conflict was Temp/ Brig.-Gen. (later Colonel) David F.H. Logan, who would subsequently serve with the Commands and Staff. During the Boer War (1899-1902) he had been the Adjutant of the Cape Garrison Artillery, and he had trained at the Royal Military Academy (RMA) during the early 1880s, making him an officer of much experience. By the time of the First World War, he had made his home at Woodlane Crescent in Falmouth, and had been on the Western Front since the beginning of March 1915. His son, 2nd Lt David Herbert Hosken Logan, had recently applied to attend the RMA, listing three regiments he desired to join in order of preference: the Borders, due to his Scottish 'ancestral claims'; the Duke of Cornwall's Light Infantry, as he had lived in the county for five years and could claim 'several Cornish relatives'[23]; followed by the Dorsets. Born in Bristol on 4 August 1897, he attended Wellington College in Berkshire, and turned seventeen on the day war was declared, patriotically requesting an officer's commission just a month later, when he signed up in Kensington on 23 September 1914. He married Dora in October 1915, and towards the end of the following May, he was able to fulfil his initial wish by becoming a Second Lieutenant 'in the field' with the 2nd Border Regiment of the 7th Division.

At 7.27 a.m. on the morning of 1 July, numbers 3 and 4 Platoons began to move forward in a direction to the west of Mametz, with the 9th Devons on their right, but due to the slightly different route taken by the Scottish troops, No Man's Land was crossed with significantly less casualties than their English counterparts. However, once the enemy lines had been reached, small groups of Germans began resisting the attack at close quarters, with the War Diary admitting '… the position seemed to be rather serious'.[24] This was due to the battalion on their right flank – the 9th Devons – being cut down at Mansel Copse instead of providing the intended support.

British artillery shells then began landing precariously close, and the Borders lit flares to warn them off, but this only served to draw *German* fire onto their location. Urgent requests for more ammunition were sent back with runners, and the necessary items were eventually brought back, enabling the assault to continue. Still encountering pockets of snipers and grenadiers in the '... innumerable large shell-holes,'[25] these had to be out-flanked individually before the objectives were taken. The role of the gunners was praised, after much of the wire had been cut by explosives, thus reducing the number of casualties, with another contributing factor being the fact that '... the advance was very close behind the artillery barrage the whole time'.[26] Homage was paid to the resilience and coolness of the battalion which had carried out its orders under a '... heavy sprinkling of hostile shrapnel'.

Second Lieutenant Logan receives only one mention in the War Diary's 1 July narrative, confirming that he was one of three officers to lose their lives in action. A further six were wounded – one later died – whilst seventy-nine in the ranks were dead, 240 injured (ten of whom fatally), and four were missing. His former college produced a 'Yearbook' throughout the war, and the publication for 1916 included the contents of a letter written by 2nd Lt Logan's Platoon Sergeant to Col Logan:

> Your son was very young, the youngest in the battalion. We all liked him, he was a good and brave young officer, cool and collected under fire. The day before he was shot, he and some of his men were buried by the explosion of a 5.9 shell. On the morning of the attack, I said to him, 'Shall I stand near you, sir?' He said, 'Your place is on the left of the platoon, mine is on the right'. Your son would not allow anyone to go in front of him, but went first into the [German] dug-outs.[27]

The Sergeant added that his officer was killed as they advanced between the first and second enemy lines (Shrine Alley was reached at 7.50 a.m.), and the latter's body was later interred at the Citadel New Military Cemetery, Fricourt (II.D.12). He was just nineteen. His widow, Dora, received a telegram at her Folkestone home informing her that her husband had been killed in action, whilst the death was also announced in Cornwall.

The ranks of the 2nd Borders were boosted by over 250 new recruits on 9 July, plus another 132 the following day. Twelve officers joined just under two weeks later – such were the losses on 1 July. Approximately 300 prisoners of war were taken by the battalion on this date, including two colonels, along with heavy howitzers, field guns and a wide array of military hardware. More than 3,400 men of the 7th Division had become casualties – yet another statistic in a war which created so many horrific numbers – although the British press inevitably seized upon the positives:

> A battalion say they had a good time at Mametz. One lad said it was the best scrap he had been in so far [as] it seems to have turned into a super-rat hunt ... 'We didn't find many of them in Mametz, but the few who stayed had the time of their lives. They looked like great big rats running from hole to hole ...'[28]

Another told the newspapers:

> ... on my way back from the front I came upon a high-walled enclosure bearing a deal board upon its portal with the inscription 'prisoners of war' with a very business-like sentry. There was a bunch of about 100 inside, most of them just brought in from Mametz Wood ... They were a trench-weary bunch, caked with clay and in many cases bandaged about the head and hands ... They all had the same story of not having received any rations for five days owing to the intensity of our barrage ...[29]

Col Logan was created a Companion of the Order of Bath and Commander of the Order of St Michael and St George for his services during the First World War. He and his wife, Ethel, had also lost their teenage son in the trenches.

8

21st Division

The 50th Brigade of the 17th (Northern) Division moved up from its reserve position near Albert prior to the advance and linked up with the 21st Division at Fricourt. Comprising of the 10th West Yorkshires, 7th Yorkshires (Green Howards), 7th East Yorkshires and 6th Dorsets, it was to be the regiments from the north of England which would experience the worst tragedy on 1 July. The plan was to advance upon the flanks of Fricourt in the hope it would fall under severe pressure, but in the event of this not happening, the 7th Green Howards would be ordered to attack full on. Soon after the main offensive began, 'A' Company, of the latter, on the extreme right, was sent forward in error, and 108 men were cut down within minutes. The War Diary for the 7th East Yorkshires, waiting in reserve at the time, would later note: 'Guides say one Company went over without orders … This is only a rumour'.[1] Sadly, it was true. The hamlet was still in German hands by the afternoon, so the decision was taken to launch a frontal assault at 2.30 p.m., engaging a combination of Companies from the 7th East Yorkshires and 7th Green Howards. At 2.33 p.m., with no significant preliminary artillery barrage, the men went 'over the top' and did not even get 20 yards before most had been hit. The 7th East Yorkshires' War Diary notes that there was only one ladder with which to climb out of the trench, and at 3.15 p.m. added: 'Have had probably 150 casualties of first six platoons going over.'[2] The combined total from both Yorkshire battalions was around 400 for an operation which achieved precisely nothing in terms of ground gained. Those who were able to crawled back as best they could, while being subjected to snipers' bullets and having to leave most of their stricken comrades behind.

Pte Stephen Bishop, of the Green Howards, was one of the dead. Born at 'Perran Park, Cornwall', according to the SDGW, his precise place of birth was actually Perranzabuloe ('St Piran-in-the-sands') near Truro. The 1901 Census records the six-year-old living at Perranporth Villa with his father, Benedict Bishop (forty), a Helston-born butcher, and his mother, Maria (thirty-two), who was also a native of Perranzabuloe. Benedict, like his father before him, had the grand middle name of 'Palamountain', and Benedict senior was a former tailor and draper who ran a business in Coinage Hall Street, Helston. The 1881 Census records his son as aged twenty-three in this year – his age differs by three years to the 1901 survey – and was already plying his trade as a butcher. (The Bishop household in 1881 also contained a number of boarders – German-born males who are described as 'Travelling Bandsmen'.)

In the years before the First World War, the Bishops moved to the north-east of England, settling in Stockton-on-Tees where Pte Bishop enlisted, and the town was still the residence of his mother, Maria (his father is not mentioned) when the CWGC later compiled its Debt of Honour Register. The latter also reveals that the Cornish-born soldier (twenty-one) was in 'B' Company at the time of his death, so it is far more likely he lost his life in the disastrous attack in the afternoon, as only 'A' Company went forward in the morning. He could, of course, have been the victim of shelling at any time of the day. Pte Bishop's name is to be found on the special memorial within Fricourt British Cemetery, as his body is known to be buried here, although the grave could not be positively identified after the war. The burial ground is situated on the old No Man's Land, and contains many men from the 7th Yorkshires who fell on 1 July.

Memorial to the 7th Yorkshires, Fricourt.

There was to be no ambiguity with regard to the orders for the 10th West Yorkshires, whose War Diary reveals:

> At 7.30 a.m. the Battn. took part in the grand assault. The Battn. assaulted in four lines, two lines got through the German position to the fourth line and were cut off, the attack on our left having failed. Casualties were very heavy, chiefly caused by machine-guns which enfiladed our left flanks and were so deadly that the third and fourth lines failed to get across No Man's Land.[3]

By the end of the day, twenty-two officers had become casualties (including the CO, Lt-Col Dickson, who was dead), along with 688 men in the ranks. These were the highest figures of any single unit along the entire Somme Front, and included another soldier with Cornish connections. Pte Francis Arthur Grylls Nowell was a native of Devonport who joined up in Penzance. His mother, Mary, had been born in Newlyn, whilst his father, Francis – a bargeman in 1901 – also hailed from Devonport. Pte Nowell, who had at least two siblings – Nicholas and Susan – is commemorated at Thiepval (2A, 2C and 2D). One of the reasons for the failure of the 10th Battalion's attack was the state of the German barbed wire, which had been partially destroyed in some sections, but found to be almost completely intact in others. Those who did reach this far noted how the defenders stood almost shoulder to shoulder, loading and re-loading their rifles to repel the British onslaught. Despite the gains of the 7th, 18th and 30th Divisions to their right, the attack was now floundering, with many dead strewn across No Man's Land, and isolated parties still stranded in enemy territory.

The 96th Brigade of the Royal Field Artillery, which had been targeting positions in and around Fricourt during the previous week, had been issued with its final orders for 1 July, concentrating its fire upon the German front lines prior to the infantry assault. 'As the attack progresses this barrage will lift'[4], noted the War Diary, which added that the next target would then immediately be focused upon.

This 'rolling barrage' had been carefully calculated to allow the infantrymen to cross exposed areas *behind* a curtain of their own shells, but close enough to prevent the enemy from re-grouping once the explosive shield had passed. This was also very much dependent upon the total destructive power of the cavalcade, as any survivors could then establish themselves in the battered trenches and open fire on the soldiers marching towards them. As the 10th West Yorkshires discovered, the wire and the men which opposed them combined to enable an awesome depth of weaponry to be unleashed upon the Tommies in No Man's Land.

In mid-July, the *Royal Cornwall Gazette* informed its readers:

Much sympathy is extended to Mr And Mrs A. Colmer and family of Hannafore, Newquay, on the death of their only son, 2nd Lt. Arthur Cecil Colmer, R.F.A., who was killed in action on 1 July. The gallant manner of his death is best set out in the following letter which Mrs Colmer has received from her son's superior officer:- 'Dear Mrs Colmer – It is with deep regret that I have to tell you of your son's gallant death. His duties took him into the trenches yesterday morning, and in a gallant attempt to bring in a wounded man he came under German machine-gun fire, and was killed. He was brought back into the British trench immediately and the body was buried in Dartmore [sic] Cemetery. Your son was an excellent officer, popular with his brother officers, and considerate with the men. His loss will be felt both in the Battery and in the Officers' Mess. One cannot be sorry for the gallant young soldier who dies the finest death a man can die, but it is to those who are left that one's heart goes in sympathy. – Yours sincerely, E. JOHNSTONE, Capt., A Battery, 96th Brigade, R.F.A.' Further comment would be superfluous. Lt Colmer was 23 years of age. He joined up at the beginning of the war. Being a motor cyclist, he was desirous of becoming a motor despatch rider, but when he went to enlist he found there were no vacancies. Nothing lost, he joined at once as a private in the D.C.L.I. Afterwards he was transferred to the Despatch riders, doing duty in this capacity [on the Western Front] for eleven months. Then he was recommended by his commanding officer for a commission. He chose the Royal Field Artillery, having friends in the same branch of the service, and was gazetted in September, 1915. After going through a course of training he again went to France, and was home on leave only three weeks ago. His friend received letters and field cards from him after he was killed so that it was an even greater shock when the wire came to say he was dead. Deceased was very popular in Newquay and district. He was an enthusiastic motorist and a prominent member of the local club. Lt Colmer was well-known in the Liskeard district, with which his family have had such close associations for many years.

The CWGC lists the officer as being a 'native of Liskeard', but the 1901 Census differs by revealing he was born at Hornsey in London. The family address is, however, Pike Street in Liskeard, where thirty-three-year-old local man Arthur May Colmer★ was working as a 'Draper, Outfitter and Tailor', along with his wife Annie (a Londoner), and their two children, Arthur (eight) and Dorothy (six), who were also local to Liskeard. It can therefore be deduced that they moved from the capital back to Arthur senior's home town between 1893 and 1895. (★Back in 1881, Arthur M. Colmer's father, Oliver – originally from St Austell – was also trading as a 'draper' in Pike Street.) Arthur Cecil Colmer was associated with the Liskeard Wesleyan Sunday School, and a Roll of Honour was later established depicting all of its old scholars who subsequently joined the Colours during the First World War.

Spending a short period with the 8th DCLI (which had been formed in Bodmin in September 1914, where the new recruit enlisted from his former occupation as an 'outfitter'[5]), A.C. Colmer soon switched to the Royal Engineers and became a corporal, serving for nearly a year with the BEF in France performing '… useful work as a despatch rider'.[6] Following his commission, he

West of Fricourt, 2007. Inset: 2nd Lt A. Colmer.

underwent a course of training in Ireland and at Shoeburyness before returning to France. His body now lies at the Dartmoor Cemetery at Becordel-Becourt (I.F.44), the name of which was changed at the request of the 8th and 9th Devons during May 1916. There are ninety-one men of the Royal Field Artillery interred here, including a father and son named Lee who served in the same Battery. Also close by is VC recipient Pte J. Miller, of the King's Own Royal Lancaster Regiment, who was fatally wounded whilst successfully delivering an important message under heavy fire on 30/31 July 1916.

2nd Lt Colmer's parents later moved to Bournemouth, and were residing in a dwelling called Restormel House by the 1920s. The Newquay residence known as 'Hannafore' was on the Headland Road, while his sister, Dorothy – who is almost certainly the 'Mrs Hooper' referred to in the officer's service record[7] – was living at 'Clovelly' in the town's Harbour Crescent by 1916. Arthur Cecil Colmer had written a will just two days before he died.

The remainder of the 21st Division attacked to the north of Fricourt, with one of the leading battalions being the 8th Somerset Light Infantry (SLI). At 6.30 a.m. on 1 July, trench ladders and bridges were put into position just as the British bombardment intensified, and an hour later, the '… men advanced in quick time … Officers and men were being hit and falling everywhere [but] the advance went steadily on'.[8] Casualties were caused by the inevitable machine-guns, and the Somersets were held up at the enemy wire until the initial resistance was overcome, allowing entry into the German forward systems. These first crucial stages of the fighting were described to the *Taunton Courier* by a wounded Sergeant of the SLI:

I shall never forget the few hours before the battle. The Somersets were dead game to have a straight thrust at the Germans, and some of the young officers became very impatient at the delay. Suddenly the order came to mount the parapet of our trenches, and you never saw anything equal to the sprint … Helter skelter we peltered across the ground which was intervening, and as we drew up to the German defences we met a hellish machine-gun fire. Bullets whizzed in all directions. One after another I saw my pals fall, there was no chance of helping any of them. It was a case of every man for himself ... Into the thick of the fire we plunged, and then there came a man to man fight with the Germans ... [who] appeared to be strong in numbers. [They] shouted out 'Surrender, Surrender', but our officer – who I may mention is only 19 years of age – would have none of it. He yelled to us, 'Stick it. Somersets!', and we did. The enemy put up an awful fight. I made for my man, when suddenly I was pounced upon by two of the Prussian Guard, great fierce-looking fellows. They gave a yell of delight as they thought they had got me, but my luck was in. I dodged first one and then another thrust until I manoeuvred in such a way as to be able to use the butt-end of my rifle. I got in a terrific blow safe and sure, which sent one reeling to the ground. Immediately the other put his hands up and begged for mercy with the usual cry 'Camerade, Camerade'. Just then some more Prussians appeared. It looked as if the Somersets were to be surrounded. Somehow they were not quite, and our officers still shouted words of encouragement, and we went for the blighters until there were no more left alive. The fellow who surrendered to me died with the rest, for they were a traitorous lot.

Approximately 100 men consolidated a position in the afternoon, and repulsed a bombing attack from the direction of Fricourt. 'The enemy's barrage of shrapnel prevented further advance'[9] recorded the War Diary, but reinforcements and rations were sent up to the new front line at 8 a.m. the following morning. Forty-eight hours later, the survivors were withdrawn. Eight officers and 107 men in the ranks had been killed during the initial assault, with many more wounded, and once again, there were Cornishmen amongst the dead of the 8th SLI.

L/Cpl Hedley Bennett, a St Austell lad according to the SDGW , was one of them, however his identity took a while to fully establish. The *Cornish Guardian* described him as being aged nineteen and a half in 1916, yet in 1888, the birth was registered in the St Austell district of a 'Hedley Bennett', creating a difference of eight years. The latter was the son of Daniel, a 'clay labourer' in 1901, and Emma, with the family living in nearby St Dennis, yet the *Guardian* also added that the parents of the fallen soldier were Mr and Mrs F.H. Bennett, of 'Moorland Road, St Austell', leading to the assumption there were two separate individuals who may be mistaken for one another. A look at the war memorial plaque within St Austell's Holy Trinity Church provided the conclusive proof, where a certain Frederick Hedley *Bennetts* is listed amongst the names. Returning to the 1901 Census, four-year-old 'Frederick H. Bennetts' is confirmed as living in the town, and his age tallies with the known casualty, although both Rolls indicate his name to be either 'Hedley' or simply 'H', and there is no 's' to be found at the end of 'Bennett'. (The surname Bennetts seems to be predominant in Cornwall rather than elsewhere in the country.)

The original article reveals that he enlisted on 18 June 1915, into the 9th Somersets, which were stationed in St Austell at the time [see page 88], and he was apparently the only local man to join up. 'He made himself extremely popular with his comrades,' continued the *Guardian,* 'and so proud were the Somersets at having secured one St Austell recruit that he was claimed as the "pet of the Regiment"'. He was previously employed for four years at '... Mr Ed. Broad's★ St Austell establishment, and by those associated with him and all with whom he came into contact he was a young fellow generally respected'. [★In 1901, twenty-three-year-old Edward Broad was working as a 'cooper'.]

Proceeding to France in February 1916, having already been promoted, L/Cpl Bennett was in line for a second stripe, but lost his life on the Somme battlefields. Pte Havens, who was a close friend of the family, wrote to the fallen soldier's parents: 'I am sorry to tell you that your son Hedley was killed in action on 1 July. I did all I could for him. He was shot through the head.' (This is almost certainly Albert Henry Havens, service number 16188, who survived the war.) Other letters of condolence were sent to the Bennett family, all expressing their regret '... at losing one they esteemed so highly'.

German front line, Fricourt, 2007. Inset: L/Cpl. H. Bennett[s].

Several Cornish newspapers reported his death, although one stated that he enlisted in January 1915, rather than June. (The 9th Somersets were based at St Austell from December, 1914, until May of the following year, when the battalion moved to Wareham, so it seems likely the January date is accurate.) The CWGC does not add any more personal data, and only reveals that L/Cpl Bennett's grave is located at the Gordon Dump Cemetery (X.N.1), Ovillers La Boisselle. This location is actually some distance to the north of where he fell, so his body was most likely taken here from its original site of burial after the war.

Pte Donald Claude Glenfield Hick was another fatality, and although he was born in Redruth at the beginning of 1899, the 1901 Census reveals a subsequent change of location. Residing in what appears to be either 'Vine' or 'Pine' Cottage, next to the Winchester Building in Falmouth, is Barnett Hick (forty-three), a 'laundry proprietor' from Lelant, along with his thirty-nine-year-old Truro-born wife Kate, a 'laundress'. They had six sons, ranging in age from eighteen years down to two, with Donald being the youngest. William was a butcher, Ernest worked for his parents, and Horace was an errand boy, with the other two, Fred and Lionel, being of school age. Pte Hick – who is remembered at Thiepval (2A) – enlisted in Stratford, Essex, and he was aged just seventeen when he fell. Combat soldiers had to be nineteen or over to fight overseas, so he would have undoubtedly lied about his true span of years to enlist. His name appears on the Falmouth war memorial, but in the absence of a place of residence listed in the SDGW, it is possible he had moved to East London by the time he joined the army.

This geographical chain of events can be positively verified in the case of Pte Richard Ernest Miners (15695), whose similar service number to that of Pte Hick (15612) suggests that they were in the same batch of new recruits with the Somersets. The former, however, had previously served in the Northumberland Fusiliers, and had signed his attestation papers in Cramlington, to the north of Newcastle-upon-Tyne. By 1901, he was a fifteen-year-old 'coal miner driver below ground', and as his father's occupation was a 'coal inspector', it is clear why the family moved from their one-time home in Padstow, where Richard was born. (With the Cornish mining industry declining, many of its employees were forced to move elsewhere in search of similar work.) William Miners (sixty) hailed from Cramlington originally, although his wife, Louisa, was from Devon, and all four of their children were natives of Cornwall, with the two youngest, Elizabeth and Alfred, giving 'Callstock' as their places of birth. Agnes (fourteen) came from the same coastal town as her brother, Richard. The latter would have been aged around thirty when he died, and he is also commemorated at Thiepval (2A).

Each Brigade was assigned a Company of Machine Gun Corps (MGC), and the 64th – on the extreme left of the 21st Division – was to accompany the attack launched by the 9th and 10th King's Own Yorkshire Light Infantry. On 1 July, half of the 64th MGC was assigned to the assaulting battalions, whilst the remainder would advance with the supports – its role, clearly, to provide heavy duty covering fire when and where needed. After crossing No Man's Land, it was noted that a number of troops '… beyond the left flank of the Brigade'[10] were retiring [probably the Royal Scots of the 34th Division], and guns were established in this area. Seven weapons were known to have been placed in position, whereas it was believed others had reached the front lines. 'Hearty congratulations to all ranks M.G. Co. in the splendid way in which they brought up their guns yesterday', the War Diary was informed by senior officers on 2 July, 'General stated that he had heard good things said of the M.G. Co. on all sides'[11]. The 64th Brigade had made good ground by the afternoon, and set about consolidating its gains over the next few days, by which time the MGC could assess its losses. Much smaller than an infantry battalion, the personnel numbered just forty-five, including two officers, forty-eight hours after the assault had commenced. Three officers were dead and three wounded, whilst in the ranks, four were known to have lost their lives, thirty-four had been injured (one fatally), two were suffering from shell-shock and twelve were missing. Miltary Medals were awarded to a Sergeant and two Privates.

Pte Frederick Osborn Greenslade had fallen. Although born in Willesden, Middlesex, he clearly had connections with Cornwall, as he enlisted in Redruth was formerly in the DCLI. The *Royal Cornwall Gazette* would later reveal: 'Mr Frederick Greenslade, of Pennance, Lanner, has been informed that his son, Pte F.O. Greenslade, D.C.L.I., was recently killed in action.' The newspaper had not been informed that the soldier was, in fact, serving with the MGC at the time of his death. He can be found in the 1901 Census still living in Willesden, although his place of birth is given as 'Harlesden', and he was aged three in this year. Both his father and mother, Elizabeth, were Londoners, and moved to Lanner (also known as 'Lannarth', a one-time tin and copper mining village near Redruth) in the intervening years. Pte Greenslade is commemorated on the village war memorial (which gives his first name as 'F. Osborn'), and also on the larger monuments at Redruth, and Thiepval (5C and 12C).

★★★

Both flanks of Fricourt had been occupied by dusk on 1 July, and overnight, the Germans quietly withdrew from the hamlet, leaving the British to occupy it virtually unopposed the following day. Thus, the catastrophic charges by the 7th Green Howards and 7th East Yorkshires had been in vain. Once the 8th Somerset Light Infantry had gone over just to the north, the 10th Green Howards followed, but were met with a hail of machine-gun bullets, causing the lines to waver. Upon seeing this, Maj. Loudon-Shand leapt up onto the parapet and began urging his men forward, in full view of the enemy, and was soon mortally wounded, but then he insisted on being propped up in the trench so he could cheer them on until he died. The Major was awarded a VC for his supreme self-sacrifice.

Voluntary recruitment in Britain had now slowed considerably, and this trend had been recognised for some time by Lord Derby, the Government Minister responsible for filling the ranks of the armed forces. The so-called 'Derby Scheme' required that men of military age would give their consent to be requisitioned into uniform *if necessary*, and various factors such as age, marital status or the importance of their occupation would determine how likely an individual was to receive his call-up papers. This process did not produce nearly enough manpower during 1915, and so it was decided to introduce the Military Service Act in January 1916, which brought about conscription. In July 1916, when Britain's volunteer army was going into battle on the Somme, Lord Derby – now the Under Secretary of State for War – explained his aims of the Allied strategy:

> The offensive is proceeding in logical accordance with the British policy of wearing down the enemy. An advance along 20 miles of difficult country, defended by masses of enemy troops equipped with every deadly device known to modern warfare cannot effect a sudden collapse of resistance to our attacks. The war will not be ended by spectacular assaults on detached sectors of the German line, but by putting as many German soldiers out of action as lies within the power of the Allied armies. To that end the British Army is now contributing a splendid effort; an effort meeting with full measure of expected success.[12]

34th and 8th Divisions

The straight Roman road from Albert to Bapaume passed through the positions held by the 34th Division, crossed No Man's Land and continued beyond the heavily fortified German positions at a steady incline until it reached Pozieres Ridge, some three miles away from the British front line. This was the objective on the first day of operations, assisted by the Divisions on either side, who were expected to assist the main thrust of the assault by capturing their own territorial gains in conjunction with this most strategic of infantry advances. Therefore, the men of the 34th Division were tasked with the supreme and most daunting prospect of all on 1 July – smashing the German defences and manpower (which had been strengthened to the point of being virtually unassailable) during daylight hours. The enemy had calculated that this sector would witness the launch of the British army's most concerted effort on the Somme, and their methodical approach to ensuring that the initial offensive would have every chance of failure was not overlooked. Either side of La Boisselle were the infamous 'Sausage' and 'Mash' Valleys, funnelling would-be attackers into an ever narrower killing zone swept by machine-gun and sniper fire, while the village itself was yet another example of a stubborn fortress, fiercely armed with many weapons of war.

The 34th Division was part of the New Army, made up of three Brigades – 101st, 102nd (Tyneside Scottish) and 103rd (Tyneside Irish) – all of which would be committed to the attack at the same time. Whilst the flanks were the responsibility of the 101st and 102nd Brigades, the Tyneside Irish would be following on behind to punch a hole through the middle. To assist the advance, two mines would be blown at 7.28 a.m. – at 'Lochnagar' on the northern edge of 'Sausage' Valley, and at 'Y Sap', closer to La Boisselle and at the bottom of 'Mash' Valley. These had been secretly under construction for months, dug out by the Pioneers and Sappers of various units, and placed directly beneath the German forward trenches. It should, however, be remembered that grave doubts had already been cast as to the state of the barbed wire in front of the enemy parapets, and observers were convinced it was still intact in most places. Yet there was no option but to press on with the timetable, as everything hinged on this one portion of the Western Front – barely a mile across – and if the assault crumbled here, any breakthrough elsewhere might be rendered obsolete. The volunteers of Kitchener's Army were about to carry a huge burden.

On the right flank, the 15th and 16th Royal Scots – some of whom were already in No Man's Land – advanced at precisely 7.30 a.m. and immediately met a hail of machine-gun fire from three sides of 'Sausage' Valley, decimating the ranks, yet the survivors somehow managed to enter Scots Redoubt, where they grimly held on. The southern line of the Valley had been broken, but parties of various battalions, trying to storm into 'Sausage' Redoubt at the head of the Valley, suffered dreadful losses before finally retiring. The number of *dead* amongst the 15th and 16th Royal Scots by the end of the day was approximately 450, and the fate of forty-five-year-old Maj. Harris Stocks, DSO, of the 15th Battalion, gives some indication of the desperation of the fighting. 'I was out with him', noted one eyewitness, 'the last I saw of him he was wounded in the arm and bleeding, but he was still carrying on and encouraging his men'. Another stated: '… he was hit, I think, in the leg … This was beyond the third line of German trenches, when we were trying

Aeriel view/Lochnagar Crater.

to capture the fourth line. I heard afterwards that he had been taken prisoner and died of his wounds … He was lying down and appeared as though he could not move much'. Capt. Lodge stated that the Major had received a shot through the arm, and then the body, whilst attending to his 'batman' [servant] Pte Bishop, who had been mortally wounded. The Major – who was described as 'always completely fearless under fire'[1] – then conducted the defence of the con-solidated territory. Despite claims that he was 'wounded and missing', possibly a POW, it is a fair assumption he was already dead by dusk on 1 July.

One of the fallen in the ranks of the Major's battalion was twenty-seven-year-old Pte Eric Gibb, who was born in Lancashire and enlisted in Manchester. The SDGW gives his place of res-idence as 'Bude, Cornwall', and the soldier's service record[2] – one of a minority to have survived at the National Archives – reveals his father, Walter, was the owner of the resort's Grenville Hotel during the First World War. In 1901, Walter and his wife, Sarah – both natives of Manchester – were in the same trade, running a business in Cheshire, and by the 1920s, they were in charge of the Imperial Hotel in Barnstaple, North Devon. There is no sign of Eric in 1901, who would have been aged twelve and probably at school. He joined the army as a Kitchener recruit on 24 September 1914, at the age of twenty-five years and eight months, from his employment as a 'commercial traveller'. At 5ft 9in in height, he left Southampton bound for France on 8 January 1916, and his death is presumed 'for official purposes' to have occurred on 1 July 1916 after he had been posted as 'missing'. Serving with 'B' Company at the time, several of Pte Gibb's personal items – such as letters, photos, cards, diaries and coins – were returned to his family, although his body was not recovered to be identified, and he is now remembered at Thiepval (6D and 7D). Before the attack, soldiers were told to place non-essential accessories and sentimental keep-sakes in safe-keeping, ready to be re-claimed at a later date. Of course, many knew that a percentage of the bundles containing pictures of loved ones and special ephemera would soon be making the sad journey home without their owners.

The 10th Lincolns (Grimsby Chums) and 11th Suffolks (Cambridge Battalion) witnessed the Lochnagar mine being detonated at close quarters two minutes before the assault began, and were showered with debris as 60,000 pounds of explosives blew up across No Man's Land. Tales of the advance up 'Sausage' Valley came back with wounded Cambridge soldiers:

> We had been in the trenches five days when we were told that we were to go over the top next morning (1 July). The boys started singing and cracking jokes, and laughing themselves hoarse… We were due to go over at a certain time in the morning, and I can tell you it was a sight to see us go over in a storm of shell, rifle bullets and machine-gun bullets. You could never have thought we could have gone a yard without being hit, but we managed to get to the German trench. I got dropped just in front of it with a shrapnel bullet in my stomach, but most of the boys got there, as I could hear the Germans howling at them. While the wounded were on the ground the Germans searched it with big shells to try and polish us off.[3]

Another recalled how he used his rifle as a crutch when he received a leg wound, hobbling back across No Man's Land whilst '… the shells were bursting around like rain and their machine-guns were firing from all parts'.[4] Sgt Newman, injured in both ankles, declared: 'Our men [marched] onward through the greatest and most terrible hell that our boys will ever know; but, thank God, it was through hell to victory.'[5] Yet the Sergeant's optimism was sadly unfounded, because the 11th Suffolks recorded over 500 casualties by nightfall, and most of the survivors were back where they had started, unable to breach the German defences. The Grimsby Chums had also been torn apart, as predicted by their CO, Lt-Col Cordeaux, several days previously.

To the left of the 11th Suffolks and 10th Lincolns stood the men of the 21st Northumberland Fusiliers – 2nd Tyneside Scottish – who were to advance between the crater caused by the Lochnagar Mine and the southern edge of La Boisselle. The opposing trenches here were at a much shorter distance than those which were situated within 'Sausage' and 'Mash' Valleys, but the resistance from the Germans was just as ferocious. The Tynesiders were led over the top by pipers, and Willie Scott proudly advanced at the head of the 2nd Tyneside Scottish, being one of the first in the enemy trenches, but his body was later spotted by his comrades, bagpipes still gripped in his arms. Company Sergeant Major J.E. Patterson took charge of the 21st's bombers, and was awarded a Distinguished Conduct Medal (second only to a VC for men in the ranks) for his leadership and gallantry, whilst Capt. J.M. Charlton was noted for the way he brought a Lewis gun into action until the weapon jammed, whereupon he was killed trying to storm a German strong-point.

Once again, casualties were high. The combined number of fatalities for the 21st and 22nd (3rd Tyneside Scottish) which went forward together was close to 300, with many more wounded. Private William James Rowe★, a native of Penzance, was one of the former. Aged twenty-nine, he was the husband of Bridget, who lived in Newcastle-upon-Tyne, and the new recruit had enlisted in nearby Wallsend. His parents, James and Alice, were also residents of Northumberland by the 1920s (according to the CWGC, which also records his age), and the surname is prevalent both in Cornwall and in the north-east of England at this time. Pte Rowe is commemorated at Thiepval (10B, 11B and 12B. The Northumberland Fusiliers have the most names of any one regiment at Thiepval – nearly 3,000). [★There were a number of individuals with this name whose births in Penzance were registered during the 1880s, so he is *possibly* the same William James Rowe born at Penwith Street, in the heart of the town, on 18 April 1888. His father, William James, was a 'Carrier Master', although his mother's name is given as 'Frances'. His age and details of his parents do not match, but a 'James Rowe' married Alice in Newcastle during 1906, and if this was 'William James', the Carrier Master from Penzance, then his son may well be the Somme casualty, whose home residence in 1914 was Worthy's Court, Newcastle.]

The two other Tyneside Scottish battalions – 1st and 4th (20th and 23rd Northumberland Fusiliers) endured a disastrous day, advancing along the southern edge of 'Mash' Valley, to the north

Grenville Hotel, Bude, post–First World War.

of La Boisselle, only to be cut down in their hundreds by machine-guns firing at them from three sides. This attack is focused upon in more detail in the 8th Division narrative.

A mile *behind* the British forward trenches stood the 103rd (Tyneside Irish) Brigade on a position known as the Tara–Usna line, which looked down the exposed slopes of the Avoca Valley leading to La Boisselle and the valleys of 'Sausage' and 'Mash' either side. The 1st, 2nd, 3rd and 4th Tyneside Irish battalions were spread out across much of the width of the 34th Division, and therefore the regiments they were expected to pass on their way to delivering a knockout blow beyond the enemy's defensive systems ranged from the Royal Scots on the right flank to the 1st and 4th Tyneside Scottish on the left. At 7.30 a.m., 3,000 men rose promptly to time and began their march down the hill, straight into a barrage of fire from numerous machine-gun positions in and around La Boisselle. Once again, the earlier British bombardment had not succeeded in its task of flattening the German lines, and most of the 2nd and 3rd Tyneside Irish – advancing either side of the Albert-Bapaume Road – were cut down before they had even reached No Man's Land. On the right, however, following in the path of the 11th Suffolks and Royal Scots, the 1st and 4th Tyneside Irish kept going across ground which was not quite so open as the topography to their left. Five hundred yards now separated them from the Germans, so on they went, still subjected to the hostile attentions from emplacements which had not yet been overrun, but now the ranks had thinned dramatically, and only a handful penetrated the maze of enemy barricades, accompanied by small numbers from other battalions. Barely fifty soldiers from the original 3,000 of the Tyneside Irish Brigade reached a point 700 yards within enemy territory, and now they pondered their next move. Consolidation was, perhaps, the most likely course of action, even if their strength would not be sufficient to establish a competent stronghold, but these were not their initial orders. In the distance was Contalmaison, the Brigade's final objective, fortified – inevitably – by yet more Germans as it contained the HQ of one of its Divisions. In between were further trenches and barbed wire, but the decision had already been made. The remnants of the Tyneside Irish were last seen setting off towards Contalmaison, a staggeringly brave act on a day of unparalleled disaster.

The 103rd Company of the Machine Gun Corps accompanied the Tyneside Irish into action, and because of the widespread nature of the Brigade's alignment at 7.30 a.m. on the morning of 1 July, it is impossible to establish precisely where on the battlefield all of its casualties occurred. Capt. Millar, the CO, was killed, as were two more officers, with a further six wounded. The Company Sergeant Major had been hit; eight sergeants were missing (seven of whom were known to have been injured); two corporals were down, and at least one private was dead. Fifteen soldiers were incapacitated, and forty-three were unaccounted for, with a proportion of these already confirmed as requiring medical assistance.

Pte William Verran is listed in the SDGW as having 'died of wounds' on 1 July, although in all the confusion of this day, he was originally reported 'missing' forty-eight hours later. The *Royal Cornwall Gazette* revealed in mid-August 1916, that Mrs Verran, of Simmons Street, St Day, had received this devastating news from the War Office. It also noted that the soldier was formerly in the 3rd Devons, which is corroborated by the SDGW , and in addition it notes the soldier joined up in Tiverton, although his place of residence is given simply 'Devon'. The location of his birth is given as 'Genorap, Cornwall', which, upon closer research, is actually Gwennap, near Redruth. In 1901, the family was living in the village's Scorrier Street, and thirty-one-year-old Alberta, from St Agnes, is listed as the mother of William (seven), who has the same birthplace, and Amy, from Gwennap itself. There were a number of families named Verran associated with this area, with one owning a farm in the 1880s, whilst several others were involved with mining. Pte Verran's father, William, had passed away by the 1920s, and the soldier himself is remembered at Thiepval (5C and 12C).

The valiant attack of the 34th Division had failed. Having ordered his entire strength forward at the same time, the Divisional Commander, Maj.-Gen. E.C. Ingouville-Williams, had no reserves at his immediate disposal to deploy and assist the battalions which were struggling the most, but it has to be ventured that these men, too, would probably have suffered the same fate, as the German defences were just too strong. All four of the commanding officers of the Tyneside Scottish fell in the advance, and many officers of all ranks were killed or wounded alongside their men. Over 6,300 soldiers were classed as casualties by the end of 1 July; an estimated three-quarters of the entire Division, and only minimal gains had been achieved on the right flank. Pozieres Ridge, the first day target, was not reached until the end of July, and only then after the bitterest struggle.

Maj.-Gen. Ingouville-Williams expressed his deep pride in the exploits of the Tynesiders, and his Division as a whole, as well as sympathising with the huge losses. He volunteered to look for wounded at nightfall, searching through the carnage at 'Sausage' Valley to see if any of his stricken men could be saved. Clearly a senior officer of great compassion, he often shared the dangers of the ordinary Private soldier, and on 22 July he was close to Mametz Wood – the scene of many 1 July casualties for the 8th and 9th Devons – when he was killed by a shell. Undeniably, the Somme did not respect rank or humility.

8TH DIVISION

More formidable defences have seldom been assaulted than the German lines against which the British hurled themselves on 1 July 1916. If the weapons at the disposal of the attack had increased ten-fold in power since the days of Badajoz and Sebastopol*, in barbed wire, in deep dug-outs and, above all, in the well-protected machine-gun, the defender had the field engineer. That any defences could have existed under the gained a full equivalent. Naturally a strong position, the German line had been strengthened by unremitting labour, by lavish expenditure of materials, by skilful turning to account of every natural feature, by the employment of every device known to hammering to which the British bombardment had subjected them was almost incomprehensible; that any defenders would

Men of the 2nd Devons, pre-First World War.

survive to offer any opposition, let alone a vigorous and effective resistance, seemed hardly possible, and before the attack there seemed nothing absurdly ambitious in assigning Pozieres as [the] objective to the Eighth Division.

[★The Spanish town of Badajoz was besieged by an Anglo-Portugese Army in 1812, during the Peninsular Wars, and eventually overrun by the Duke of Wellington's men, whereas Sebastopol witnessed a similar scenario in the Crimean War (1854-56), with the Russians finally capitulating to the British.]

This description of the Somme fortifications from the Official History of the Devonshire Regiment aptly sets the scene for the task which faced the three Brigades of the 8th Division at 'Mash' Valley, as well as the left flank of the 34th Division, to the north of La Boisselle. Four Companies of the 2nd Devons left their forward positions during the last ten minutes of the British barrage and were within about 100 yards of the German trenches by 7.30 a.m., but just before this hour a thin mist drifted across the battlefield, which, added to the smoke and dust caused by the shelling, rendered observation very difficult. Capt. Andrews, who was in command of the front line, gave the order to advance, yet was felled by a bullet almost immediately. The Devon men, with the 2nd Royal Berkshires and 2nd Middlesex on either side, received horrific fire from the front and both flanks of 'Mash' Valley, and only a small number gained entry through the enemy wire. After a short period of consolidation, German counter-attacks drove the survivors back into No Man's Land, where they were the targets of German artillery-men, machine-gunners and snipers. British wounded began crawling back towards their own trenches, and a fresh attack was called off due to the alarming number of casualties. At 8 p.m., what was left of the 2nd Devons withdrew to bivouacs near Brigade HQ, minus approximately 450 men from all ranks.

Several of the fallen officers had close associations with the Devon/Cornwall border, such as Plymouth-born 2nd Lt Edward Jago, and 2nd Lt G.S.D. Carver, whose father lived at Whitchurch near Tavistock. Carver was originally reported 'missing', and testimonies from his men were gathered following his disappearance: '[He] went with [his] platoon into the German trenches', noted Pte Osborn, whereas Pte Home recalled that both he and the officer were wounded near the German wire, and both began inching their way back to the British lines, although the 2nd Lt died 20 yards from safety. Pte Burge '… recognised 2nd Lt Carver's face' as he passed the corpse in No Man's Land, and others in the battalion were in no doubt the latter was dead, although there were expressions of surprise that his body had not been retrieved if it was so close to the Devons' wire. Pte Goddard reported Carver had '… died of wounds in the field', and Pte Cox added he had last seen the officer '… in the first German trench [when we] were advancing. He [Cox] had to go on …'[6] Second Lieutenant George Carver has no known grave.

The *Cornish Times* announced in mid-July that: 'Capt. A. Preedy, Devon Regiment, second son of Revd Canon and Mrs Preedy, of Saltash Vicarage, was killed in action on the 1st inst. The deceased officer obtained his first commission in October, 1914, and was given temporary ranks as captain in February last.' Alban Preedy was born in Plymouth in August, 1892, and attended Allhallows School in the city before studying at Cambridge University. His service record[7] reveals that two of his brothers were also army officers during the war, and the captain's death was reported via telegram to his mother, Beatrice, almost immediately. J. Coyle, of the 2nd Devons, told his superiors: 'Capt. Preedy was killed on 1 July at La Boiselle. Sergeant Small, of my Company, told me this is a certainty,' whilst Chas Chad, of 'A' Company., added: 'In the big advance on 1 July (7.20 a.m.) … as I crawled back wounded, I passed Capt. Pridy [sic] lying dead [in No Man's Land]. It was after 8 a.m.' J. Sene believed the hour to have been much later: '… about 3 p.m. Capt. Priddy [sic] was killed in front of German lines.' Aged twenty-three, the officer is now remembered at Thiepval (1C).

In the ranks, Pte Samuel James Bailey was one of five Cornishmen to lose his life in the advance. Born in Hayle, he was the twenty-nine-year-old son of Samuel John and Kate, from Mount Pleasant in the town. The 1901 Census finds the family in the same district, with Joseph Northey (eighty-one), a retired 'engine-fitter', the Head of the household, living with his 'son-in-law' Samuel Bailey – also an 'engine-fitter' – and Kate, both of whom were natives of Hayle. Samuel J. junior, Joseph's grandson, was the eldest of four children, and he is now commemorated at Thiepval (1C). Pte Edward Bickford is listed in the SDGW as having 'died of wounds' on 1 July. Hailing from Millbrook, near Saltash, he is likely to be the seven-year-old Edward living at 'Blindwell', Millbrook, in 1901, with his parents Henry and Hannah. The CWGC of the 1920s indicates he was the brother of Mrs Alice Page, of Cornwall Street, Devonport, but the only sister mentioned in 1901 is four-year-old Mary. Pte Bickford, who was residing in his home village when he joined up in Plymouth, is another whose name is to be found at Thiepval (1C).

Pte Thomas Henry Davies also enlisted in Plymouth from his residence at Torpoint. A native of Camborne, he was the son of Richard, and was aged twenty when he fell. (Thiepval 1C). Pte William Peter Northey Gilbert was, by coincidence, another born in Camborne and living at Torpoint when he joined the army, this time in Devonport. The 1901 Census indicates a William Gilbert, aged fourteen and employed as a 'tin dresser', in the same house at Penpounds, Camborne, with his father, William (forty-four), who has the occupation 'tin worker' crossed out on the form and replaced by 'diseased legs'. His mother, Susan, was a locally-born 'charwoman'. One of at least six siblings, Pte Gilbert is once again among the long list of 'missing' at Thiepval (1C). Pte Arthur Petherick, who is remembered on the same monument, completes the quintet. The SDGW lists him as being born at Stratton, near Bude, and he enlisted in Holsworthy from his Devon home in nearby Bridgerule, right on the county border with Cornwall. He is not immediately identifiable in the 1901 Census, although there is a Petherick family living in Bodmin Street, Holsworthy at the time – Arthur (thirty-six), a 'tailor and cutter', his wife, Mary (thirty-eight), and their five children, all of whom were natives of the town. One of the youngsters is eight-year-old Francis A. Petherick, who is almost certainly the same Francis Arthur Petherick whose birth was registered in the Okehampton district during 1892, but there were also Pethericks born and bred in the Stratton area – although individuals called 'Arthur' do not feature prominently – so his precise details are unclear. This may be one of those cases where the soldier's place of birth is inaccurate, or perhaps he was known by a different Christian name.

'No accurate information could be ascertained as to the exact number of casualties the Battalion had suffered', noted the 2nd Devons' War Diary, 'although it was clear that there were very few left who had not been hit …'[8] Those who had survived were bestowed with three months' respite from the horrors of the Somme, whilst some of the injured returned home for recuperation.

The question asked most often of many of the wounded at Southampton is: 'Well, what did you feel like?', and this simple query in nine cases out of ten is answered by just 'Oh, all right'. A sergeant in the Middlesex agreed that he, too, felt all right, but added: 'I felt as if I could do with a drink'[9]

32nd and 36th Divisions

In the south of the 32nd Division's sector, near Authuille Wood, stood the German-held Leipzig Redoubt, jutting out into No Man's Land close to the British lines, and at 7.30 a.m. on 1 July, two battalions of the Highland Light Infantry (HLI) overran the salient before the enemy could emerge from their dugouts. Reserves being brought up to support the assault, however, were soon mown down by machine-guns in a position known as the Nord Werk, leaving the defenders able to re-group and launch a concerted effort to dislodge the invaders, which they achieved by nightfall. During the day, Sgt Turnbull, of the 17th HLI, captured an outpost which was immediately counter-attacked by the Germans, and remained under heavy fire for many hours, wiping out the small garrison – except for Turnbull himself – several times. He maintained the position almost single-handedly, and was later killed whilst engaged in a fierce exchange of grenades. The Scotsman was awarded a posthumous VC for '… displaying the highest degree of valour and skill in the performance of his duty'.

Further north, the capture of the village of Thiepval was handed to the 16th Northumberland Fusiliers and the 15th Lancashire Fusiliers, from Salford, with several units in support. 'D' Company of the latter was under the command of Capt. E.C. MacLaren, whilst a Lt Hampson is also mentioned in the War Diary as being '… detailed to lead one of [the] platoons'.[1] The summary below differs from most equivalent accounts as it is somewhat subjective, making comments and observations rather than merely delivering the cold, hard facts, although it does begin by reciting the now all too familiar remarks about the battalion suffering heavy casualties whilst crossing No Man's Land. It goes on:

> … certain officers, NCOs [Non Commissioned Officers] and men penetrated the [German] line and passed into the third line trench where it is almost certain they were seen later by our aeroplanes – in an isolated position. It is presumed that they gave a good account of themselves, and hoped that some were taken prisoner, probably after being wounded, and received good treatment.[2]

As at the Leipzig Redoubt, the Germans launched a number of determined counter-attacks, whilst at the same time targeting British reinforcements as they crossed No Man's Land. 'It was obvious by 9 a.m. that further efforts in this direction were a useless waste of life … Including stretcher bearers, the result at 8 p.m. was 3 officers and 150 men remaining out of a total of twenty-four officers and 600 men who attacked in the morning.'[3] The *Salford Reporter* would soon record how the likes of Capt. Heald – who found war 'distasteful' but nonetheless volunteered in August, 1914 – and 2nd Lt Quentin Smith – rejected twelve times before finally being accepted by the army – were both 'missing presumed dead'. A captain by the age of twenty, Heald was severely wounded in the advance, but kept going, shouting: 'Come on Salford, in at them!' Smith had only been with his new regiment since 19 June. The bodies of both men were not found for another four months.

The *West Briton* would announce in mid-July: 'The War Office has reported Lt Edgar Hampson, nephew of Mr J.H. Hirst, of Saltash, to be missing and probably a prisoner of war. He received his commission in September, 1914, when only eighteen years of age, having previously been in the Manchester O.T.C. [Officer Training Corps]. He has been at the Front over twelve months.' (A Manchester newspaper report differs by stating he had arrived in France during November, 1915.)

The 1901 Census reveals a thirty-seven-year-old Carlisle-born John H. Hirst living in Saltash and employed as a school master, whereas the same survey indicates Edgar Hampson (aged five) was a resident of Manchester's Broughton district along with his parents, Peter – the future proprietor of the *Salford Reporter* – and Edith. A former pupil of the city's Grammar School, Lt Hampson's service record[4] contains several eyewitness accounts of his fate on 1 July, including one from Pte J. Roberts, who recalled that both Hampson and Capt. MacLaren '… were last seen fighting in the streets of Thiepval with about 200 men'. Another testimony revealed:

> Informant [Sgt Nelson] states that on 1 July at Thiepval, Sgt Holman of B Company. saw both Capt. Heald and Lt Hampson killed in the charge. He told informant this and that both were killed instantaneously. Beyond this informant knows nothing as the Battn. was relieved that night'. Pte Jos. Appleyard concurred on 21 August 1916: 'He [Hampson] was shot in the stomach by a machine-gun in the German front line trench at Thiepval, and died at once. I was about 20 yards from him at the time. We hold these front line trenches now.'

The enemy forward defences were situated on the edge of Thiepval itself, so whether the lieutenant actually advanced as far as the streets of the village – as claimed by Pte Roberts – or if he fell on the outskirts of the fort, is unclear. In November 1916, the officer's body was found, identified and buried in Thiepval Wood, upon which confirmation was sent to his family. Peter Hampson's own newspaper would then reveal a further 1 July account from one of his son's lance corporals: 'The last I saw of Lt Hampson he was cheering the men forward and was himself leading. He was a good officer … and well liked by the men in his platoon.' Pte Hall added: 'He always was a gallant officer [even] under the most trying ordeal … He was a true English gentleman and not afraid of dying.' The grave was subsequently lost, and Lt Hampson (twenty) is now remembered on the Thiepval Memorial to the Missing (3C and 3D), which was built after the war close to where he fell. The monument and the clump of trees are within sight of each other.

The 15th Lancashire Fusiliers were also known as the 1st Salford Pals (Lt Hampson had the distinction of being the first applicant for an officer's commission in its strength), and there were a number of similar units in the 32nd Division, including the Newcastle Commercials (16th Northumberland Fusiliers), Glasgow Boys' Brigade (16th HLI) plus the Glasgow Commercials (17th HLI). Many regions of the United Kingdom and Ireland were beginning to experience losses on an unimaginable scale.

36TH (ULSTER) DIVISION

Ulster at the time of the First World War comprised the six modern counties of Northern Ireland, plus Donegal, Cavan and Monaghan, which are now situated in the Republic. This Division had been assigned an awesome proposition on 1 July – to secure the German Front trenches between Thiepval and the River Ancre (plus the removal of enemy positions on the north bank of the latter), storm one of the biggest strong-points on the entire Front (the Schwaben Redoubt), and then capture the *second* line German positions further to the rear. One advantage they possessed over many of their contemporaries was their position on the morning of the attack, which was situated on the edge of Thiepval Wood, and therefore their movements prior to the assault were largely hidden from the Germans. During the early morning build-up, hostile shells were launched in the general direction of the Ulstermen, although pin-point precision could not be established due to the lack of observation. In one of the narrow assembly trenches, boxes of grenades were being distributed when one fell to the floor, dislodging the pins from two of the small bombs, whereupon Private Billy McFadzean, of the 14th Royal Irish Rifles, flung himself upon the explosives to smother the blast, which killed him instantly. His courage and self-sacrifice prevented multiple loss of life, leading to a posthumous award of the VC.

At 7.30 a.m., buglers sounded the charge, and the Ulstermen swarmed across the intervening ground at great speed – unlike the regimented slow walk of their counterparts elsewhere – and soon the first objective had been secured. Others swept on towards the Schwaben Redoubt and surrounded it, having advanced nearly a mile under a heavy bombardment in an hour. The 107th Brigade was then ordered to attack, in pursuit of the German second lines, but received enfilading machine-gun fire from the flanks as both the 32nd and 29th Divisions were faltering either side. This Brigade originated entirely from Belfast, and had a strong Loyalist identity, with many men wearing their orange sashes as a reminder of the Battle of the Boyne. The War Diary of the 15th Royal Irish Rifles (North Belfast) continues:

> Casualties very heavy. Called for reinforcements but none available. About 10 a.m. large quantities of prisoners, maps, papers, etc., began to come in. Communication completely broke down owing to German barrage for five hours. Our Company. alone sent fourteen runners back only one of which got through … Capt. Chiplin was severely wounded ditto Capt. Tate and Capt. O'Flaherty killed also Lt Hind …[5]

Survivors of several battalions, including the 15th RIR, reached Stuff Redoubt and found it devoid of defenders, prompting some to press on even further into enemy territory. As the day wore on, the Germans launched their characteristically strong counter-attacks from the flanks, which the British had no chance of supporting with fresh troops, so the gains were gradually and systematically driven back, but not before some outstanding bravery from the Ulstermen was recognised. Capt. Eric Bell, of the 9th Royal Inniskilling Fusiliers, attached to a Trench Mortar Battery, displayed supreme courage throughout the day, leading bombing attacks on his own, resisting counter-strikes, rallying his men and organising fresh initiatives. He was killed near Schwaben Redoubt. By the end of 1 July, Pte Robert Quigg, of the 12th RIR, had already advanced three times with his platoon in the attack on the north banks of the River Ancre, but could not get through. The following morning, he went out into No Man's Land on seven occasions, each time returning with a wounded man, and was prevented from going out again by sheer exhaustion. In the same area, Temp/ Lt Geoffrey Cather, 9th RIR, performed similar acts of mercy in the evening of 1 July and into the next day, when he was shot dead by a sniper whilst bringing water to the casualties still stranded out in the open. The trio were all bestowed with VCs – a total of four awarded to the Ulster Division as a direct result of the first day of the Somme offensive. (The Schwaben Redoubt was reinforced by men of the 49th (West Riding) Division on 1 July, and one man of the 1/7th West Yorkshires – Cpl George Sanders – held on to an isolated portion of the strongpoint with a small group of comrades for thirty-six hours, without food or water, resisting all attempts to re-take the position. Cpl Sanders, who organised the defence and survived the rest of the war, also received a VC.)

Several Cornish newspapers announced in their obituary columns: 'O'FLAHERTY – Killed in action on 1 July. Capt. Douglas Hill O'Flaherty, Royal Irish Rifles, elder son of the late F.H.H. O'Flaherty, Esq., Belfast, Ireland, and Mrs O'Flaherty, Aughnanure, Newquay, Cornwall.' (Aughnanure Castle, in County Galway, was once the seat and fortress of the 'ferocious O'Flaherties', who formerly dominated large territories in west Connaught.)

Above: Thiepval Memorial/German trenches, 2007. Inset: Lt E. Hampson.

Left: Drawing of Capt. E.N.F. Bell gaining the VC.

Born in 1880, Douglas O'Flaherty was an Old Boy of Elstow School, Bedford (which closed in April, 1916 – O'Flaherty is mentioned in the school register for 1895, belonging to 'Russell' house). He married Beatrice in 1912 (the same year he and 500,000 of his contemporaries signed the Ulster Covenant, which opposed Home Rule), and his widow was informed of his death via telegram several days after it had occurred. Rifleman J. Spalding later provided confirmation to the War Office by stating:

> At Thiepval on 1 July 1916 at about 10 a.m. in the third German line trenches Capt. Chipman★ was shot by rifle fire and died shortly after. Capt. O'Flaherty was struck by a shell and killed instantly. I was close to Capt. Chipman when he was shot, and Capt. O'Flaherty was about 50 yards away. I was wounded shortly afterwards and had to crawl back to our lines which took me 7 hours under fire the whole time[6]
>
> [★Capt. W.H. *Chiplin*]

It is probable that Capt. O'Flaherty lost his life close to the Stuff Redoubt, which was reached just after 10 a.m. in the morning. His body was not recovered, and he is now remembered at Thiepval (15A and 15B), one of approximately 2,000 dead from the Division which recorded a total of 5,100 casualties. The stunning initial success of the Ulstermen could not be sustained, and having achieved one of the most significant advances of the entire day – equal to the gallant march of the Tyneside Irish – the subsequent loss of much of the ground gained was a bitter reversal.

After the war, Ulster Tower was built on part of the German front line taken by the 36th Division. It is an exact replica of Helen's Tower at Clandeboyne, near Belfast, and oversees the passionate commemoration of Irishmen on the Somme every 1 July. The view from the top provides a stark reminder of how exposed the ground was when many infantrymen tried to cross No Man's Land on their way to supporting their comrades already engaged in hand-to-hand fighting. Capt. O'Flaherty is commemorated on the Newquay war memorial, as well as at his old school in Bedfordshire, plus nearby Elstow Church – the tablet of the latter being erected in October 1922.

One wounded second lieutenant of an Irish regiment was asked the particular part he had played in the assault, to which he replied: 'Oh, I did nothing. Never got the chance, worse luck, but the men were fine. No men in the world could have done better.'[7]

29th and 4th Divisions

An often-shown piece of movie footage from the First World War depicts the huge explosion which occurred at Hawthorn Ridge, in front of the German-held town of Beaumont Hamel, on the morning of 1 July. 40,000 pounds of ammonal had been placed beneath the enemy Front trenches by 252 Tunnelling Company of the Royal Engineers, but the timing of the detonation was to have disastrous consequences for the attacking force in the immediate vicinity. There were many underground tunnels and quarries built into the chalk, some being hundreds of years old, having once been used to house medieval refugees during religious wars, and these constructions were utilised by the British in the run-up to the offensive, just as the ones in enemy territory had been by the Germans since the start of the war. One, accessed via the basement of a local bake-house, was used to house men and corn during the Franco-Prussian War of 1870, and was pressed into service once again during the First World War. Utilised first by the Germans in 1914, it was noted that the cavern could be accessed via a hole in the Serre Road which '… opens up after heavy rain', whilst '… heavy traffic … has for long caused trembling'.[1]

The British recruited local men to act as guides, and the utmost secrecy was required when digging towards a position directly beneath the German trenches. By its very nature, it was extremely hazardous, and the working conditions were pitiful, but the morale of the men was kept up by the knowledge that they would soon be delivering a very nasty surprise to the enemy above them. At 7.20 a.m. on 1 July, the Hawthorn Mine was blown a full ten minutes prior to the attack, as the plan was to rush and hold the crater before the main bulk of the infantry advanced. As it turned out, it only served to alert the Germans of the pending assault, and a ferocious fire was opened up with machine-guns, trench mortars and larger shells. To the south of Beaumont Hamel, and far enough away to be unaffected by the explosion, the Germans defending 'Y' Ravine subjected the 87th Brigade of the 29th Division to a horrifying cannonade ten minutes later, with men of the 1st King's Own Scottish Borderers and 2nd South Wales Borderers being mown down before they had gone even a short distance. The 1st Borders were also decimated, so the 1st Newfoundland Regiment – the only Empire battalion in the entire line on 1 July – moved forward from its reserve position and crossed the exposed ground to avoid the congestion now occurring in the communication trenches. With no artillery support, the Newfoundlanders were caught by the machine-guns which had already found their range, and as the men bunched to squeeze through narrow paths cut in the British wire, they were slaughtered in their hundreds. Within forty minutes, 91 per cent of 750 soldiers had been killed or wounded – the second highest casualty figures of 1 July – and the attack was called off. (On 28 June, Major-General H. de B. de Lisle, the General Officer Commanding 29th Division, had referred to the Somme offensive as the '… most important battle in which British troops have ever fought'[2], and expressed his supreme confidence in the outcome of the opening day.)

Following the Hawthorn Mine explosion, men of 'Z' Company, 2nd Royal Fusiliers, moved quickly to occupy the crater and immediately faced a devastating enemy barrage, whilst those trying to reinforce the forward lines were cut down in No Man's Land. This was due to the

British artillery '… persistently shelling the second and third line of the enemy's first system'[3], thus enabling the survivors in the German Front trenches to focus upon the attack, and at midday, the few remaining 'Tommies' out in the open were forced to withdraw.

Pte Henry Charles Walker is included here because he enlisted in Falmouth, although he was born and lived in Southall, Middlesex. The twenty-eight-year-old son of Henry and Helen, he was married to Anne at the time of his death, and is remembered at Thiepval (8C, 9A and 16A). Falmouth has links with the Royal Fusiliers, as the 16th (Reserve) Battalion was raised here in October 1914, whereas the 7th (Extra Reserve) RF spent a considerable time in the port before embarking for France in July, 1916. Pte Walker may have been visiting relatives in the Cornish town when he joined up, or been here due to his employment.

The 16th (Public Schools) Battalion of the Middlesex Regiment went up in support, only to be confronted by the same hostile machine-gun fire, and none of its men were known to have breached the German wire, which was largely uncut. Dead and wounded were strewn around the area of the new crater, and at nightfall, a number of the latter were removed by the enemy before being taken into captivity. One who escaped the fate of death or becoming a prisoner was Alfred Turner, of the Lancashire Fusiliers, who lay in a shell-hole close to the German trenches for two days and three nights, and one of the many bodies in the vicinity was that of a Middlesex officer, who had been shot through the skull. Turner noted the man's name – Barker – before crawling back to safety, whilst in the meantime, a Pte Allen had told his superiors of Lt Barker's death, adding he felt the latter was '… too far gone to do any good'.[4] Having been observed to fall at 8.15 a.m., the lieutenant died twenty minutes later, despite Allen's rendering of basic medical attention. A number of corpses around the Hawthorn Redoubt were not recovered until the following November, when Beaumont Hamel finally fell to the British and Commonwealth troops – yet another first day objective which took months to secure.

German soldiers would later recall how, on 1 July, the 16th Middlesex walked slowly towards them with their bayonets glinting in the early morning sun, only to lose over 500 of its strength before dusk, with most – like Lt Barker – having fallen within the first hour. Unable to retrieve many of the casualties due to No Man's Land being subjected to constant machine-gun and rifle fire, the best that could be assumed was that those who were unaccounted for had been taken prisoner, and messages to this effect were sent to many homes across the UK and Ireland. One such telegram arrived at the dwelling of Mrs Katherine Painter, of Killigrew Road in Falmouth, who was informed that her husband, locally born Company Sgt Maj. George Herbert Painter had not been seen since going into action on 1 July.

The *Falmouth Packet* revealed that the senior NCO was married to a:

> … Miss Thomas, of Penryn, and has two children, a boy and a girl. He volunteered for service when the War broke out, and the training he received in the old Falmouth Artillery Volunteers stood him in such good stead that he was soon appointed sergeant-major of his Battalion. Naturally, his young wife, mother and relatives are in a state of great suspense and the inhabitants of Falmouth and Penryn deeply sympathise with them in their anxiety.

The Duke of Cornwall's Royal Garrison Artillery was reorganised by the Territorial Act of 1908 and assigned to defending ports, with its HQ in Falmouth. In 1901, the Painter family was living at Snow's Court in Falmouth, where George★ (forty-four) – a 'mariner' born in the town – and his wife Elizabeth (forty-five), from nearby Crowan, were looking after their five children. Sixteen-year-old George Painter was the eldest, employed as an 'apprentice pattern maker'. (★In 1861, George senior was aged four, residing with his parents in Stills Yard, Falmouth. His father, listed as 'John Paynter', was a 'ship's carpenter'. Snow's Court, apparently one of the largest of the town's residential enclaves, was situated behind the shops in the main street. In 1912, nineteen houses, plus a bakehouse and a paint workshop, were demolished to make way for the St George's Cinema.)

CSM Painter's service record[5] is still in existence at the National Archives, and indicates that he joined up in Kempton Park (the SDGW states that it was 'Harrow, Middlesex') on 12 September 1914, from his occupation as an 'engineer's pattern maker'. He had been apprenticed at Cox & Co., the owners of Falmouth Docks, for six and a half years, and was aged thirty at the time of enlistment, having already served as a sergeant in the 10th (Falmouth) Company of the RGA Volunteers. His two children, mentioned in the newspaper clipping, were born in 1905 and 1907 respectively, and his mother's address in 1914, along with some of his other siblings, is given as 'Wellington Terrace, Falmouth'. (The SDGW gives his place of residence as 'Wembley, Middlesex', but this is not mentioned in the *Falmouth Packet*.) Still 'missing' in mid-August 1916, CSM Painter's death in action was finally deemed to have taken place on 1 July previously. He is commemorated at Thiepval (12D and 13D) and Falmouth.

Another Cornishman of the 16th Middlesex whose official military documents[6] *also* survived the Blitz in 1940 was Pte William John Button, who was born at St Mabyn and enlisted in Marylebone, London, during February 1915, from his employment as a 'footman'. He was aged nineteen years and 245 days, his mother's name was 'Annie' [Lostwithiel-born Susan Ann in the 1901 Census], and under the column 'defects' is added: '… some curious teeth'. The new recruit – whose home address is noted as 'St Tudy, Bodmin, Cornwall' – was unmarried, and had a number of older siblings. He contracted German measles in the spring of 1916, necessitating time off to recuperate, but rejoined his battalion in June, and took part in the advance on 1 July which would claim his life. Being another man whose whereabouts could not be ascertained after the advance, his effects were later returned to his mother, who also received his 1915 Star in 1919, his British War Medal the following year, and finally the British Victory Medal during 1921. (These were the standard campaign medals issued to millions of servicemen who were engaged by the British armed forces in a foreign Theatre of War between 1914 and 1920. The 1914 Star was awarded to the 'Old Contemptibles' of the opening skirmishes, whereas its 1915 counterpart was the domain of many Kitchener volunteers.) Pte Button is remembered at Thiepval (12D and 13D), and St Tudy.

On 2 July, the War Diary of the 2nd Royal Fusiliers noted: 'Salvage of dead and wounded still remaining in our own trenches actively carried on.'[7]. Four days later, the equivalent narrative of the 1/2nd Monmouths, from the same Division, recorded: 'A dog (spaniel) was found in No Man's Land and brought in.'[8] By this date, it seemed, only creatures with four legs could survive out in the open.

4TH DIVISION

Two German strong-points – the Ridge Redoubt and larger 'Quadrilateral' – dominated the 4th Division's sector between Beaumont Hamel and Serre. The 1st East Lancashires advanced to the south of Ridge Redoubt at 7.30 a.m., followed closely by the 1st Hampshires, but both suffered heavy casualties, and when the leading Companies of the 2nd Royal Dublin Fusiliers began to receive the same hostile fire, the remainder of the latter did not proceed beyond the British front line due to the carnage and congestion ahead of them.

At the end of July 1916, the *Royal Cornwall Gazette* announced:

> Mr And Mrs W.S. Watson, of 'Trevose', Capetown, have been informed that their elder son, 2nd Lt Charles Edward Stephens Watson (grandson of the late Revd Edward Watson, Newquay), has been reported 'Missing, believed killed' since 2 July. Immediately on the outbreak of war Lt. Watson was

called to serve in the South African Naval Defence Force at Simon's Town. From this he obtained a transfer, at his own request, to military service in the regular army in England, and spent a few months at Sandhurst. Last August he obtained a commission in the East Lancs. Regt, and was stationed at Laira Battery, Plymouth, until he left for France six weeks ago. He was in his 21st year, and was educated at South Africa [Rondebosch High School] and at Kent College, Canterbury, as was also his brother, Ewart, who is in training at Pontenstroom for service in German East Africa.

The service record[9] of 2nd Lt Charles E.S. Watson – known as 'Charlie' – reveals some interesting and equally patriotic facts about the mind-set of young men living in outposts of the British Empire at the time of the First World War. His father, William, wrote to the War Office in London at around the same time the officer's tragic circumstances were being revealed in Cornwall: 'My son was a great grandson of one of the 1820 South African settlers and was proud to return to the home of his ancestors to fight for his King.' After the Napoleonic Wars had ended on the battlefield of Waterloo in 1815, European migration increased dramatically, with many leaving for the New World across the Atlantic, whilst other destinations for British families seeking a fresh start inevitably included the locations of a burgeoning Empire – Australia, New Zealand and South Africa. Cornish miners were especially in demand, searching for the elusive gold and diamonds around the globe, but maritime skills were also required, both for transporting the prospective labour as well as running the fledgling ports when they arrived. Tens of thousands of Cornish folk left their home county during the nineteenth century, sometimes out of choice, but others from necessity, when famine or lack of employment forced them to re-locate on foreign shores. (Rondebosch would later record how 'Charlie' was '… a worthy descendant of those pioneers'.)

By 1914, the Boer War of 1899-1902 was still fresh in the memory, and although it pitted the Afrikaners (from predominantly Dutch ancestry) of the Transvaal and Orange Free State against Queen Victoria's Imperial army, these turbulent years inevitably affected the whole of South Africa. Cape Town, where 2nd Lt Watson was born in September 1895, remained a base for the British forces, as well as providing many hospitals to cope with the wounded and diseased servicemen.

The permanent 1915 UK address of 2nd Lt Watson – a keen sportsman – is given as 'c/o Mrs Watson, Hirundo, Tower Road, Newquay, Cornwall', and from piecing together other sources of research, it would appear that the officer's grandfather, Revd Edward Watson, mentioned in the *Royal Cornwall Gazette*, was a Wesleyan Methodist Minister for a decade from the mid-1880s, with his widow continuing to live at 'Hirundo' after his death.

The loss of 2nd Lt Watson in action was witnessed by a number of his men, all of whom agree more or less as to how it happened, but there are two curious statements to be considered first. Pte Spirring noted: 'Watson was wounded in the back by shrapnel at about 7 o'clock in the morning, half an hour before we started. I saw him taken away …' This is consistent with the effects of the retaliatory shelling by the Germans as they responded to the fierce hour-long British bombardment before the infantry went over. Spirring does not indicate how badly injured 2nd Lt Watson was – whether he was removed on a stretcher or walked to receive medical attention on his own. (The school records at Rondebosch contain a letter written by Revd W.H. Jefferies, attached to the 1st East Lancashires, to the second lieutenant's family: 'He was killed by shell-fire, and did not suffer.' This ambiguous report does not, of course, give a specific time of death.)

However, Pte Warren recalled that Pte M. Manion, of 'A' Company, told him: 'Mr Watson took two stars off his shoulders to come up into the trenches. He had lost a brother earlier in the war and wanted revenge. He was [a] captain in the 3rd Army School of Instruction …'

According to both Casualty Rolls – SDGW and CWGC – Watson was a second lieutenant, and therefore would have displayed one 'pip' on his shoulder denoting his rank. A lieutenant has two 'pips' and a captain three, so the reason for this discrepancy is puzzling. Had he actually been wounded and was returning to the front line against the advice of a doctor, or was he originally detailed to remain behind with other battalion officers – as was the case with every unit in the event of heavy casualties – but was determined to go forward into the attack? Was Pte Spirring mistaken in his identity of the man he saw being 'taken away', or equally did Pte Manion make an error in his observations of the individual removing two of his 'stars'? (It is highly likely that Pte Manion was, indeed, at fault. He testified that 2nd Lt Watson's brother had been killed earlier in the conflict, and therefore wanted 'revenge', but the former only had one male sibling – Ewart – who was still undergoing training by July, 1916.)

The remaining testimonies leave little doubt as to the last moments of 2nd Lt Watson. Pte Warren's memory of Pte Manion's account continues: 'He [Watson] got as far as the German first line barbed wire and was then struck full in the face with a bomb and was killed instantly'. From Pte Pilkington, who recorded that the officer was leading 'A' Company at the time came this: '[He] was shot through in the mouth [and] bleeding badly, and before he could be helped, [I] saw him shot again and killed.' (Pilkington added that the territory was relinquished and Lt Watson's body was not seen again, although a search was made.) Pte Parry revealed the latter had been seen '… fighting with revolver and dagger in German trenches, and his men say they saw him hit in the face by a bomb'. Pte Rochford wrote: 'I think he was with the bombers, almost in the German trench, he was hit twice in the face and I saw him fall [at] about 7.45 or 8 o'clock'. L/Cpl Harrington said: 'He was hit by shrapnel in the face. I saw him hit. He died and was buried in the ground'. Another account by Pilkington ran: 'Near German trench, I saw Lt Watson, a few yards to my left, carrying a revolver and a dagger. He was shot first in the mouth, and then in the head. The second shot killed him outright. He trained us at Plymouth before we came out. He was very brave; stuck at it very well and all our lads gave him a good name'. Pte Jepson recalled: 'Mr Watson was in a shell hole with L/Cpl McGee of B. Co … He told me that Mr Watson had had his face partially blown off by a bomb and that he had died. I do not know whether his body was ever got in'. Finally, Pte Hobson said: 'I saw Lt Watson on the parapet of the 1st German trench fighting with two or three Germans. He was shot and fell backwards, dropped over and lay still. We were in front of the trench for some hours.'

Rondebosch archives also contains the thoughts of a brother officer, who later remarked: 'It will be a great consolation to know that he died fighting and leading his men. We are all very proud of him … After all, 'Who dies, if England lives?'

Pte Upsdell remembered that the bodies of three officers were brought in some time afterwards, and he was convinced that one of them was 2nd Lt Watson; however, the South African is yet another to have his name inscribed at Thiepval (6C). His private effects were returned to his parents in his native country, who were also told by Revd Jefferies: 'All officers had come to form a very high opinion of him. The men of his platoon would go with him anywhere … He was keen on his work, and on more than one occasion proved himself a gallant soldier … [He] told me more than once that he had no fear of death'. Described by Rondebosch High School as '… manly, affectionate and lovable …', his former teachers and fellow pupils were stunned that 'Charlie' had lost his life '… amid such furious struggle', but commended his '… high and noble spirit with which he faced the chances of that fateful day'.

Nearby, the 1st Rifle Brigade and 1st Somerset Light Infantry were preparing to advance, five minutes before the appointed hour, when a German shell exploded in the front line. Lt Morum, of the 1st RB, who was standing on the fire-step with his watch in his hand, was blown to pieces, thus leaving his comrades in no doubt what they were about to face. The attack by the 1st SLI has already been discussed while examining the personal diary of Sgt Cook, but another account, spoken to the press by a lance corporal upon his return to England on a Hospital Ship, was printed in the *Somerset Guardian* later in the month:

Our fellows were only too anxious to get over the parapet, and there were several mouth organs going. Our brigadier-general [Bertie Prowse, DSO] had given us some encouraging words. He said: 'Remember, the old Somersets have always had a good name; keep it, and no lagging behind. Remember Plug street, the Aisne and the Marne. If anything wants shifting the Somersets will do it.' We had a sing-song and sort of feast before going up to the trenches, and all the boys were in excellent spirits. When the order came they were up over the parapet and making for the German front line…

The lance corporal subsequently makes references to the prisoners who were brought back, commenting they had not eaten for four days due to the severity of the British barrage. Having then temporarily lost his rifle, he was set upon by a bayonet-wielding German close to the enemy second line, and only managed to avoid serious injury by kicking his assailant hard in the stomach. The portion of the trench they had captured, near the 'Quadrilateral', was suddenly raided by another party of Germans, and the attack duly stalled, with vicious hand-to-hand fighting continuing into the evening. (When the author of the above arrived in London, he added: 'We had a splendid reception … and were nearly covered in flowers'.)

Holding out into the early hours of 2 July, the survivors of the 1st SLI were finally withdrawn under cover of darkness, and CSM Percy Chappell was the highest rank of the battalion to return to his own lines unscathed. (For his gallantry, CSM Chappell was awarded a Distinguished Conduct Medal plus an officer's commission.) Brig.-Gen. Prowse, DSO, the CO of the 11th Infantry Brigade and former officer of the Somersets, was the most senior officer to lose his life on 1 July when he was mortally wounded whilst re-locating to the newly captured German lines. 'The shell that killed our CO [Lt-Col Thicknesse] and Capt. Ford also killed Brig.-Gen. Prowse,' noted Sgt Cook, 'this cut short the career of a very brave officer'.[10] (The first statement is almost certainly untrue. Thicknesse and Ford – the Adjutant – are reported in the War Diary as losing their lives '… before our trenches were passed,'[11] suggesting it occurred early on in the advance, around 7.30 a.m. The widespread consensus of opinion regarding the death of the Brigadier-General is that he received his fatal wounds at around 10 a.m., when he was in the process of moving Brigade HQ closer to the fighting line. His high rank would have prevented him from going over with the first attack.)

The entire complement of twenty-six SLI officers who had formed up in the assembly trenches prior to the assault were either killed, wounded or reported missing by the end of the day. 2nd Lt Marler, who was in charge of the Brigade Dump in Vallade Trench, and 2nd Lt Roseveare, performing an identical role at the Divisional Dump, plus Capt. Acland, of the Royal Army Medical Corps, escaped injury, although the two second lieutenants did not advance. Ronald Chard Roseveare was attached to the 1st Battalion from the 9th, and was the son of Alfred and Ethel, who lived at 'The Dunes' in Daymer Bay, near Wadebridge. The nineteen-year-old was killed in action on 8 August 1916, near Ypres in Belgium, and his body was buried at Essex Farm Cemetery, which was made famous by John McCrae's poem 'In Flanders Fields'. After toiling in a Field Dressing Station for several days with hardly a break, McCrae temporarily left his task of tending to the hundreds of wounded men in his care and stepped outside for some fresh air, only to be confronted by many more graves which had been filled since he last saw daylight. In May 1915, following the death of a friend in action, he felt compelled to write about the poppies which were growing amongst the rows of crosses which had sprung up all around. Fifteen months later, 2nd Lt Roseveare – whose 'good moral character'[12] was certified by the Revd M.A. Bucknall, of St Minver, when the former received his commission – became yet another inhabitant of the ever-growing burial ground, which now contains 1,199 British and Commonwealth interments. The Cornish officer is also commemorated on a plaque in St Enodoc Church, later made famous by the Poet Laureate, Sir John Betjeman.

One of the 151 men from the ranks of the 1st SLI to lose his life on 1 July was, according to the combined data of the SDGW and CWGC, thirty-two-year-old Truro-born Pte Samuel George

Price, who was married to Margaret, of Notting Dale (Notting Hill), in London. His parents, Thomas and Charlotte, who were both deceased by the 1920s, also had residential links to the same area of the capital. Having enlisted in Bath, the soldier is now commemorated at Thiepval (2A), but the official records are partially erroneous, as no individual with this exact name was born in the Truro district between 1882 and 1886. Samuel George Price came into the world at East Hill, St Austell, on 14 May 1884, at a time when his father was working as a 'cutler', although it was his mother who registered the birth. The family evidently moved around the county, as Samuel's siblings have varying home towns listed in the Census returns, including Launceston, Bodmin and Penryn, and by 1891 the Prices had settled in Smithick Hill, Falmouth. The reason for the subsequent relocation to London is unclear, although a fair assumption is the quest for employment, as back in 1881, Exeter-born Charlotte was a 'street lace seller' in Tavistock, while the long-term trade of her husband, a native of Launceston, could rarely be described as lucrative. Samuel's occupation when he joined up is unknown (he was almost certainly a Kitchener volunteer, as he arrived on the Western Front during June 1915, after training), but whatever his job in peacetime, he may have been one of the unfortunate victims described in detail by Sergeant Cook in Chapter Five, caught by enfilade fire, or frozen in bizarre tableaux of death, perhaps seated at the rim of a shell hole apparently tending to his puttees. His Medal Index Card has the added entry: 'assumed died, 1 July 1916'. Evidently, no one who came back alive could verify his last moments.

Two Territorial battalions attached from the 48th (South Midland) Division – the 1/6th and 1/8th Royal Warwickshire Regiment, who were both based in Birmingham at the outbreak of war – took part in the 4th Division's attack on 1 July, advancing to the left of the 1st Somerset Light Infantry. Led by the 1/6th, with the 1/8th close behind, the Warwickshire men soon reached the 'Quadrilateral' (known as 'Heidenkopf' to the Germans, who placed a mine under the position should it be overrun), and some continued on towards the 'Feste Soden', in the second line, whilst others even penetrated further to a distance of 2,000 yards into German territory, but inevitably became isolated. Back in the main area of fighting, the defenders were engaged with bombs and grenades until the supplies ran out, with the War Diary for the 1/6th RWR adding: 'Enemy machine-guns and snipers were doing a great amount of damage all the while.'[13] Virtually surrounded at the 'Quadrilateral', the survivors from different regiments were eventually ordered to return to their own lines as best they could, but not before the two Warwickshire battalions had lost over one thousand men between them.

The *Falmouth Packet* would later record:

News has been reached by Mr and Mrs E.H. Moon, of Market Street, Penryn, that their son, Sergeant S.H. Moon is wounded and missing. Before joining the army, Sergeant Moon, who enlisted in the Royal Warwickshire Regiment in September 1914, was an assistant schoolmaster at St Mary's School, Birmingham, his first period of education being spent at the Falmouth Grammar School. He was extremely well-known in local football circles having played at one time for the St Gluvias Debating Society XI★, also the Grammar School. The young man, who is only 26 years of age, had been at the Front seventeen months, and the inhabitants of the ancient borough sympathise with the parents and relatives in their distress.

(★This football club seems to have been in existence from around 1900 until 1936, based in and around the vicinity of St Gluvias Parish Church, with the vicar usually taking on the role of president. Several pieces of relevant ephemera are held at the Truro Records Office, indicating Sidney Moon paid his 1s- subscription in the successive years of 1907, '08 and '09, and there is also the additional information that he scored one goal in both 1907 and 1908.)

Public Schools Battalion, 1 July 1916. (Imperial War Museum)

The Quadrilateral, 2007. Inset: 2nd Lt C. Watson.

In the SDGW, the residence of Sgt Sidney Herbert Moon is given as 'South Yardley, Birmingham', although his 'place of birth' is left blank. The 1901 Census finds him living in Lower Street, Penryn, with his locally born fifty-nine-year-old father, Edward, an 'outfitter, clothiers', and mother, Sarah, who was originally from London. The couple's six children were Reginald (twenty), an 'outfitter', Elsie (nineteen), 'manageress, bookshop', plus Ethel (seventeen), Violet (fifteen), Sidney (twelve) and Gwendoline (eight), all of whom were natives of the Cornish town. Back in 1881, Edward – a tailor – and Sarah were residents of the same address, this time marked as 'St Gluvias', and a two-year-old named Edward is present, along with Reginald. Edward is possibly the young man of twenty-two in the 1901 Census, living in Canterbury, although he has the rather peculiar birthplace of 'St Julvers, Cornwall' – possibly a corruption of 'St Gluvias'.

Sgt Moon was still reported to be 'wounded and missing' in mid-August 1916, and later presumed dead. He is commemorated at Thiepval (9A, 9B and 10B), as well as on the war memorial at St Gluvias Parish Church in Penryn.

Once again, despite early initial progress, the momentum of the 4th Division could not be maintained, leading to a devastating withdrawal. Once again, the dead and wounded were stranded out in No Man's Land, with the latter's only hope of salvation being the cover of night, when those who were able could attempt to get back at an agonising pace, whilst those who could not waited for the brave medics and stretcher-bearers to venture out into the hellish cauldron of sudden German flares and the attention of snipers. For some, inevitably, this mercy came too late.

The Rest of the Somme Front on 1 July

At the village of Serre, one of the most enduring legacies of the entire conflict took place on the morning of 1 July, when 700 men of the 11th East Lancashire Regiment – the Accrington Pals – walked slowly in the bright sunshine across No Man's Land and were mown down in their hundreds within twenty minutes. It was noted that: 'Not one man wavered or went back.'[1] A small group was last spotted heading towards Serre, hopelessly outnumbered, and never seen again. The attack was soon suspended, and the entire losses of the 29th, 4th (including the two Warwickshire battalions of the 48th) plus the 31st Divisions exceeded 14,000 officers and men by the end of the day, yet the assault had been repulsed at every juncture in these sectors.

A wounded officer told the press back in England he was '… jolly glad to hear Serre was captured after staring at Serre Wood for four months from the trenches'. (He was sadly mistaken.) The account went on:

> Many Germans were said to have come to this neighbourhood to rest, but they fought very hard for tired men. Their machine-guns, which they concealed cleverly, were very deadly. When our shells were giving them different kinds of hell they hid the machine-guns in concrete emplacements, and they had them out in no time when we advanced …[2]

To the immediate north of Serre, men of the 48th (South Midland) Division were holding the line between here and Gommecourt, but they were not issued with orders to advance on 1 July, and although their artillery and machine-gunners harassed the enemy throughout the day, the Germans holding the opposing trenches were able to concentrate on the British flanks without having to deal with a frontal assault from infantrymen.

Gommecourt itself – the so-called 'diversionary' manoeuvre to prevent the Germans from sending its reserves south to the Albert-Bapaume Road – was to be taken in a 'pincer' movement, with the 56th (London) Division enveloping the 'underbelly' of the salient to link up with the 46th (North Midland) Division, which would be carrying out similar operations on the northern fringes.

The units which the two wounded Cornishmen – Lt J.A.R. Reeves, from Tregony, and Pte A.G. Williams, of Truro – had been forced to leave due to their injuries received in the build-up to the offensive, were part of the 168th Brigade of the 56th Division. One of the narratives contained within the War Diary of the 1/12th London Regiment (Lt Reeves' battalion) recorded on 1 July:

> The whole of the Company was held up by uncut wire in front of the German first line and came under enfilade fire from a machine-gun on their left. This Company opened rifle fire on the Germans who were standing with their heads and shoulders above their parapets throwing box-shaped hand grenades. After about ten minutes nearly everybody in the Company was wounded … There was a gap of about 20 yards in the German wire through which Maj. Jones led a party of about eight men until he fell wounded about 2 yards in front of the enemy's parapet and was seen to crawl into a shell hole …[3]

Pte Williams' comrades in the 1/4th Londons advanced behind a smoke barrage, and by 10.25 a.m., reports were received that the leading Companies had reached the German second line, but subsequent contact was lost, leading to the employment of runners to establish the situation. At 1 p.m., it was disclosed that 'D' Company in reserve had suffered 50 per cent casualties, and half an hour later an urgent request came over for more grenades to be sent up to an isolated group holding out in the enemy trenches. A bombing squad was sent across No Man's Land, although none of the soldiers reached their destination, and when the dugout containing Battalion HQ was blown in, causing several fatalities, the immediate outlook for the assault looked increasingly untenable. An order to reform in the British assembly trenches was issued, and from a 'fighting line' of twenty-three officers and 700 other ranks who had formed up in the morning, only seven officers and 356 men answered the next roll call.

The London Division's determined assault on Gommecourt was finally driven out as daylight faded, with the survivors being bombed and sniped as they stumbled back to their own trenches. The 46th Division, meanwhile, was largely unable even to break the German forward system, and also lost heavily in the killing ground of No Man's Land, contributing to the combined casualty total in this 'diversion' of nearly 7,000 dead, wounded or missing. (At Fonquevillers on 1 July, Capt. J. L. Green, of the Royal Army Medical Corps, was attached to the 1/5th Sherwood Foresters of the 46th Division, and although wounded he rescued a stricken officer from the enemy's wire entanglements before dragging him to a shell hole where he dressed his injuries, despite being the target of numerous grenades thrown at the two men. Capt. Green then began bringing the casualty back to safety, and had almost succeeded when he was killed, leading to another posthumous award of the VC.)

Individual but often unrecognised stories of gallantry occurred up and down the line. Rifleman Perkins, of the Rangers, stated that he reached the German trench where '… he was seized by two Germans but managed to [fight] them off by striking them in the face with a bomb he was holding in his hand. He then got back on to the German parapet and was seen by other men of the Company standing there throwing his bombs into the German trench …'[4]

A week after the assault, two men of the Rangers were rescued by a night patrol, having been sustained by putrid water from the base of a shell-hole, yet – as incredible as it sounds – a private from the 1/4th Londons was found stricken in mud fourteen *days* after going into action at Gommecourt, extricated from his gruesome predicament and sent home to recuperate. He apparently survived.

The traumas which human beings sometimes have to face are quite staggering.

★★★

The first day of the Battle of the Somme was over, and the decisive breakthrough had not occurred; indeed, in some parts of the line where entire units had virtually been wiped out, a concerted German counter-attack was very much feared by senior officers. One Brigade Commander was dead (Brig.-Gen. Prowse, DSO), as were thirty-one battalion commanders plus other officers of all rank from major down to second lieutenant, in a total of approximately 2,500 killed, injured or unaccounted for. These numbers were carefully compiled over the following months, and the initial returns revealed that for the soldiers in the ranks, a horrifying 35,888 had been wounded, with a further 17,419 missing, in addition to the 7,449 already known to have lost their lives on 1 July. Therefore, in the twenty-four hours after midnight on 1 July, it was estimated that 62,000 men had been hit by machine-gun bullets, blown up by shells, or struck down during the ferocious fighting.

As time went on, the statistics of those 'killed' and 'missing' began to change dramatically, as the latter category included those still out on the battlefield (either incapacitated or dead), as well as the individuals waiting for salvation or identification. Some of those who survived eventually returned to their own lines, inevitably having missed the next roll call, and only rejoined their original battalions later – if they were fit for duty.

For those who advanced deep into enemy lines, however, their chances of regaining the British trenches were often very slim, and all were overpowered due to the lack of support. As we have seen with many of the individuals, they were still officially 'missing' weeks, months or in some cases even over a year later, as various eyewitness accounts were assessed and verified. Particulars of individuals who were not seen to fall dead were circulated amongst the neutral Red Cross organisation in the hope they had been incarcerated, and every effort was made to contact the various camps which existed in Germany. (The final number of British POWs taken on 1 July was put at 585, which is a very small total compared to the tens of thousands who attacked, but it does indicate, if any more proof was needed, the ferocity with which the Germans defended their lines, and the determination of the British to eliminate them. The *Royal Cornwall Gazette* revealed at the end of July: 'News reached Mr Charles Webber, of Newlyn East, on Tuesday, that his son is a prisoner of war in Germany. He was in the "great push" of 1 July, and believed to have been killed'. The 1901 Census reveals a forty-six-year-old Newlyn-born Charles Webber, who was still living in the town and working as an 'Elementary school teacher'. His wife, Elizabeth, and two children, Irene R. (fourteen) plus Samuel L. (twelve) were all natives of 'Newlyn E.', and a look at the Medal Index Cards in the National Archives reveals two possible matches for the latter – Cpl Samuel Webber, of the Welsh Regiment, and Pte Samuel Webber, who served with the Hampshires. Assuming the son of Charles Webber was, indeed, called Samuel, he is more likely to have been taken in captivity whilst advancing with the 1st Hampshires, part of the 4th Division near Serre, as this unit suffered heavy casualties in No Man's Land before being forced back, losing every one of its officers in the attempt. The 9th Welsh [Welch] Regiment was in reserve with the 19th (Western) Division on 1 July, although a small number were killed on this date, possibly whilst attached to other regiments, as the War Diary gives no indication of any deaths.)

The 'band of brothers' ethos was as strong as ever during the First World War, with comrades promising each other that they would contact their respective families should anything happen to one of them during an advance. In the case of the Somme offensive, with whole battalions committed to the attack, tight-knit platoons of men were often lost within minutes, leaving no one to tell the tale to their loved ones back home. Another factor to be considered is that over the next few months, the British and Commonwealth troops inched forward across a proportion of the 1 July battlefield, therefore finally securing ground on which the corpses lay, although the effects of Nature and subsequent shelling often rendered the remains unidentifiable.

Finally, the sobering list was complete. A total of 19,240 had been killed or died of their injuries as a result of action on 1 July; 35,493 were wounded, and 2,152 unaccounted for. In addition to the 585 POWs, this totals 57,470 individuals for one day's fighting. (The 2,152 unaccounted forincludes the men of the Tyneside Irish, last seen heading for Contalmaison, or the small group of the Accrington Pals and their equally doomed march on Serre. Whether 'missing' or 'not yet found', the devotion to duty of these men was extraordinary.)

When the family of Capt. Millar (the CO of the 103rd Company of the Machine Gun Corps which included Gwennap-born Pte William Verran) enquired about the delay in the return of his personal items, the War Office informed them: 'Some 35,000 letters are being sent weekly in connection with the effects of deceased officers and men.'[5] The parents of 2nd Lt P.J.F. Dines, who fell on 1 July whilst serving with the 9th Devons at Mametz, were soon informed of their own, private tragedy, and responded: 'Your letter of the 5th inst. informing us of the death of our dear son … has caused us great sorrow. However, we have the consolation that he died nobly for his country …'[6]

Original First World War graves and Ovillers Military Cemetery.

From the German perspective, their losses were astonishingly low considering the gargantuan army which was launched at them on 1 July. Although more prisoners were taken by the British, the number of dead and wounded was disproportionately far less for the Kaiser's men, and an example of this can be found in the 8th Division, which included the 2nd Devons and its Cornish contingent, at 'Mash' Valley. The British infantrymen in this sector lost over 5,000 on 1 July, whereas their enemy recorded less than 300. Despite the Allied gains made in the south of the line, around Fricourt, Mametz and Montauban, the remaining German redoubts and village fortresses, armed with their lethal machine-guns and protected by barbed wire, had repelled an attacking force estimated to be seven times larger than its own.

Even by the blood-thirsty standards of the First World War, the losses on this one day were appalling, and actually surpassed the totals for previous entire wars. Yet there was no question of the offensive being called off, and fresh reserves would have to be swiftly brought in to perpetuate this nightmarish battle of attrition.

Cornish Casualties and the Plight of the Wounded

Once the attack on Ovillers had failed in 'Mash' Valley, the injured of 8th Division – like so many on 1 July – were caught in the open, still subject to the murderous fire of machine-guns and marksmen within the German lines. Pte Cyril Jose, of the 2nd Devons, who had enlisted underage and trained in Bodmin, would later famously quote he was '… alone in a field of dead men',[1] lapsing in and out of consciousness for over twenty-four hours before he finally began to make his way back, having endured a night avoiding enemy patrols. His own battalion's War Diary reveals that in the afternoon of the first day that the British trenches were too narrow to allow stretchers to pass, and in addition many defences had been blown in so as to expose them to enemy fire. Such were the numbers of casualties, that Regimental Pioneers '… carried the wounded back to the Aid Post on their backs and in waterproof sheets'.[2] One of Pte Jose's stricken comrades, Truro-born Pte John Teague, reached the Casualty Clearing Station at nearby Heilly, but succumbed to his wounds five days later.

Capt. W.J. Gilpin, the former Truro College student who later joined the Royal Garrison Artillery, passed on his own observations about this relevant subject matter to his former school:

> Our infantry are magnificent, but the people to whom every honour should be given, and of whom one hears so little, are the stretcher-bearers. As a class they stand out miles ahead of everyone. In the middle of a scrap the cry: 'Stretcher-bearers this way', goes up; off they double to where they are needed. The wounded are coolly patched up and carried off under the heaviest fire … [The stretcher-bearers] went out at a run and back at a walk. One takes his hat off to [them]. All their work is walking about in the open where everyone else is hugging the ground and taking cover wherever they can find it[3]

One of the many hardships confronting the medical teams at the end of 1 July was the lack of available men to assist them, and although there were normally no shortages of volunteers, on such a day as this, when entire battalions were decimated and the able-bodied survivors had just endured a day's heavy fighting out in the field, most were in no fit state to spend the hours of darkness searching No Man's Land for their fallen comrades, however determined they were to do so.

Meanwhile, the newspapers back in the UK were also faced with a problem. They were obliged to report at least a proportion of the deaths and injuries on a local and national level to their readers, but at the same time too many grim stories of carnage and suffering had the potential for public opinion to turn against the War Effort, even though there had been much support for it back in August 1914. With conscription now underway on a large scale, any major setbacks on the Somme and elsewhere might seriously jeopardise the compulsory recruitment drive, so caution had to be exercised. Even so, the horrific losses on the Western Front could not be hidden forever, and the media began to tread a very fine line, reporting some stories with almost a 'Boy's Own' approach of adventure and daring:

> Falmouth Corporal Wounded. How a German Sniper Was Bluffed. Corporal M.J. Dalton, of 11, Clifton Crescent, Falmouth, a member of the 1st Hampshires*, has had one of his ankles smashed through a

German sniper's bullet. He is now an inmate in one of the hospitals in England. It appears that the corporal took part in the great attack, when he had the misfortune to be hit in the ankle … He thought the best way to bluff the German was to lie quite still and to pretend that he had been killed. The ruse succeeded and the sniper left the young Falmothian alone. The next thing Cpl Dalton knew was someone tugging at his coat sleeve and saying to him 'Come on chum, get in while you have a chance'. He looked up and found it was a lance corporal of the Dublin Fusiliers, so they started together to crawl back to their lines, where they arrived without any further mishap[4]. [*In the same Brigade as the 1st Somersets.]

Other headlines declared: 'CHEERFUL WOUNDED' and 'NOTHING TO WORRY ABOUT'.

Several train-loads of wounded came into London on Monday, and the men were very cheerful. They regard the advance in the light of an irresistible forward movement which will continue for many weeks … All the men had the usual adjectives to describe the noise of the tremendous preliminary bombardment. They state that the great shells altered the face of the landscape, and in places, it seemed that nothing could live there. That this was not so, however, was proved when the advancing infantry went past some trench or fortification that had still existed after the storm of high explosive …

An injured Major added:

You can't hope to move a yard on the Western Front without casualties, and the front lines of your advance absolutely must stop a lot of lead. There's no other earthly way of doing the trick, but it doesn't matter a hang so long as you get your objective or you enable fellows behind to come up, and so long as you give as good as you get … His machine-guns did the Boche priceless service. It was these, and not his infantry, that enabled him to hold our men at all …[5]

But the entries made in the War Diaries at the time are much more pragmatic. The CO of the 2nd Borders, in the same Brigade as the 8th and 9th Devons at Mametz, noted: 'Regimental stretcher bearers and RAMC [Royal Army Medical Corps] personnel rendered devoted service. The wounded were evacuated under very heavy shell fire and very great credit is due to the officers and men concerned.'[6] As has already been established, the retrieval of the injured was a huge risk, and often led to more fatalities amongst the rescuers, although there are documented instances of a humanitarian ceasefire in certain parts of the line to allow the medical teams free access amongst the casualties. Generally, however, there was little mercy shown, and even in the sections of No Man's Land which were not especially prone to hostile fire, the mere fact that many stricken men could not be reached in time contributed considerably to the inevitable slow and unpleasant deaths of a significant proportion who could otherwise have been saved by basic dressings or simply a drink of water.

The brave exploits of the three men who were awarded VCs for tending to the wounded on 1/2 July are recorded elsewhere in this text, but the tale of a Cornishman who was *recommended* for a VC is probably less well known. Capt. Robert William Michell, MD, FRCS, was the eldest son of Richard Ferris Michell, JP, from Glan Mor, Truro, and served with the RAMC from the outbreak of the First World War. When the Somme offensive began, the fifty-six-year-old was attached to a Battery of the Royal Garrison Artillery, witnessing dreadful scenes of bloodshed inflicted by the enemy upon his own men as they went forward into battle. On 3 July, he was organising rescue parties to bring in the wounded near Thiepval who had been lying out in No Man's Land for forty-eight hours, and was himself struck down by a piece of shrapnel which became embedded between his shoulder blades, paralysing him in the act of assisting one of the casualties. This was apparently his second injury in a short time, although the first had not prevented him from continuing with his duties. Now, however, he collapsed amongst the men he was trying to rescue and remained helpless for eight hours until he was spotted, leading to his subsequent return to Guy's Hospital in London, followed by a final move to a private nursing home, where he succumbed to his injuries on 20 July.

The captain's wounding and eventual death was widely reported in the Cornish newspapers, and it was rumoured that his name had been put forward to receive a VC, but in the event no gallantry medal was bestowed upon him. A Boer War veteran, he volunteered again when the First World War began, and survived an attack by a German submarine when he was on board the Hospital Ship *Asturias* (which was later sunk in 1917). A married man with a young son, Capt. Michell ran a medical practice in Cambridge, and it was here in a local cemetery where his body was laid to rest following a military funeral. (Back in 1881, the Michells were living at their 'Glan-Mor' address in Kenwyn, Truro, with forty-year-old Richard – a 'merchant' – his wife, Margaret, and their seven children, plus three servants, present in the household. All members of the family had been born close by, as had twenty-year-old Robert, although he was now an undergraduate at Cambridge.) Capt. Michell's demise was announced as far away as New Zealand, which was the home of his wife, Emily.

The 27th Field Ambulance War Diary[7] for July 1916, reveals the traumas and struggles faced by the medics on the battlefield. Private Longworth, who had received a gun-shot wound as well as suffering from shell-shock, requested a transfer from a Casualty Clearing Station back to his own unit on the 4th, whereas on the following day, Sgt Mackie was recommended for a Distinguished Conduct Medal for attending to injured men under fire. 'The bearers are in good spirits despite casualties, but had a rough time in BERNAFAY WOOD which is being thoroughly and systematically shelled'. Sgt Mackie was twice put forward to be awarded a DCM before receiving injuries himself, whilst Pte Brown was similarly singled out after working continuously for thirty-six hours after the start of the assault. It was also noted that Capt. Whitworth, the Officer Commanding the Bearer Division, should be decorated with a Military Cross.

By the middle of the month, it was revealed: 'The [stretcher-bearers] are now sadly depleted and reinforcements are urgently needed'. After the infantry advanced at 3 a.m. on the morning of the 14th, '… Capt. Whitworth and No. 1 section of bearers went out to collect wounded'. Enemy prisoners 'appeared over the rise' soon afterwards, but at 7.30 a.m., Capt. Whitworth was brought in by two *German* stretcher-bearers with shrapnel wounds to his buttocks and left arm, as it would appear the officer and his men were looking for a suitable collection post when a shell exploded close by. (Just days later, ten more of the strength were either killed or wounded, prompting the grim entry: 'This is a very heavy blow – some of my best men are gone'.)

Capt. Henry Parks Whitworth was the son of Dr. W. Whitworth, of St Agnes in Cornwall, and back in 1901, the family was living along Vicarage Road in the village. Forty-seven-year-old William was a 'Registered Medical Practitioner' who was born in the hamlet, as were his two sons, Henry P. (eleven) and George A. (seven). The boys' mother, Emily, came from Cubert in the county. After studying at Epsom College in Surrey, Henry Whitworth became a House Doctor and eventual Casualty Officer at Guy's Hospital in London, enlisting into the RAMC as a qualified medical practitioner during December 1914. Following the captain's Somme injury, his father sent a telegram from St Agnes to the War Office requesting more news, adding: 'Would you please enquire for his anxious mother?'[8], and the casualty was eventually sent to recuperate at the familiar surroundings of Guy's Hospital. Later returning to the Front, Capt. H.P. Whitworth was reported to be 'dangerously ill, g.s.w. [gun-shot wound] head'[9] on 16 October 1918, and he passed away on the 29th at the age of twenty-nine, having recently been awarded a Military Cross. He lies buried at the Duhallow Advanced Dressing Station Cemetery near Ypres in Belgium.

Now that the events on the battlefield have been dealt with, the role of the facilities further back from the fighting can be focused upon in more detail. Pte C.M. Barnes, an Old Boy of Truro College serving with the RAMC, noted later: 'At the commencement of the "Push" we had one lively day. Our total for the first twelve hours being just over twelve hundred …'[10] At Mametz, in the sector held by the 7th Division, the 22nd Field Ambulance War Diary reveals for 1 July that its Advanced Dressing Station (ADS) began receiving casualties at 7.45 a.m., where the walking wounded were given medical attention, food and hot drinks. Stretcher cases provided more of a problem, as their numbers blocked one of the trenches set aside to bring more reserves up to the firing line. The Main Dressing Station had been set up in the Church Army Hut, and a large flare lamp was commandeered as darkness fell to enable '… the dressings to be done outside all through the night'.[11]

By 2 p.m., the congestion had become a real problem, and was only relieved by the requisitioning of German prisoners to assist with carrying stretchers, although the amount of items available to transport the patients was a major drawback. Requesting a further fifty stretchers at 10.30 p.m., only half that number were received six hours later, and the cramped trenches were now overflowing with patients. Only five motor ambulances had reached the ADS by the early hours of the 2nd, but this service was improved as the day wore on, and by midnight, the battle ground had been cleared of its disabled combatants. (Having secured Mametz, this task was much easier to accomplish than at other parts of the line which had not moved at all, such as around La Boisselle and Ovillers. Here, the Casualty Clearing Stations were overwhelmed with blood-stained men, and even had to close at one stage because the staff just could not cope.)

The more serious cases were placed on trains and transported away either to one of the many Base Hospitals behind the line (depending on the severity of the wound), or back home to 'Blighty'. This evacuation chain became hugely efficient during the Somme offensive, and required extensive organisation, leading to scenes such as the following:

> When a train arrives at a railhead it is met by the R.T.O. [Railway Transport Officer] or other officer sent from the [casualty] clearing station, who arranges with the O.C. [Officer Commanding] of the train the number of lying down and sitting up cases to be taken. The RAMC orderlies from the clearing station bring the patients in cars to the railheads where they unload them, stretcher cases being laid on the platform. One of the train's M.O.s [Medical Officers] quickly inspects them, and gives orders to train orderlies as to the coach and compartments in which each patient is to be placed, while the other two train M.O.s superintend the actual loading of the train … The train filled and the line clear, we started for our 'base' [hospital]. No one who has not witnessed it can imagine the care and skill with which our RAMC orderlies can load a train of men suffering from extremely severe and painful wounds, and the ingenious devices by which they continue to make the journey less painful[12]

In public, the casualties were said to be 'cheerful', but in reality, of course, the situation was grave in the extreme. As the Somme offensive ploughed on, and thousands of bloodied, broken men returned home in the manner described above, the authorities screened off a number of platforms at major railway stations which were disembarking the wounded in order to prevent prying eyes from seeing the horrific consequences of the battle raging on the Western Front.

For those who did reach 'Blighty', the next huge logistical task facing the War Office was where to send this colossal, incapacitated army of men in khaki and bandages. The Territorial Forces Act of 1908 recognised the need for the care of casualties in the event of war, and plans were initiated to requisition civilian hospitals for the treatment of military personnel right across the country, with the largest in the South West being the 4th Southern General Hospital in Plymouth, which would be required to set aside beds for a capacity of 193 officers and over a thousand men in the ranks. Other, smaller sites in each district were also ear-marked, but when hostilities finally began, the scheme was found to have been grossly underestimated, leading to all manner of large public and private buildings in the form of lunatic asylums, country estates and civic halls becoming centres for the treatment of the sick and injured.

A stricken serviceman was not necessarily sent to his home-town or county to convalesce, so men of all regional accents ended up being taken to parts of the country they may not have even heard of before they joined the army, but even so, the local population made every effort to welcome these beleaguered strangers who had endured untold horrors on the battlefield. Under the heading 'Wounded Soldiers Entertained', the *Falmouth Packet* announced in August 1916: 'Through the kindness of a number of the ladies of Flushing, twenty-six wounded soldiers were entertained to tea and games at Trefusis Fields on Wednesday. Cigars and cigarettes were provided, and the excellent climatic conditions prevailing allowed of a very enjoyable time being spent.' A letter signed by a 'Visitor' sent the following proposal to the Editor of the same publication:

> Sir – may I suggest through the medium of your widely read paper that during this very fine, hot weather, it would be a great kindness if owners of gardens in and near Falmouth would open them for the use of convalescent soldiers? I feel sure they would be very grateful to be allowed to sit quietly under the shade of trees, and, of course, if tea was given to them it would add to their pleasure.

The following Cornishmen, or those with a connection to the county – listed in order of rank – were all wounded on or around 1 July 1916 and the brief details found in newspaper articles have been subjected to further research, although some is merely speculative.

'Lt E.F. Boultbee of the Machine Gun Corps was severely wounded in the British advance on 1 July, and is lying in a hospital in England. He married fourteen months ago the only daughter of the late Colonel Bolitho, of Kenegie, and she died of appendicitis four months ago.' Born at Woburn Sands, Bedfordshire, in 1883, Edward Boultbee was working as a bank clerk in Hammersmith, London, by 1901, and joined the army in 1914, serving first with 'A' Squadron, 4th Troop, of Lord Strathcona's Horse on Salisbury Plain, followed by stints with the London Scottish and a Canadian infantry unit before receiving his commission with the Northamptonshire Regiment. He went to France in March 1916, transferring to the MGC two months later, and the circumstances of his injuries were later revealed to a Medical Board by the officer himself:

> On 1 July 1916, trying to take over machine-guns with the first part of the attack, to the German lines, I was severely wounded ... struck by a bullet in upper third of left arm on outer side: this passed through making its exit on inner side ... At the time of being hit I was in No Man's Land ... the artery being severed and the nerves injured ...[13]

The War Diary indicates that Boultbee moved out at 7.30 a.m. behind the 4th Middlesex, but he along with many of the gun teams were brought down out in the open. His hand paralysed, Lt Boultbee – who went forward with the 63rd Company, MGC, of the 21st Division near Fricourt, along with the 8th Somersets and others – was treated at No. 34 Casualty Clearing Station before being repatriated, spending many months at the Northumberland War Hospital and an equivalent in Brighton, where he underwent at least two operations. Desiring to be appointed a machine-gun instructor at Grantham (the HQ of the MGC), his medical report indicates '... progress is very slow'[14], and he eventually transferred to the Royal Air Force in the final year of the conflict, after which he moved to Canada.

The officer's service record reveals he was 'unmarried' when he joined up at the start of the war, and he wed Gertrude Bolitho in Penzance during the spring of 1915. She was born at 'Poltair', Madron, near Penzance, in February 1894, the daughter of Lt-Col (retired) Otho Glynn and Mary Bolitho. Her father, who was also a native of Penzance, was formerly in the 3rd Dragoon Guards, and came from a family of distinguished army officers. Lt-Col William Bolitho, DSO, a Boer War veteran, commanded the 1st Devon Yeomanry during the First World War, and lost a son, Lt W.T.M. Bolitho, of the 19th Hussars, on active service in 1915. 2nd Lt Geoffrey Bolitho, of the Royal Flying Corps, died in France on 25 October 1916, and a number of the descendants of Bolithos who emigrated to Australia during the 1860s returned to fight with the Empire forces on the Western Front during the 1914-18 conflict.

Different members of the Bolitho family were influential in Gulval, Trengwainton, Polwithen, Trevelloe and other areas of Penzance, with St Pol de Leon Parish Church in nearby Paul containing several memorial windows and plaques to the family. The war memorial in Mousehole was unveiled by Mrs Bolitho, the widow of Col W.E.T. Bolitho, who died after a long illness in 1919. Many of the properties which were once owned by the Bolithos are now holiday homes or flats, including 'Kenegie', which was bought by Thomas Simon Bolitho – father of Otho – during the nineteenth century.

'Lieut. John Jenkyn, wounded in the Somme battle, is a son of the late Mr John Jenkyn, of St Ives, and is attached to a Welsh Regiment'. Once again, the 1901 Census provides a probable match – thirty-seven-year-old John Jenkyn, a builder living in Belmont Terrace, St Ives, with his wife, Catherine, and their two children, Kate (seven) and John (six), all of whom were natives of the seaside town. In the absence of a service record, the Army Officer's List of June 1916, reveals that a Lt J. Jenkyn was serving with the 3rd Monmouthshire Regiment at this time, although the War Diary of the latter is *also* unavailable, so precise details are not to hand. The 3rd Monmouths were performing the role of the Pioneer Battalion for the 49th (West Riding) Division on 1 July, when the latter – in reserve – sent two Companies of the 1/7th West Yorkshires to assist the 36th (Ulster) Division at Thiepval. Men of the 49th were subjected to an enemy bombardment on 8 July, and fought off an attack on the Leipzig Salient a week later, whereas the SDGW reveals the first Somme fatality of July for the 3rd Monmouths occurred on the 4th, with several more dying of their wounds later in the month.

> Lt Ronald Trounce, of the East Yorks, elder son of Mr and Mrs S.P. Trounce, of Culroy, Truro, was wounded in the great advance on 1 July. He was shot through the left knee by a machine-gun just as he had mounted the parapet of a German trench. The knee-cap has been removed and Lieut. Trounce is in hospital in France, making satisfactory progress.

Born in Sidmouth, Devon ('St Mary, Truro' is crossed out in his service record[15]), he was working as a bank clerk when he enlisted into the Devon Yeomanry in Cornwall's cathedral city during March, 1915, aged twenty-one years and seven months. His one time address was 'Bank House, Truro', but when he received his commission into the 3rd East Yorkshires, the residence 'Culroy' is given instead, and he later transferred to the 1st Battalion, which had been in France and Flanders since September 1914.

Just before 7.30 a.m. on 1 July, to the north of Fricourt in the 21st Division sector, the fierce British barrage of the first German trench system was lifted, and the infantry moved forward. The 1st East Yorkshires, following behind the 9th and 10th King's Own Yorkshire Light Infantry, noted: 'Although our bombardment had been very severe and the German trenches were badly damaged, there were still a few machine-guns untouched and these took a heavy toll on the battalion. In spite of heavy losses, the Brigade pushed on and seized the first objective …'[16] Lt Trounce is noted as one of eleven injured officers (the CO, Lt-Col Stow, later died of his wounds, whilst another was 'missing believed killed'), and his service record indicates: 'patella fractured', which was later removed at No. 34 Casualty Clearing Station.

Asked the following questions, the replies of the doctors treating Lt Trounce are revealed after each: 'Was the injury in the first instance very severe?' – 'Yes'; 'Are the effects likely to be permanent?' – 'Yes'. 'He is fit for duty at home in an office only …' At Falmouth Hospital, it was declared: 'The left knee is almost completely rigid and seems likely to remain so. He is in consequence unable to walk any distance. The disability unfits him for any military service except office work'. In November 1916, the officer wrote from an address 'Trewinnard', Penarth: 'I have been fitted for a hinged splint which I am to wear for the rest of my life.' The following month, when his period of sick leave was due to end, he informed the War Office he would be returning to Truro, and that he had received no news about a possible wound gratuity. In 1917, he applied for a position in a shipping firm, and the CO of the 3rd East Yorkshires – Trounce's original battalion – implored the War Office: 'There are so many officers now, unfortunately, who are only capable of admin work owing to their wounds that I beg to recommend that this officer's request is granted, namely that he be allowed to retire'.

'Sgt Thomas W. Keskeys, R.E., son of Mr Robert Keskeys, Germoe, was wounded within ten minutes of the beginning of the great fight on 1 July'. The Sergeant's service record[17] is still in existence at the National Archives, revealing he was born at 'Germoe, Helston, Cornwall' and working as a 'wheelwright', employed by Mr Jewell, when he joined the Cornwall Royal Garrison Artillery in 1910, aged seventeen. He became a Regular with the Royal Engineers three years later and went abroad with the first contingent of the BEF in August 1914, becoming an 'Old Contemptible' in the process. Serving with the 9th Field Company, RE, he was part of the 4th Division near Serre on 1 July 1916, with different sections allocated to all parts of the line, re-wiring and restoring damaged defences and trenches. The War Diary indicates that two men in the ranks were killed on this date, and nine wounded, with the Sergeant's documents stating he was admitted to the 20th Field Ambulance on 2 July. The papers also declare that he had been awarded a Military Medal for gallantry prior to the Somme attack; he stayed on active service until May 1917, and his father ran the Post Office in Germoe. (The service record of a John Keskeys is in the same batch, and this is almost certainly Sgt Keskeys' brother, who was aged nine in 1901 when the family was living at Bal West, Germoe. The former also joined the RE from his trade as an 'acid carrier', working at the Bute National Explosive Works in Hayle from his home address of 'Ashton, Helston'.)

Sgt Keskeys spent the remainder of the war in the UK, but went to Hong Kong in 1920, and died in Preston Military Hospital on 3 March 1925, having reached the rank of staff sergeant. His death was reported in a Cornish newspaper, stating he was the '… beloved youngest son of Robert and the late Susan Mary Keskeys, of Bal-west, Germoe', and that he was thirty-one years old. He was the father of Cecily and Nelson.

Corpl. Claude Symons, R.E., eldest son of Mrs T. Symons, 100, Kenwyn Street, Truro, has been wounded in action, and is now in hospital at Cardiff. In a letter to his mother, printed in the *Royal Cornwall Gazette*, he states: 'On our arrival at Swansea the station was packed, and the people cheered us as we drove away in cars to our destination. I was wounded on the first day of the great advance, about an hour or so before our lads attacked. I have been told I shall be here about six months, but I hope to be about a bit sooner than that. I have had two fingers removed from my right hand (the little finger and the ring finger), which is not so bad considering what the others got. I think I got off lucky, because there were eighteen killed and twenty-five wounded by the same shell that got me. We came away so quick that I lost everything, even my watch which father gave me …' Corpl. Symons is 26 years of age.

British dead on the Somme. Inset: Capt. R. Michell.

Aged ten in 1901, Claude Symons was living in Calenick Street, Truro, with his mother, Amelia, and numerous siblings, although there is no mention of his father, who may have been serving in South Africa at the time, as his wife is listed as 'married' rather than a 'widow'. Cpl Symons arrived in France on 1 August 1915, and survived the war.

> Pte O. Zimber. Second son of Mr C.F. Zimber, of Fore Street, Bodmin, who was in the taking of Montawban [Montauban, 1 July] and came through without a scratch. He was also in the recent Trones Wood attack [14 July], where he first received a bayonet wound in the right hand, and was later shot in the shoulder by a German officer with his revolver. He is now in a Manchester hospital.

Listed in the 1901 Census as eight-year-old 'Oscar', born in Bodmin, his father, Charles – a jeweller – was, ironically, a German national. Although there is no match in the Medal Index Cards, Pte Zimber was almost certainly serving in the 18th Division on 1 July, as his comrades were also later detailed to attack Trones Wood. Charles Zimber and his brother, Roman (another Bodmin jeweller and previously classed as a 'watchmaker' in his native land) were undoubtedly registered as 'aliens' when war broke out, yet at least five men with this surname served in the British army between 1914 and 1918 – four of whom, it would seem, were linked to Cornwall. The fifth, a 1915 casualty, came from another branch of the family based in Ireland. 'Zimber Bodmin' watches are still turning up at auctions to this day.

'Pte Vibart, the county wicket-keeper, of the Middlesex Regiment, who was wounded at the Front, has been recuperating at Camborne.' This particular individual – Ronald Francis Vibart – had an interesting, varied and ultimately tragic life, which, according to the cricketing publication *Wisden Almanac* started with great promise, being educated at Harrow and having played at Lords in 1893 at the age of fourteen. He apparently won the Ebrington Cup three times, and also became the Public Schools heavy-weight boxing champion in 1896 after taking on five opponents on

Queen Mary visits wounded soldiers, 1916.

Pte Oscar Zimber.

Hawthorn Crater, 2007. (Susan Thornicroft) Inset: Ronald Vibart.

the same day. (The Harrow School Register notes he attended the College between 1892 and 1896, where he also represented the football XI.) Following a stint in the Argentine, he returned to England and enrolled as a professional cricketer for Cornwall, being equally adept at batting, bowling and keeping wicket, turning out at club level for Truro, Troon, Camborne, St Austell and Falmouth – the latter location paying him £18 for his services in 1912.

His first two names appear as 'either/or', depending upon different sources, with a Frank Ronald Vibart being born in the Honiton area of Devon in 1878, and the same combination is to be found in the 1881 Census, where he is residing with his grandparents, John and Elizabeth King, plus his mother, Evelyn, who is described as the wife of 'Capt. Vibart, R.A. [Royal Artillery]'. Twenty years later, Capt. John Vibart (sixty-six), now retired from the army, was living in Bideford, Devon.

The actual war service of Pte Vibart is somewhat sketchy. The *Wisden Almanac* claims he served with the 16th (Public Schools) Battalion of the Middlesex Regiment – the same unit which witnessed the deaths of Cornishmen CSM Painter and Pte Button at the Hawthorn Crater, near Beaumont Hamel, on 1 July 1916 – but this is not corroborated in the Medal Index Cards, which reveal no matches for a Frank Ronald or Ronald Frank Vibart/Vibert, yet his wounding was clearly stated in the newspaper under this surname. It should be borne in mind, however, that the MIC collection is incomplete, as a small number were lost in transit a number of years ago. (The Harrow Register only denotes 'Great War, Middlesex Regt'. It also states his mother was a Mrs Akroyd, of Wavendon House, Woburn Sands, in Bedfordshire.)

After the conflict, he returned to cricket, and was actually selected to play for the North of England against the touring Australians in 1926, but personal problems had plagued him for some time, and in the event he did not turn up. Three years later, he was back in Cornwall, undergoing a very public divorce from his wife, the details of which were reported at great length in various newspapers. By 1934, he was living at Taunton, having formerly played professional cricket for the

Somerset town, as well as nearby Chard, and suffered an especially gruesome death by his own hand at the end of July. Aged fifty-five, he was described as being of 'no fixed address', and had taken poison which led to his death an hour after being admitted to hospital. There is no mention of his time in the army in the *Taunton Courier*, although the article, which goes into graphic detail as to the proceedings of the subsequent Coroner's Inquest, also added that the deceased was a 'well-known sportsman' who had played cricket for a number of distinguished sides, as well as playing in goal for several football teams in the Exeter area when he was younger.

Having attended Harrow, it is highly likely that he was with the 16th Middlesex on 1 July 1916, although there is no definite evidence to support this. The 16th, it is to be remembered, recorded over 500 casualties on this one day – most in the opening hour – and did not even reach the German front line. Quite how much those battlefield experiences contributed to Pte Vibart's future tormented state of mind will probably never be known.

Military Lessons Learned from 1 July, and the Progress of the Rest of the War

The two most glaring and tragic legacies of 1 July have been reiterated time and again in the personal stories of Cornishmen within this text: the British artillery bombardment had failed to obliterate the German defenders and their weaponry, while also leaving sections of the enemy wire firmly intact. Yet there were other factors in addition which all contributed to the huge loss of life. Number 3 Section of the 63rd Machine Gun Corps, at Fricourt, took up position during the last ten minutes of the barrage, between 7.20 a.m. and 7.30 a.m., '… from which fire could be brought in enfilade and oblique upon the German front line and supports', and although the men were able to inflict 'considerable casualties' upon the Germans manning the front line, the advancing infantry still met with 'fierce opposition'[1], with the eventuality that those following behind could not launch their own attack as per the timetable due to the continuing cannonade which they faced in No Man's Land. In this particular area, however, good communication was maintained between the Company Commanders in the firing line and the Section Commanders further back, thus enabling the replenishment of reserves, ammunition and water when required, so here, in the 21st Division, a certain amount of successful momentum could be maintained. One of the many problems which arose centred around the lack of transport, and gun limbers were used to carry essential equipment up to the forward positions. 'This is a most important question', noted the 63rd MGC's War Diary, and suggested an officer with the sole responsibility for transport should be appointed.

At Gommecourt, grave concerns were raised about the machine-gun teams being 'knocked out' as they crossed to assist the infantry, and in many cases failing to reach their destination. It was put forward that the number in each squad was doubled from four to eight in order to increase the chances of a heavy-duty weapon being brought to bear upon the enemy, whilst the actual gun itself was described as '… bulky and inconvenient to carry'[2], adding that the magazine drum was also easily prone to damage. 'As none of the Lewis Gun Teams have returned I am unable to give authentic information on this point …'[3]

Two important issues were again raised with the benefit of grim hindsight; namely the effectiveness of the artillery barrage prior to, and during, the assault, plus the insufficient numbers of bombs, and qualified bombers, brought up to maintain the efficiency of the attack.

Working to a strict timetable, the High Command and Royal Artillery observers had worked out how long it would take for the infantry to reach its primary, secondary and further objectives, thus setting the lifting of the bombardment at precise junctures. For any soldiers held up by unexpected resistance, there was no time to report this delay to the gunners, who simply followed orders and adjusted their range according to the established pattern. This sequence of events clearly afforded the Germans the opportunity to re-establish themselves in defences which were in danger of being overrun, and even when one attacking line of British infantry had passed over them, the Kaiser's men knew their fortifications further back would deal with the initial attack, leaving them to face the next onslaught.

The Battalion [7th Queen's] suffered considerably from enemy in dug-outs sniping and throwing bombs. Many surrendered after such acts, some falling to their knees in surrendering. Speaking generally, the enemy showed a very decided disinclination to fight hand to hand, and only did so when they could obtain an advantage by some unsportsmanlike act.[4]

The War Diary for the 12th York and Lancasters, which took part in the abortive attack on Serre alongside the Accrington Pals, gives one of the most damning conclusions to the events of 1 July. It slammed the policy of containing troops in the assembly trenches, which were subjected to frequent enemy shells and caused many casualties even *before* they had gone over, stating that more 'bombardment slits' should have been dug to shelter the soldiers from the explosions. Once the first wave had moved up into the front line, a similar scenario occurred, yet all of this could have been largely negated – according to the author of the narrative – if the following observations had been addressed prior to the launch of the offensive, namely: the assault needed to begin just after dawn, in double time, whilst in reality, the successive waves suffered by being too slow and far apart. With over four hours' of daylight to prepare, the Germans were more than ready for the assault, and British survivors who reached the enemy lines reported they could see every movement from the positions they had just left: '… this being so any attack by day was scarcely likely to succeed'.[5]

In addition, it was believed that officers, NCOs and machine-gunners were 'marked men' as they crossed No Man's Land. Surprise was expressed at large numbers of Germans '… apparently appearing from nowhere' when the British went forward, and only scant information regarding enemy dug-outs came back with the survivors, who noted one '… not damaged by our fire', was situated close to a machine-gun post. (The French had not adopted the 'wave' system in their attacks, preferring to send small groups of men forward at pace with the result that Gallic gains were far more extensive than the British on 1 July.)

In a Special Order Of the Day on 2 July, Brig.-Gen. H.C. Rees, DSO, revealed his admiration for the men of the 94th Brigade, adding he saw '… no man turn back or falter. I bid goodbye to the remnants of as fine a Brigade as has ever gone into action'[6] (Rees succeeded Brig.-Gen. Prowse, DSO, as CO of the 11th Infantry Brigade. The latter had been mortally wounded several miles to the south of Serre on 1 July.)

The structure of command in the British army must also take some of the criticism for the failings of 1 July 1916. Orders were rigid and expected to be followed to the letter, even in the heat of battle when circumstances instigated various unforeseen obstacles, short-comings and sudden changes to the assault's direction. Desperate pleas for advice and strategy were passed back to senior officers, but in some parts of the line, communication wires via telephones had been destroyed by shelling, whilst 'runners' tasked with delivering vital information were often never seen again. Meanwhile, German tacticians and commanders in the firing line were encouraged to use their initiative, dealing with situations and eventualities as they saw fit at the time, with the result which now confronts every historian who pores over the British disaster of 1 July 1916. The mines, too, were not utilised to their maximum effect, despite months of careful digging and planning. The time between the explosions and the launch of the assault – mainly two minutes (or ten in the case of the Hawthorn Crater at Beaumont Hamel) allowed the Germans to win the race for the craters, as all had been logically placed under the enemy front lines. Instead of preparing 'saps' venturing into No Man's Land to keep the infantry partially sheltered, many Divisions were too reliant on their artillery, thus condemning the battalions to hundreds of yards of exposed ground and the ravages of enemy machine-guns.

It should be noted, however, that some Divisions *did* secure their objectives – notably the 30th, 18th and 7th in the south of the line (the 18th, for example, though inexperienced was greatly influenced by two highly competent commanders – Lt-Gen. Congreve, VC, and Maj.-Gen. Maxse), whilst the neighbouring 21st was instrumental in the capture of Fricourt on the night of 1/2 July.

The charge of the 36th (Ulster) Division at Thiepval also deserves a special mention. Recalling one of the 12th York and Lancasters' observations: 'The attack should have been made in double time' – this was certainly the approach of the Irishmen, who practically ran headlong towards the Germans and overwhelmed them, only to be gradually pushed back by superior numbers due to a lack of support. Whether the cavalry should have been deployed here, or elsewhere, has been hotly debated ever since, but the terrain was not best suited to horses – a rapidly obsolete form of warfare amid all the mechanised horrors of shrapnel and machine-gun bullets – and, when all aspects are considered, it may not have secured the breakthrough the valiant infantry had prepared. In the event, the cavalry was not sent in, as neither sectors where breaches were made in the enemy lines were perhaps close enough to the axis of the attack – the Albert-Bapaume Road, where the 34th Division was being beaten back with astonishing barbarity.

The apportioning of 'blame' for the slaughter of 1 July has gone on ever since, and is probably best left to other texts, as entire books on this subject can be scrutinised at the reader's leisure. Suffice to say, however, that mistakes were *undoubtedly* made which sent thousands of men needlessly to their deaths, whereas other military decisions, taken for the wider success of the war, had to be sanctioned which led to regrettable casualties but nonetheless crucial territorial and strategic gains. Let us return to the personal aspect of the book, to the individuals who formed the whole. Sir George C. Marks, MP for the Launceston Division, commented at St Germans soon after the offensive began: 'Don't imagine this war is over. There's much yet to be done. Don't imagine that we have victory just ahead of us. We are just beginning, only beginning. We have immense sacrifices yet to make, I speak what I know'[7]

The famous 'Song of the Western Men', written by Robert Stephen Hawker, the vicar of the desolate parish of Morwenstow on the North Cornish coast, contains the lines: 'Here's twenty thousand Cornishmen will know the reason why.' It has to be ventured whether the 20,000 who fell on 1 July 1916 asked themselves the same question.

★★★

At the end of August, 1916, the *Royal Cornwall Gazette* reported:

> Much anxiety is felt concerning the safety of Ptes. Ralph Oates, Albany Road, Redruth, and H. James, Basset Street, Redruth, both of the Sportsman's Battalion. They were in the big push of 1 July, and were last seen going over the parapet into a bayonet charge. The only communication since received by the worried parents is an intimation from the War Office that their names have not appeared in the casualty lists. Pte Oates was formerly on the local post-office staff, and returned to the Front two months ago after a rest at home following wounds received [in action].

The 23rd and 24th Battalions of the Royal Fusiliers (RF) became known as the 1st and 2nd Sportsman's, with both serving in the 5th Brigade of the 2nd Division by July, 1916, whereas the 7th Northamptons was also a Sportsman's Battalion, having been raised by Edgar Mobbs, a Northampton and England rugby union player who rose to the rank of Lieutenant-Colonel, commanding 'Mobb's Own'. The latter was killed whilst storming a German machine-gun post in July 1917. Neither of the 23rd or 24th RF was involved in a 'bayonet charge' on 1 July, whilst the 7th Northamptons – 'Mobb's Own' – were at Ypres on the same date, and not in action either. It is more likely that the date in the newspaper report is an error, and should have read '31 July', by which time the 24th Royal Fusiliers had moved south to the Somme, taking part in a major assault in the area of Delville Wood, to the north-east of Montauban. According to the SDGW, fifty-eight men in the ranks lost their lives on this day, including a number who had connections with Devon and Cornwall – notably Pte Alfred Harold Oates, who was born and enlisted in Redruth. The CWGC lists him as being the son of Thomas and Elizabeth, of 10, Albany Road, in the Cornish town, so this is almost certainly 'Ralph'. (The fighting in Delville Wood also led to the report that Lt Frank Eathorne, of the 24th RF, was 'missing, believed killed', and it was later confirmed that the twenty-four-year-old from Camborne, who had attended Redruth County School, was, indeed, dead.) Pte H. James is not included in the official Casualty Rolls, so it is possible that he was taken prisoner.

On the same page is a sad item, indicative of how far-reaching the consequences of the conflict were to ordinary men and women back home:

> At East Kerrier Petty Sessions, yesterday, Hester B_____, married, was charged with being drunk and incapable at Perranwell. She admitted the offence, and Supt. Nicholls remarked that the defendant had a son in the Army, and she gave way to grief at the thought of his being at the Front. Since this occurrence she had been a teetotaller. The defendant was the wife of a labourer, and was in poor circumstances. A fine of 5s was imposed.

THE REST OF THE SOMME CAMPAIGN AND BEYOND

As we have seen, 2 July was very much a day for consolidation – either attempting to retrieve the thousands of wounded still out on the battlefield (for most), or restructuring new gains in the south of the line. Gen. Sir Douglas Haig, in overall command of the British offensive, was told of the initial casualty estimates – put at roughly 40,000 – but he was of the opinion that the enemy should be 'pressed hard' with the least possible delay, so the next phase of the Somme campaign began. Thiepval, Beaumont Hamel and Serre would not be targeted again for some time, whereas La Boisselle – on the all-important Albert-Bapaume Road – was attacked with venom on the afternoon of the 2nd, employing new tactics of short, sharp barrages and more effective smoke-screens. Overnight into the 3rd, the village which had proved virtually impregnable in daylight was finally stormed, falling into British hands by the 5th, although at a heavy price.

> Second-Lieutenant J. Owen Thomas, 1-5th Duke of Wellington's West Riding Regt, son of the Revd J.H. and Mrs Thomas, Grampound Road, was severely wounded on the 4th inst., somewhere near La Boisselle, having both legs badly fractured below the knee through the bursting of a shell in the trench where he was. He is at present in hospital … He had only been on active [service] about six weeks. Prayers were asked at Truro Cathedral on Saturday for Lieutenant Thomas …[8]

Thousands more British and Commonwealth troops died in the capture of La Boisselle, whilst neighbouring Ovillers – the scourge of the 2nd Devons on 1 July – fell by the 17th, having proved to be particularly stubborn. Systematically, this part of the line was slowly edging forward, almost inch by inch, and a different proposition now confronted the attackers – a series of strongly-held copses which would become infamous in the wider aspect of the First World War – Bernafay Wood, Mametz Wood, Trones Wood, High Wood, Delville Wood – all had to be taken with horrific loss of life on both sides. Mametz Wood, for example, was attacked on the 7th across a muddy battlefield, but was not completely secured until over a week later. One of many fatalities here was Lt John Russell, of the 9th Duke of Wellington's Regiment, whose father lived in Newquay. The officer's immediate superior informed Mr Russell: 'Your son was my second in command. He was a pillar of strength. He was always in front and cheered the men on. I think they would have followed him anywhere …'[9]

So it went on. In mid-July, the 1st DCLI entered the Somme cauldron, only to find a veritable Hell.

Fricourt and Mametz were now but heaps of debris with scarce one brick standing upon another. In each village a mound of white stones marked the site of the church. The opposing defensive systems, once clearly defined with trees and grass lands in between as if to cloak the terrible significance of those rows of sandbagged trenches and deep excavations, were now one vast expanse of shell-torn ground, the earth gashed and tumbled, pitted with deep shell-holes and craters. It was as if a terrific storm had passed that way, shattering trees, tearing off the branches and flinging them in all directions, leaving the stumps naked and bare – the awful witness to the power of modern artillery-fire. Unexploded shells, rifles, equipment, bombs and debris of every kind, strewed the battlefield: here and there a huddled corpse clutched the earth in mute appeal for rest beneath its troubled surface.[10]

Of the Somme offensive, the *West Briton* would announce:

After ten days and nights of continuous fighting our troops have completed the methodical capture of the whole of the enemy's first system of defence on a front of 14,000 yards (eight miles). This system of defence consisted of numerous and continuous lines of fire trenches, support trenches, and reserve trenches, extending to various depths of from 2,000 to 4,000 yards, and included five strongly fortified villages, numerous heavily-wired and entrenched woods, and a large number of immensely strong redoubts. The capture of each of these trenches represented an operation of some importance, and the whole of them are now in our hands.

The 10th (Pioneer) Battalion of the DCLI was a new arrival on the Western Front, disembarking at Le Havre only eleven days before the Somme battles began, and their progress was eagerly charted by Cornish folk back home. Observers from the media attached to the various regiments noted that, in common with virtually every other unit, the West Country men were '… feeling for the first time the loneliness … from being in a foreign land and the separation from home associations and customs', so it was suggested in various newspapers that locals should send regular 'parcels of gifts' to the servicemen now braving the dangers abroad. 'D' Company had a strong connection with St Austell, and contained many of its sons, so the town was urged *en masse* to dig deep.

On 20 July, at High Wood, Lt Saville and a party of the 8th Devons – survivors of the 1 July assault on Mametz (Saville advanced at 3.30 p.m. and avoided the fire from 'The Shrine') – were involved in another assault on the German lines, but the officer was injured in a cornfield just 50 yards from the enemy trenches. Upon hearing this, Pte Theodore Veale volunteered to go to his assistance and firstly dragged the casualty into a shell-hole before returning to fetch some water. Veale made the perilous journey a number of times, with his valiant attempts thwarted on several occasions before the lieutenant was finally brought in after Veale had held the Germans back with a Lewis gun. Both men survived the war, and Dartmouth-born Veale was awarded a VC for his supreme bravery.

Matter-of-fact letters came back from injured Cornishmen, including the following written by Pte Edward Barnicoat, DCLI, of Tregony, who implored his parents 'not to be anxious', whilst adding:

The Germans were very liberal with their shells in my case, as they hit me in various places such as head, right hand, right foot, left breast, little finger, left hand and right thigh. That is quite enough for one, don't you think? However, I might have been much worse, as some poor chaps have arms and legs blown off, and one man I heard of had two legs and right arm blown off. I was wounded up in Delville Wood on 26 July by a high explosive, as far as I can make out, but I cannot say for certain, as it knocked me down with terrific force when it hit me.[11]

Inevitably, some communications contained the worst possible news:

> Dear Mrs Maunder – I very much regret to tell you that your husband was killed early in the morning of 30 July by [a] shell explosion while gallantly doing his duty … I shall feel his loss to the platoon very much indeed, and offer you my sincerest sympathy in your terrible loss. I can appreciate what it means to you, as I have a wife and children myself. – Yours sincerely, J.D. Stroud.[12]

Pte James Maunder, from Truro, was the son of a city postman, and formerly worked as a mason for Mr W. Lobb. A keen footballer, he was aged twenty-six, and left behind a two-year-old son. By the time of his death, the village of Pozieres had finally fallen, exactly a month after its intended capitulation on the first day, yet the offensive was still less than a quarter of its way through the bloody campaign. August rolled on, and Delville Wood was still swallowing lives, including that of 2nd Lt Arthur Bennett, from Camborne, on the 18th:

> Arthur led his platoon right into the enemy trenches, through a heavy barrage of shrapnel and machine-gun fire, and, though they suffered terribly, they succeeded in inflicting great losses on the enemy, besides capturing several prisoners. Arthur himself cleared the way into the enemy sap, where the wire was practically impassable, by blowing a way through with rifle grenades. He was killed instantaneously … on the German parapet by a shrapnel bullet … The other Cornish officers who fell are Tyack, Paull, Higman and Collins … Our casualties were awful that day …[13]

Newspapers were now full of casualties – dead, wounded, missing, prisoner of war, 'shock-shell' – from Launceston, Delabole, Falmouth, Helston, St Just, and seemingly everywhere in between. September and into October were the same, a grim nightmare of a war where every yard had to be fought for by men desperate to secure it from an equally determined foe. (Pte Reginald Grose, who fell on 25 August 1916, at Colincamps, near Serre, whilst serving with the 10th DCLI, was but one of many. A native of St Stephens, the official documentation relating to his death is now in the possession of his grandson, who still lives in Cornwall. The legacies transcend the decades.) With the weather failing, the campaign limped into November, although the battlefields around the River Ancre, which had not seen any major fighting since the British were so spectacularly halted on 1 July, were opened up once more, leading to the capture of some territory which still bore the corpses of that ill-fated morning back in the distant summer.

> The British troops have made excellent progress on the Western Front during the past few days. Following upon the advance on a five-mile front along both banks of the Ancre, and the capture of the strongly-fortified village at St Pierre Divion, Sir Douglas Haig reports a further advance. The heavily-fortified village of Beaumont Hamel has been stormed, and the British troops have occupied, in addition, the village of Beaucourt-sur-Ancre …[14]

This article, published in a Cornish newspaper on 16 November 1916, is headed by the words: 'THE BRITISH VICTORY', and sub-titled by the astonishing claim: 'BRITISH LOSSES "HAVE NOT BEEN HIGH"'. The latter was clearly passed on by the War Office, and may have referred solely to the final few days of the Somme campaign rather than its entirety, but the implied information is, at best, ambiguous. The final casualty toll will never be known, yet its most conservative estimate for British and Commonwealth servicemen begins at 400,000 for an advance which, at its furthest point, reached six miles, still four miles from Bapaume, which was the first day target. The term 'victory' is also open to debate, although the British had, more or less, achieved their bed-rock aims of confronting the Germans toe-to-toe in a grisly war of attrition, relieving the pressure at Verdun and convincing their enemy once and for all that the United Kingdom and its Empire would not back down. Yet the negatives of such an offensive need no great dissection. Losses were horrendous, a decisive breakthrough was never remotely possible, and the volunteer army – Kitchener's Men – had been decimated. The territory gained was of no strategic value, other than its significance in the psychological battles of mind over matter – the possession of German lines which had once seemed unassailable. The Somme offensive was officially over.

★★★

Mrs Bray, from Bodmin, wrote and told me:

> My brother [Leslie Martin Pearce] was 18 years my senior … Leslie once went over the top and managed to drag a soldier back to safety – he was supposed to have a medal, but like many others, it didn't come about. He was very young at the battle of the Somme as he put his age on to enlist. I remember him and a friend coming home with tin hats, but very vaguely.

1917

The biting, raw winter of 1916/17 was tragically apt for the utter horrors on the Somme which had preceded it, and both armies attempted a period of rest and recuperation before the fighting would, inevitably, begin in earnest once the big freeze had thawed. Behind the lines, 'normality' was strived for, epitomised by a report in the *West Briton* of a football match between Cornishmen in the Royal Garrison Artillery, and their opponents from the 1st (Devon) Royal Engineers, which the latter won by two goals to one. 'The … game was very keenly contested, the men evidently remembering the old rivalry between the two counties'. Sgt Hodge, from St Just, was the referee, and a gunner named Rushworth, of Truro, scored his team's solitary consolation with a 'beautiful shot, after a free kick.'

But the war was never far away. Lt Melville Hastings, serving with a Canadian Infantry battalion, disclosed one particular encounter which stuck in his mind:

> Here's a little story … Our party left Neuville St Vaast to wire about 200 yards of the firing line in front of Avion, a distance of about four miles over Vimy Ridge. It was a wild, bitter night. Coming home I lost my party, and very soon myself also. Wet through and dog-tired I was meditating sitting down to await daylight when I fell into a C.T. [communication trench]. A short distance along I espied a dim light proceeding from a miserable sort of lean-to on one side of the trench. Seated on a biscuit box and by himself was an old clergyman, whom I should like the people of St Thomas, Launceston, to know was their vicar. He had with him a case of Huntley and Palmer biscuits, some cigarettes, and also an urn of cocoa, with a prime stove underneath. This old priest was not in a comfortable bed in Launceston that night, [because] he was dishing out home comforts to troops …[15]

At the end of February, a significant event occurred when the Germans tactically withdrew from many positions on the Somme which the British and Commonwealth troops had battered and pummelled unsuccessfully the previous year, thus practically negating the entire Somme battle. It is wholly unjust and insensitive to claim the thousands of men therefore died 'in vain', but after the initial euphoria of occupying ceded territory turned to vexed concern that the new enemy defences – known as the Hindenburg Line – now appeared even *more* formidable than before, these thoughts must have passed through the minds of the battle-weary survivors at some stage as they cautiously moved forward over the former battlefields.

In April – despite near blizzard conditions – the Allies launched a new offensive at Arras, and the Canadians stormed the strategic Vimy Ridge, whilst in June, Messines Ridge was also taken after adopting the new 'bite and hold' tactics, whereby small gains were systematically stormed with swiftness and efficiency under a lightening artillery barrage. As French morale faltered, the British and Commonwealth troops now bore the brunt of the campaigns on the Western Front, and launched the Third Battle of Ypres on 31 July – an offensive destined to become even more horrific and pitiless than its Somme equivalent. 'Passchendaele' lasted until November and became an unforgiving quagmire after the natural drainage had been obliterated by shells, leaving heavy rains to flood the low-lying hills and valleys around the Belgian town.

Pte John Key, of the 1st Royal Marine Light Infantry, enlisted in October 1916, and soon became a sniper for his accuracy with a rifle, but on 26 October 1917, he received a gunshot wound in his right shoulder, smashing his watch and tearing his service papers. He soon returned to Passchendaele and was once cut off by a German counter-attack, being one of only twenty from a strength of 200 to walk away unscathed. Pte Key recalled how, after one British attack, the bodies of the enemy were piled four or five high on the wire. His son later informed me from his St Austell home:

> I hate to think what a terrible time they had having to march up to 40 miles on duckboards surrounded by a sea of mud and shell-holes full of water. He said one of his friends was blown to pieces a few yards away. A man called Keast died quite young – he was gassed. [In 1918, my grandparents] received a letter saying he had been killed in action [Pte Key had actually been taken prisoner]. After the Armistice he was in poor health and down from about 11 stone to about 7 stone after his release. By some means he got back to Belgium where a Belgian family called Landennie in a place called Huy nursed him back to better health. I don't know how he got to Belgium or how long he was there, he didn't talk a lot about it. There was no after-care, he just had to come home and take up his job and get on with it. [He] worked a Beam Engine on the clay pits in later years and had a passion for steam.

A British tank attack at Cambrai during November 1917, yielded some success, but the year ended as it had begun, in virtual stalemate. Each side knew that hostilities could not go on indefinitely, and 1918 would undoubtedly be a decisive period of the entire conflict.

1918

Events were now moving at an urgent pace. The Eastern Front had collapsed due to the Russian Revolution, releasing thousands of experienced German veterans to join their comrades in France and Flanders, whereas the Americans were finally starting to deploy in significant numbers, having declared war on the Kaiser the previous April. Their reluctance to assist the Allies militarily has complex issues, not least her attitude that it was primarily a European war which did not involve her citizens, but the targeting of American shipping in the Atlantic by German U-boats gradually hardened the once placid stance of isolation.

The Germans themselves were well aware of the implications of the seemingly endless supply of men, equipment and supplies which the United States could undoubtedly provide, so they decided to strike first at the battle-weary British, Commonwealth and French forces still holding the fragile front lines. Knowing the assault was imminent, but unaware of its exact focus along the Western Front, the British Government dispatched the Revd Frank Edwards to America in order to inform all sections of US society of the dire crisis which was over-shadowing the future of Europe. Before he left, Revd Edwards visited a relative of the late Lt Frank B.V. Thomas, who had been shot dead by a sniper at Laventie on September 21st, 1916, whilst serving with the 1/5th DCLI, and in a curious premonition, the officer had confided to one of his comrades twenty-four hours before that he did not think he would still be alive by night-fall the following day. A native of Penzance, Lt Thomas was the twenty-year-old son of a solicitor, and was himself studying law when he felt compelled to join up. Just days before he died, he wrote to his father back in Cornwall:

> I am more proud than I can say to do my little bit … but, please dad, don't think of me as a hero, for I am only a British Tommy, and proud to be one… I am very happy … Whatever the future has in store for me you will at any rate have some satisfaction from the knowledge that I have tried my best to do my duty … My Mother is worth fighting for … If it is to be my lot to 'go under', don't worry, Dad, dear – just 'carry on' …[16]

Requesting a copy of the communication in order to help him promote his mission across the Atlantic, Revd Edwards would later acknowledge the part the Cornishman's words had played in his quest:

> In its sincerity and complete abandonment of self for the good and safety of others, the letter typified the spirit of thousands of brave and noble English schoolboys. I found myself amongst people who, although kindly disposed in the main towards England's cause, had as yet no conception of the spirit, straits and sacrifices of the British people … I have no hesitation in saying that one of the most powerful and convincing instruments in bringing home to the heart of the American people the true spirit of the British nation was the letter written by young Frank Thomas to his father on the eve of his death. That letter thrilled America. It broke multitudes into tears. Strong men sobbed like children again and again under the reading of that brave, sincere, high-souled message from a British boy to his loved ones at home. It gave the American people their truest insight into the heart and spirit of the British nation. It was printed and circulated in its hundreds and thousands. Young Thomas, in that letter, did glorious work for England.[17]

Just 5ft 7in in height when he was alive, the subsequent stature of the young Penzance-born officer in death appears to have been immense. On 21 March the Germans launched their great offensive in the West, smashing through British lines from Cambrai to St Quentin, over-running positions and virtually annihilating entire battalions which stood in their way before sweeping across territory on the Somme in a matter of days which had taken the Allies four long months of torture to secure back in 1916. Even the town of Albert, which had witnessed the attack of the 34th Division along the road to Bapaume on 1 July, had fallen within less than a week, yet the advance was losing momentum, and eventually came to a standstill in April. Other, smaller attempts to break the Allied lines failed – some only just – and now defence could turn into attack as the Kaiser's final gamble crumbled away.

The casualty list for these final months of the war, however, was astonishingly high – over 160,000 alone for British forces in just sixteen days following the 21 March assault by the Germans. Fighting throughout the summer was brutal and unrelenting, with neither army contemplating yet another winter shivering in the trenches, and August saw the Somme battlefields fought over yet again, although this time round, there was to be no repeat of the agonisingly slow progress recalled so vividly by the survivors of 1916. Past woods and shattered cemeteries, disturbing the dead who had already fallen to take this grotesque landscape, the Allies ploughed onwards, eventually reaching German-held territory which could only have been dreamed of two years before. This was modern warfare – tanks, aircraft, mobility – all combining with lessons learned from previous First World War campaigns to drive home the advantage. Military tactics put into practice during 1918 are still being used today.

On 18 October, at Le Cateau – scene of a desperate rearguard action by the BEF on 26 August 1914 – Sgt Horace Curtis, of the 2nd Royal Dublin Fusiliers, was attacking with his platoon when

Somme landscape. Inset: four Cornish soldiers who fell during 1916.

it came under heavy machine-gun fire. Realising the necessity to eliminate the source, the Sergeant advanced through the enemy bullets and shells from the British barrage before killing or wounding two gun-teams, resulting in the surrender of four more. Turning his attentions to a nearby troop train loaded with reinforcements, he captured 100 prisoners, and for his gallantry, he was awarded the only VC bestowed upon a Cornishman on the Western Front during the First World War. Born at St Anthony-in-Roseland, he enlisted into the DCLI at Bodmin on 12 September 1914, but soon switched to the 7th Royal Dublin Fusiliers, serving in Gallipoli, Salonika and Egypt before joining up with the 2nd Battalion in France during August 1918. (This unit had, in fact, taken part in the 1 July 1916 attack on the Somme, being in the same 4th Division as the 1st Somerset Light Infantry.) Curtis, who lived at Fiddler's Green, Newlyn East, from an early age, received his medal from the King at Buckingham Palace the following year, and re-enlisted in 1920, reaching the rank of Company Sergeant Major with the 4/5th DCLI. His father was a former gamekeeper at the Place House Estate, and young Horace – who was educated at the National School under Mr Webber – won many trophies for cross-country running in Cornwall. He returned to his former occupation of clay-pit labourer, and died in Redruth during 1968 – by coincidence, on 1 July.

When the Armistice was finally signed on 11 November 1918 (marked in Cornwall by whistles of ships in various harbours, peals of church bells, hooters blasting out from the foundries, factories and mines, plus a general state of rejoicing across the entire county), the British army was virtually unrecognisable from the one which had taken to the field way back in August 1914. Many of the front-line troops in the 'Old Contemptibles' were dead, wounded in body, scarred mentally, or captives of the Germans. Kitchener's Men were also greatly reduced in number, but not in pride, as the Official History notes:

The lengthy Roll of Honour … shows how nobly the Regiment gave of its best, for love of England: for the patriotism of West Countrymen is well known … 'One and All' is the motto of the [DCLI] – *for* 'One and All' was the spirit in which officers and men of the Regiment fought and suffered – even unto Death.[18]

Lt F. Thomas and Sgt. H. Curtis, VC.

The 2nd Devons finished the war near Mons in Belgium, where the BEF fought its first battle of the conflict on 23 August 1914, whereas the 9th Battalion was positioned at Landrecies in France, having recently returned from Italy, where its sister unit, the 8th, still remained. The latter was disbanded shortly afterwards, closely followed by the 9th, after some of its strength had joined the Army of Occupation in the Rhineland, whilst others received their demobilisation papers. The Devonshires' Official History commented in its resume of the conflict:

> The foe to be faced was stubborn, skilful, well-prepared and well-equipped, and there were no easy victories to be won over him, especially when it is remembered that, after the first few months, the bulk of the fighting fell on men who, before 4 August 1914, had never had any military training or had ever contemplated being soldiers … The spirit and traditions of the Devonshire Regiment did not a little for the Allied cause in the long years of the greatest contest in its history …[19]

Commemoration

The First World War took the lives of over one million British and Commonwealth servicemen, with place-names up and down the length of the United Kingdom and Ireland registering losses on an unprecedented scale. The large towns and cities, inevitably, recorded thousands each, yet there were also tiny hamlets and scattered dwellings which lost *its* men-folk, too, with Cornwall not escaping the carnage. In the 1930s, the term 'Thankful Villages' was first used to describe a particular rural location which did not – to the knowledge of the residents – witness even one of its sons go off to war and lose his life on active service, therefore it possesses no official war memorial to the dead. After much research (with the aid of, amongst others, the SDGW CD-ROM) and requests for information by the media, including a radio programme on the subject, a list of approximately forty-one can claim such status in England and Wales – a total which, when compared to the pages and pages of destinations in an average corresponding map index, is quite astonishing.

Cornwall's 'Thankful Village' appears to be Herodsfoot, near Liskeard, which apparently has a plaque dedicated to 'Those Who Served', but does not mention any fatalities. (This is corroborated by the SDGW , although it has to be remembered that the information on it is not 100 per cent accurate. A searchable database for the origins of deceased sailors and airmen – other than the incomplete data found in the CWGC – does not exist at the time of publication.) The mere absence of such a monument at Herodsfoot, however, is the strongest evidence of all – surely a grieving mother or widow would have been afforded somewhere to visit in tranquil surroundings, as so many others in this situation were granted both in Cornwall and further afield. (Gwennap, for example, has thirteen names carved on its equivalent, St John ten, eight at Lanner, and three for Mawgan.)

However poignant and meaningful the hundreds of war memorials, plaques and monuments were, depicting as they did those familiar names who had once lived in the locality but would never return, it was not a *physical* representation of a life lost (which was why a soldier's personal effects were often so eagerly sought after a death), and there was nowhere bereaved families could actually go in order to feel close to their fallen relatives. Recognising this growing need for a national focus to the immense process of mourning, a young army chaplain, the Revd David Railton, wrote to the Dean of Westminster Abbey and suggested that the body of an unidentified British soldier should be interred within the Abbey itself as a symbol of the nation's grief. After initial caution, the proposal was acted upon, and later, in France, a blindfold officer chose one from six corpses which had been removed from the main battlefields of the Western Front, including the Somme. To this day, the identity of the fallen individual has never been established, and the macabre journey took the remains across the Channel to Dover, where it received a nineteen-gun salute before travelling on to London. Interest in its progress grew, and the arrival of this strange and moving spectacle coincided with Remembrance Day – 11 November 1920. Borne to his final resting place by royalty, Admirals, Field Marshals (Haig was one) and other senior officers who had dictated the direction of the war, the Unknown Soldier was laid to rest amid the greatest public scrutiny and ceremony. 'Thousands of people of every rank and class stood with bowed heads and throbbing hearts', noted the *West Briton*, whilst captain the Revd Frank Edwards, Commandant of the Newquay Comrades, also attended the service in an official capacity.

(This was almost certainly the same individual who travelled to America in early 1918 with a copy of the letter written by Lt F.B.V. Thomas, mentioned in the previous chapter.)

VC recipients representing the three services formed a Guard of Honour, and one amongst this distinguished group of brave men was Petty Officer Ernest Pitcher, of the Royal Navy. Born at Mullion, South Cornwall, he was on board HMS *Dunraven* (a 'Q' or 'Mystery' Ship, designed to give the appearance of a Merchant vessel in order to entice a German U-boat to attack, before revealing its real purpose as an anti-submarine device) in the Bay of Biscay on 8 August 1917, when its purpose was put to the test. Pitcher was the 4in gun-layer on the *Dunraven*, and he had to stay at his post along with the crew whilst enemy shells targeted them from nearby. Subsequently, the magazine below them caught fire, so the Cornishman and his comrades placed cartridges on their knees to prevent the heat of the deck igniting them, and the men were later blown into the air by an explosion. PO Pitcher was subsequently 'Elected by Ballot' to receive a VC following the action which had seen a number of individuals performing the same act of gallantry and facing identical dangers. (Sgt Curtis, VC, mentioned in the previous Chapter, was not in attendance at the Abbey. The only other Cornish-born VC of the First World War – Pte James Henry Fynn (a.k.a. Finn), of the 4th South Wales Borderers – was decorated for bravery in Mesopotamia (modern Iraq) on 9 April 1916, when he tended to a number of wounded men under enemy fire from the Turks, carrying one stricken casualty to safety on his back. A native of Truro, Fynn moved to Bodmin as a youngster, and died of injuries on active service the year following his VC deed. He never saw his medal, which is now in Bodmin. Curtis and Pitcher both attended the VC Reunion Dinner at the House of Lords in 1929, and the former alone at a similar gathering in London's Dorchester Hotel on June 8th, 1946, to celebrate 'Victory Day' after World War Two. Chief Petty Officer Pitcher, who also served during the latter conflict, had passed away the previous February, whilst Sgt Curtis had recently involved himself with the Newlyn East Home Guard, as well as teaching local school children how to use their gas masks.)

The Cenotaph ('empty tomb' in Greek) was unveiled in London's Whitehall on the same day as the Unknown Warrior was buried at Westminster Abbey, and remains the national monument to the Dead of two World Wars. (The cinema in Truro showed footage of both momentous events from 11 November 1920, several weeks later, with Miss Doris Pengelly scheduled to sing 'Abide With Me' each evening.) For those still grieving in the towns and villages far from the capital, however, the distances involved and lack of money invariably ensured that these were never visited by a large proportion of the bereaved. Widows, parents, siblings and children of lost servicemen craved something more *tangible*, with some enshrining their loved ones' precious campaign medals and commemorative plaque (known as the 'Death's Penny') sent after the fighting had ended (a proportion of these memorabilia were later interred with loved ones), although others simply threw the items away, bitterly and angrily refusing to accept their men-folk had sacrificed their lives in such horrendous, inconceivable numbers.

Two years after the Armistice, this latter viewpoint was echoed by Revd H.W. Sedgwick (reported by the *West Briton*), rector of St Andrew's Church, Redruth, who had recently returned from a solemn visit to the British cemeteries around Ypres. Recognising the 'immeasurable debt we owed to those gallant men who laid down their lives at the call of duty, and for the freedom of the world', he told the congregation of over one thousand (including many relatives of the fallen) gathered around the 'Memorial Calvary' outside:

> During the [conflict], people were telling us about the new world after the war. I think, however, you will agree with me that if the world in which we are now living is the much talked of new world, most of us would have preferred the old, because the new world seems very much worse than the old.

As early as 1921, services for the benefit of grieving British families were being offered by French and Belgian citizens who were trying to rebuild their shattered homes and businesses on the devastated former battlefields of the Western Front. One letter which survives in the Cornwall Record Office was typed by a Jean Souillard, who described himself as a 'Graves Photographer in the Devastated Areas'. Based in Peronne, on the banks of the River Somme close to where the British and French armies went forward side by side on 1 July 1916, he wrote:

> Dear Sir – I am sending today your order of six Photographs (four of the Grave and two of the general view of the Cemetery) by post registered. I hope you will be satisfied with them and that you will receive them safely. After receipt of the parcel please forward the amount by Postal Order or Money order. If you are satisfied and if you know some friends who want similar photographs, I will be glad to receive their order and I will do my best for them. Hoping to read you very soon, I am dear, Sir, yours very obediently [signed] 'J. Souillard'.
>
> P.S. Would you kindly note that letters for France require a Five Penny Stamp.[1]

This private undertaking was overshadowed by the colossal task which faced the Imperial (later Commonwealth) War Graves Commission (IWGC), as it continued with its work of recording the final resting places of the million dead from the United Kingdom, Ireland and the Empire. As we have seen, however, many bodies were never found, and a large proportion of those which *were* had lost all identifiable features or labels due to the continuing effects of warfare, as well as Nature itself. Each and every serviceman, 'missing' or interred in a marked grave, was registered by the IWGC under the guidance of Major-General Sir Fabian Ware, whose team had begun this monumental list well before the Armistice was even signed. Now that peace reigned along the Western Front, the graveyards and cemeteries which contained the bleak wooden crosses and swiftly-constructed plaques could now be afforded a recognisable uniformity, employing architects, landscape gardeners and engravers to create the beautifully-kept structures which are now permanent features on the landscape of Northern France and Flanders.

Some families were sent a photograph of an original grave, taken by the authorities or even a comrade, and this was often the only visual evidence in their possession if the site was subsequently lost. The Somme battlefields, for example, were fought over three times – once in 1916, and twice in 1918, when the German advance was eventually pushed back – often obliterating everything in between. Pilgrimages to the place-names where loved ones had fallen began in earnest, although these were invariably embarked upon by those who could afford to do so, and even then it was a potentially dangerous excursion, with the ordnance of war still strewn hideously across the former trenches and stretches of No Man's Land, now being reclaimed by Nature. Such a trip was beyond most of the working classes, who could only read about the exploits of their men in the numerous Regimental Histories and personal accounts which were published during the 1920s and '30s. The political climate of the same era is one of turmoil and injustice – far from returning home to a land of plenty, a significant proportion of the survivors of the First World War spent the next two decades in dire poverty, with little work, and lacking in decent housing or adequate social status. In 1920, a committee in Falmouth decreed that new houses built at Penwerris should be offered in the first instance to ex-soldiers and sailors who had seen active service abroad – a sympathetic gesture, at least. Yet with the recession approaching, jobs were at a premium, and many pre-war occupations were dwindling fast. Dolcoath, for example, at Camborne – 'The Queen of Cornish Mines' which had yielded thousands of tons of copper and tin since the 1700s – finally shut down in 1921. She was not alone in her sad demise.

THE THIEPVAL MEMORIAL AND LOCHNAGAR CRATER

On 1 August 1932, the gargantuan war memorial to the Missing of the Somme was finally unveiled on a ridge at Thiepval, overlooking the surrounding countryside which had seen such destruction and loss of life between 1916 and 1918. Up close, the structure is immensely powerful, dwarfing the visitor with its awesome purpose of displaying over 73,000 names of individuals who have no known grave, including approximately two-thirds of the soldiers with associations to Cornwall included in this text. Close to this very spot, now flanked by peaceful trees, Lt Edgar Hampson, of the 15th Lancashire Fusiliers – whose uncle lived in Saltash – was last seen '… fighting in the streets of Thiepval with 200 men'[2] on 1 July 1916, whilst nearby, Capt. O'Flaherty, of the 36th (Ulster Division), lost his life at Stuff Redoubt, the news of which reached his mother in Newquay a short while later. To the north are the killing grounds of Beaumont Hamel, Serre and Gommecourt; to the south, Ovillers, La Boisselle, Fricourt, Mametz and Montauban.

The deep crater caused by the exploding of the 'Lochnagar Mine' at La Boisselle on 1 July 1916 was in danger of being filled in by the 1970s until Richard Dunning stepped in and purchased the site, thus creating the 'Friends of Lochnagar' and ensuring the location would remain a permanent reminder to men of all nationalities who fought and died on the Somme battlefields. Ninety feet deep and three hundred feet across its circumference, it is said to be the largest man-made depression ever to be created in anger, and it was witnessed by Cecil Lewis, a Royal Flying Corps pilot, whose aeroplane was blown sideways by the blast as he flew close to the column of earth which towered over 4,000 feet into the air. It was here, on the ground, that men like Pte Eric Gibb, 15th Royal Scots, a resident of Bude, lost his life in 'Sausage' Valley, and Penzance-born Pte William Rowe, of the 2nd Tyneside Scottish, fell opposite the 'Schwaben Hohe', which took the full force of the explosion.

From his position attached to the gallant 103rd (Tyneside Irish) Brigade, Pte William Verran, of the 103rd Machine Gun Corps, and a native of Gwennap, would have seen for himself the destructive power of the 'Lochnagar' detonation, but he would soon be required to advance behind the infantry towards the firing line. Whether he reached as far as the searing scar in the French countryside will probably never be known, but comparisons both stark and poignant can be drawn between this and the famous Gwennap Pit, in his home village. One of the most prominent Wesleyan Methodist destinations in the whole of Britain, John Wesley preached here as many as twenty times during the latter half of the eighteenth century, and it was estimated that around 20,000 people once gathered at this one spot to hear him speak. Allegedly formed by the collapse of an old mine works below, in Wesley's time this natural but irregular 'bowl' shape was apparently fifty feet deep and between 200 and 300ft across, although after his death it was re-modelled into a concentric circular seating area, or terracing, which continued to attract thousands to witness the legacies of Wesley's teachings, with Whit Monday becoming a particular focal point when many would walk for miles to attend. Gwennap itself was a rich mining area, abundant in minerals, although the depression of the nineteenth century forced many of its citizens to emigrate in search of a better life. Wesley was critical of poor working conditions endured by the local community, and gained tremendous respect in Cornwall as a result.

It may seem strange to equate the 'Lochnagar' crater with Gwennap Pit, but each was man-made, each is a part of history, and each serves a unique function today. Nature abides at both, as does human influence and spirit, but at La Boisselle, on 1 July 1916 the Christian and the Godless advanced in unison and were scythed down by the thousand. As the decades move on, it has become a place of hope and inspiration, as well as a monument to the immense suffering and death which gripped so many back in the First World War.

PO E. Pitcher, VC and Pte J. Fynn, VC.

Trenches around Ypres, 1920. Inset: Sgt.-Maj.
C.R. Watson, DCM, MC, MM, the DCLI's
most decorated NCO of the First World War.

The Thiepval Memorial, 2006.

Lochnagar Crater, 2006.

Gwennap Pit, pre-First World War.

Every year, at 7.28 a.m. on the morning of 1 July, a ceremony begins here at Lochnagar with the launching of a firework, imitating the exact moment the detonation occurred, and is followed by whistles being blown around the rim as a reminder of the start of the infantry assault by the 34th Division. A lone piper plays a sad lament before the formal prayers and poems are read out, and the service ends with schoolchildren releasing poppies into the crater. It is simple and deeply moving. I attended the occasion in 2001 – the same year as the last known British witness of the explosion passed away – and a strange event occurred just after half past seven, when four immaculate lines of birds flew over our position from the direction taken by the 10th Lincolns ('Grimsby Chums'), disappearing towards the quietude of La Boisselle. Five years later, I returned for the 90th anniversary, and as the village church bells rang in the distance, accompanied by birdsong, I kept involuntarily glancing over my shoulder, looking across the gently sloping fields full of agriculture and serenity, imagining the waves of soldiers advancing in perfect order. 'I'm beat; push on,'[3] flashed through my mind – the last words of 2nd Lt Gill, who had links with Treverbyn; South African 2nd Lt Watson and his connections to Newquay, fighting with two or three Germans on the parapet of an enemy trench moments before his death; Sgt Moon, of Penryn, and his carefree days of playing football before the war; nineteen-year-old L/Cpl Bennett, from St Austell, shot through the head as he was advancing. It did not seem possible such carnage had once occurred here, yet the evidence is all around, or silently hidden beneath your feet.

Tread softly o'er a soldier's grave, a Mother's love lies there[4]

The Thiepval Memorial also holds an annual ceremony beneath its dominant arches, yet for me, nothing is as emotive as standing on the front lines at the exact time the Somme offensive began. Was 1 July specifically, and the First World War as a whole, the beginning of the modern era, and the end of the 'old ways', as Redruth's Revd Sedgwick alluded to in 1920? Whatever the true answer, the legacies are undoubtedly with us to this day.

16

Conclusion

Beyond 1 July 1916, the magnitude of the first day of the Somme offensive was not scrutinised in any great detail until the conflict had finally come to an end, thus enabling the entire strategy of the war, and its different distinct phases, to be analysed separately as well as collectively. Militarily, some lessons were learned, and others laid the foundations for the future direction of the fighting. For the survivors of 1 July 1916, army life would change dramatically, as so many of their mates had been killed or badly wounded. Fresh-faced replacements were brought in, but they were not necessarily from the counties or districts as their cap badges suggested, and for some of the 'Old Sweats', the fact the former had not been there from the start went against them; at the pandemonium of the 1914 recruiting offices, the patriotic 'goodbyes' as they went off to training camps, and the camaraderie built up well before the voyage to France or the first tentative nights spent in the dangerous trenches. A peculiar guilt and shame pervaded amongst those who had gone 'over the top' and somehow returned, knowing that familiar faces were still 'out there', helpless, vulnerable, or probably dead. It was a devastating human trait most took with them to their graves.

The late Poet Laureate, Sir John Betjeman, who lies buried in Cornwall, was at school during the First World War, and later recalled how the deaths in action of Old Boys were read out to the rest of the pupils, with the orator's voice sometimes faltering when he announced the loss of a particular favourite of the staff. At Truro College, as in most equivalents around the country, the progress of its 'O.B.s' was equally resonant, and many sent letters 'back home' to be published in the collegiate magazine, alongside other first or second-hand reports: 'W.H. Jane was in the Big Push on the Somme, and was slightly gassed and had to return to Bordon Camp, near Aldershot. He called at T.C. on Sept. 16th and gave us an account of his nephew's death★ at Longueval.'[1] (★Pte Leslie Dreyer, whose aunt lived at Watering Hill, St Austell.)

Pte G. Stratford, Royal Fusiliers, wrote on 26 July 1916:

> I have been up in the line now for close on a fortnight … I think I have crowded more experience in this last week that I ever experienced in a year of my ordinary life … I have come through this battle all right, and we hope to get 'Johnny Squareface' on the run very soon. I only wish that I was back at the College once again … The guns are still on their continual strafe. It is one continual roar – from the cough of the 75s and the bark of the heavies to the whining of the Boches' shells. We are back on rest … as we have just been 'over the top' and lost a few …[2]

In April 1917, 2nd Lt F.E. Gilpin declared:

> I have just been reading last term's magazine for the second time, and find it a very interesting number. I'm longing to get a few days leave in England, and if I do I shall come home to Cornwall without delay … Our battery was mentioned in despatches for the Somme fighting, as we did some jolly good work. Will's battery is a few miles further up the line [possibly at Arras] and I am afraid he is in for a rough time … I am sick of the horrible sights and the awfulness of war.[3]

Field Marshall Haig, much maligned as a 'butcher' who oversaw the Somme campaign, eventually saw his armies triumph after learning from the legacies of 1916. He spent the rest of his life endlessly pursuing the rights of disabled ex-servicemen, of whom there were many, yet the numbers of those who died as a direct result of wounds or trauma in the years following the First World War will never be known. Officially, the Casualty Rolls end in 1921, as the majority of de-mobbed servicemen finally returned to their civilian lives leaving the Regulars to maintain the army's strength, although the strain on the health of these millions of men was incalculable. The years of standing in wet mud, exposed to the elements; the far-off, hostile climates of Gallipoli, Mesopotamia and Africa; the ghastly effects of poison gas; the lack of sanitation; the psychological horrors of war – all these factors contributed to the fragile minds and bodies of the 'lucky ones'; veterans who came home.

Having visited the Somme battlefields on a number of occasions, I have a tendency to equate certain parts of the Western Front with familiar landscapes back in the UK – as the Tommies used to do all those years ago – but nothing immediately springs to mind with the topography of Cornwall. Delville Wood cannot be found at Cardinham, and 'Mash' Valley does not resemble its counterpart at Coombe, to the north of Stratton. No building which stood in the way of the opposing armies in France pre-dates 1920, as all were obliterated between 1914 and 1918 – farmhouses, barns, hamlets and even entire towns. Everything had to be re-built after the war, and it is something of an irony that the average British soldier would probably not recognise the area as it is today, surrounded by the green of nature and peaceful copses, because the limit of his view often extended no further than the protective sandbags above eye level in the trenches, or maybe the coils of barbed wire just beyond. Their only glimpses of the wider area would become apparent during an advance across No Man's Land, when their focus was clearly upon other more pressing matters directly in front of them. Everywhere had been torn apart by the artillery shells and devastation of modern warfare, whilst the ever-growing nearby cemeteries, with their swiftly-constructed, irregular crosses and muddy mounds of earth, were unrecognisable from the uniform, immaculate and walled burial grounds which replaced them over the following decades.

It is much more conceivable that a Tommy would be better in touch with his native town or village as it is in the twenty-first century, despite the modern additions of construction and advances in technology. The basic layout of a particular location remains remarkably similar to the First World War era, with distinctive churches and the huddle of old cottages around the core of inland dwellings, or the clutter of fishermen's houses above the coastal harbours. Country estates also still remain, albeit now often converted for leisure, tourism or multiple living. So perhaps the Somme is more likely to be found *here*, in the untouched surroundings of the past which bred many of the men we have focused upon in this text. It does not stretch the imagination too much to walk across the open expanse of a field and feel the sudden rush of wind as you pass over a ridge, or be guided by the natural features which funnel you into a thicket of brambles and vegetation – yet you are only advancing through fresh air, not bullets and bombs.

An immense fear gripping the thoughts of many British soldiers as they spent the long, dreary hours of sentry duty in the trenches must have touched upon the possibility – or probability – of being killed in action and having no known grave as a consequence. As soon as they arrived on active service, the sense of adventure stopped and the harsh realities began; there would be casualties, some would die, and a significant proportion could be lost forever. These men knew where the cemeteries were, yet they also knew some of their pals had gone 'over the top', never to be seen again. This sense of unyielding oblivion must have haunted the waking hours of nearly all at some stage during the conflict, and so it proved on 1 July 1916, when Cornishmen were, and still are, amongst those yet to be found, swallowed by a foreign field which traps them to this day.

To stand on the shore at Sennen, or Bedruthan Steps, or indeed anywhere which divides the land from the sea, and watch wave after wave pound towards you before dissipating at your feet,

Launceston war memorial, 1920s.

Rough seas at Polzeath, 1930s.

Launceston recruit, DCLI, *c.*1915.

begs the questions: what has happened to the power of the wave, where has it gone, and is it still here? Maybe the memorial to the Missing of the First World War is actually all around us.

SOMME INSCRIPTIONS

When the CWGC began its gargantuan task of formalising every war cemetery and memorial on the Western Front and beyond, the authorities offered families of deceased servicemen the opportunity to personalise the headstones of their loved ones with messages of affection and pride – at an additional cost, per letter – which the dependents of the lower ranks, in particular, often found difficult due to the troubled financial and social restrictions of the 1920s. This following selection – compiled by Susan Thornicroft during the summer of 2007 – reflects the huge sense of grief and loss after the First World War which even now is touching, emotive and humbling.

'The call was short, the shock severe, to part with one I loved'

'One of the best'

'Farewell beloved, so young and brave, for King and Country his life he gave'

'Gone from our home, but not from our memory'

'We loved him in life, and we love him death'

'To have, to love, and then to part, is the greatest sorrow of one's heart'

'He did his best. Rest in peace'

'I have fought a good fight, kept the faith, finished the course'

'Pass not this stone in sorrow. May you live as nobly as he died. Mother'

Notes and References

Note: 'N.A.' stands for 'National Archives'

INTRODUCTION

1. 'The Long, Long Trail' website Forum – www.1914-1918.net
2. 'The Long, Long Trail' website Forum

CHAPTER ONE — WAR IS DECLARED

1. *Royal Cornwall Gazette*   Aug. 1914
2. *Royal Cornwall Gazette*   Sept. 1914
3. *Royal Cornwall Gazette*   Sept. 1914
4. *Royal Cornwall Gazette*   Oct. 1914
5. Located in Boscawen Street, Gill's was the largest department store of its day, and in early October, placed a prominent advert in the *West Briton* declaring: 'Britain's Motto – Business As Usual'. Christmas, 1914, at Spooners, in Plymouth, witnessed the construction of a 'War Spectacle', including a tableau which depicted British cavalrymen saving the guns in a recent skirmish on the Western Front. (Probably at Le Cateau on 26 August, when three VCs were awarded.) The scene was enhanced by the noise of explosions and the 'clever use' of electric light to give the public an impression of life in the firing line. The main attraction comprised models of the King and his senior Staff reviewing the troops at Windsor, where 'mechanical apparatus' ensured each regiment received a salute from the monarch.
6. *Royal Cornwall Gazette*   Sept. 1914

CHAPTER TWO — CORNISHMEN AT WAR

1. *Royal Cornwall Gazette* — Sept. 1914
2. *Bond of Sacrifice* (Vol. I, 1914) – reprinted by The Naval & Military Press
3. *Royal Cornwall Gazette* — Dec. 1914
4. War Diary (N.A.) — 1st Northants Regt. — WO95/1271
5. W/D (N.A.) — Royal Horse Guards (Blues) — WO95/1156
6. *Royal Cornwall Gazette* — Dec. 1914
7. *Royal Cornwall Gazette* — Nov. 1914
8. *Royal Cornwall Gazette* — Oct. 1914
9. Service Record (N.A.) — 2nd Lt the Hon. P.S. St Aubyn — WO339/19833
10.   " — " — "
11. *Royal Cornwall Gazette* — Sept. 1914
12. *Wycliffe & The War* (published by Wycliffe Coll., Glos., 1920s)
13. War Diary (N.A.) — Royal Horse Guards (Blues) — WO95/1156
14. *Royal Cornwall Gazette* — Dec. 1914
15. *Royal Cornwall Gazette* — Sept. 1914
16. *Royal Cornwall Gazette* — Dec. 1914

17. *Royal Cornwall Gazette*   Nov. 1914
18. W/D (N.A.)   1st Duke of Cornwall's Light Infantry WO95/1564

CHAPTER THREE — THE WESTERN FRONT

1. Courtesy of the Devonshire and Dorset Regimental Museum
2. Personal diary of Sgt A.H. Cook, Somerset Light Infantry. Somerset Records Office DD/SLI/17/1/39
3. Gloucester *Citizen* newspaper   July 1916
4. Courtesy of Truro College Archives
5. Courtesy of Truro College Archives
6. Sgt Cook's personal diary (S.R.O.) – DD/SLI/17/1/39
7. Courtesy of Truro College Archives
8. War Diary (N.A.)   1/2nd Monmouthshire Regt.   WO95/2295

CHAPTER FOUR — THE FINAL TEN DAYS

1. Service Record (N.A.)   Lt J.A.R. Reeves   WO374/56761
2. *Gloucester Citizen*   July 1916
3. War Diary (N.A.)   96th Bde., R.F.A.   WO95/2143
4.   "   "   "
5. W/D (N.A.)   6th Siege Battery, R.G.A.   WO95/472
6. Courtesy of Truro College Archives
7. W/D (N.A.)   63rd Coy, Machine Gun Corps WO95/2158
8. Sgt Cook's personal diary (S.R.O.) – DD/SLI/17/1/39
9. W/D (N.A.)   1/2nd Monmouthshire Regt.   WO95/2295
10. W/D (N.A.)   6th Northants Regt.   WO95/2044
11. W/D (N.A.)   7th Queen's Regt.   WO95/2050
12.   "   "   "
13. W/D (N.A.)   1/2nd Monmouthshire Regt.   WO95/2295
14. Courtesy of Truro College Archives
15. W/D (N.A.)   1/2nd Monmouthshire Regt.   WO95/2295
16. W/D (N.A.)   6th Northants Regt.   WO95/2044
17. Military Medal citation (*London Gazette*) for Sister Dorothy Penrose Foster, R.R.C., T.F.N.S. – 4/6/1918
18. W/D (N.A.)   6th Northants Regt.   WO95/2044
19. W/D (N.A.)   9th Devonshire Regt.   WO95/1656
20.   "   "   "
21.   "   "   "
22. W/D (N.A.)   1/4th London Regt.   WO95/2954
23.   "   "   "
24.   "   "   "
25. Sgt Cook's personal diary (S.R.O.) – DD/SLI/17/1/39

CHAPTER FIVE — NEWSPAPER REPORTS/PERSONAL THOUGHTS

1. *Gloucester Citizen*   July 1916
2.   "   "
3. Sgt Cook's personal diary (S.R.O.) DD/SLI/17/1/39

CHAPTER SIX — 30TH AND 18TH DIVISIONS

1. Courtesy of Truro College Archives
2. War Diary (N.A.)   2nd Royal Scots Fusiliers   WO95/2340

3. *Gloucester Citizen*	July 1916	
4. "	"	
5. W/D (N.A.)	6th Northants Regt.	WO95/2044
6. W/D (N.A.)	6th Northants Regt.	WO95/2044
7. *Gloucester Citizen*	July 1916	

CHAPTER SEVEN — 7TH DIVISION

1. Service Record (N.A.)	2nd Lt C.T. Gill	WO339/45911
2. *De Ruvigny's Roll of Honour* (reprinted by The Naval & Military Press)		
3. "	"	"
4. S/R (N.A.)	2nd Lt C.T. Gill	WO339/45911
5. *Gloucester Citizen*	July 1916	
6. *Royal Cornwall Gazette*	July 1916	
7. S/R (N.A.)	Capt. D.L. Martin	WO339/13105
8. "	"	"
9. "	"	"
10. Courtesy of the Devonshire and Dorset Regimental Museum		
11. "	"	"
12. *Cornish Times*, July 1916		
13. S/R (N.A.) Capt. G.P. Tregelles – WO339/11523		
14. "	"	" "
15. Courtesy of the Devonshire and Dorset Regimental Museum		
16. S/R (N.A.)	2nd Lt T.F. Adamson	WO339/4694
17. "	"	"
18. "	"	"
19. Courtesy of the Devonshire and Dorset Regimental Museum		
20. *Gloucester Citizen*	July 1916	
21. *The Devonshire Regiment 1914-1918* – reprinted by The Naval & Military Press		
22. War Diary (N.A.)	6th Siege Battery, R.G.A	WO95/472
23. S/R (N.A.)	2nd Lt D.H.H. Logan	WO339/240
24. W/D (N.A.)	2nd Border Regt.	WO95/1655
25. "	"	"
26. "	"	"
27. Courtesy of the Wellington College Archives		
28. *Gloucester Citizen*	July 1916	
29. "	"	

CHAPTER EIGHT — 21ST DIVISION

1. War Diary (N.A.)	7th East Yorkshire Regt.	WO95/2002
2. "	"	"
3. W/D (N.A.)	10th West Yorkshire Regt.	WO95/2004
4. W/D (N.A.)	96th Brigade, R.F.A.	WO95/2143
5. Service Record (N.A.)	2nd Lt A.C. Colmer	WO339/43653
6. *Royal Cornwall Gazette*	July 1916	
7. S/R (N.A.)	2nd Lt A.C. Colmer	WO339/43653
8. W/D (N.A.)	8th Somerset Light Infantry	WO95/2158
9. "	"	"
10. W/D (N.A.)	64th Coy, Machine Gun Corps	WO95/2162
11. "	"	"
12. *Royal Cornwall Gazette*	July 1916	

CHAPTER NINE — 34TH AND 8TH DIVISIONS

1. Service Record (N.A.)	Major H. Stocks, DSO	WO339/15563
2. S/R (N.A.)	Pte E. Gibb	WO363/G260
3. *Cambridgeshire Chronicle*	July 1916	
4. "	"	"
5. "	"	"
6. S/R (N.A.)	2nd Lt G. Carver	WO339/31056
7. S/R (N.A.)	Capt. A. Preedy	WO339/28499
8. War Diary (N.A.)	2nd Devonshire Regt.	WO95/1712
9. *Gloucester Citizen*	July 1916	

CHAPTER TEN — 32ND AND 36TH DIVISIONS

1. War Diary (N.A.)	15th Lancashire Fusiliers	WO95/2397
2. "	"	"
3. "	"	"
4. Service Record (N.A.)	Lt E. Hampson	WO339/15217
5. W/D (N.A.)	15th Royal Irish Rifles	WO95/2503
6. S/R (N.A.)	Capt. D.H. O'Flaherty	WO339/14280
7. Gloucester *Citizen* newspaper	July 1916	

CHAPTER ELEVEN — 29TH AND 4TH DIVISIONS

1. War Diary (N.A.)	1/3rd Monmouthshire Regt.	WO95/2787
2. W/D (N.A.)	2nd Royal Fusiliers	WO95/2301
3. "	"	"
4. Service Record (N.A.)	Lt H.W. Barker	WO339/37747
5. S/R (N.A.)	C.S.M. G.H. Painter	WO363/P419
6. S/R (N.A.)	Pte W.J. Button	WO363/B2624
7. W/D (N.A.)	2nd Royal Fusiliers	WO95/2301
8. W/D (N.A.)	1/2nd Monmouthshire Regt.	WO95/2295
9. S/R (N.A.)	2nd Lt C.E.S. Watson	WO339/58458
10. Sgt Cook's personal diary (S.R.O.) – DD/SLI/17/1/39		
11. W/D (N.A.)	1st Somerset Light Infantry	WO95/1499
12. S/R (N.A.)	2nd Lt R.C. Roseveare	WO339/32845
13. W/D (N.A.)	1/6th Royal Warwickshire Regt.	WO95/2755

CHAPTER TWELVE — REST OF THE SOMME FRONT

1. Official History of the Accrington Pals		
2. *Gloucester Citizen*	July 1916	
3. War Diary (N.A.)	1/12th London Regt.	WO95/2954
4. W/D (N.A.)	1/12th London Regt.	WO95/2954
5. Service Record (N.A.)	Capt. S.G. Millar	WO339/18146
6. S/R (N.A.)	2nd Lt P.J.F. Dines	WO339/30256

CHAPTER THIRTEEN — CASUALTIES/WOUNDED

1. Courtesy of the Devonshire and Dorset Regimental Museum		
2. War Diary (N.A.)	2nd Devonshire Regt.	WO95/1712
3. Courtesy of Truro College Archives		

4. *Falmouth Packet*, July 1916
5. *Gloucester Citizen*   July 1916
6. W/D (N.A.)   2nd Border Regt.   WO95/1655
7. W/D (N.A.)   27th Field Ambulance   WO95/1758
8. Service Record (N.A.)   Capt. H.P. Whitworth   WO339/21991
9.   "   "   "
10. Courtesy of Truro College Archives
11. W/D (N.A.)   22nd Field Ambulance   WO95/647
12. *Wycliffe & The War*
13. S/R (N.A.)   2nd Lt E.F. Boultbee   WO339/4880
14.   "   "   "
15. S/R (N.A.)   Lt R. Trounce   WO339/43148
16. W/D (N.A.)   1st East Yorkshire Regt.   WO95/2161
17. S/R (N.A.)   Sgt T.W. Keskeys   WO364/1995

CHAPTER FOURTEEN — MILITARY LESSONS/REST OF THE WAR

1. War Diary (N.A.)   63rd Coy, Machine Gun Corps   WO95/2158
2. W/D (N.A.)   1/16th London Regt.   WO95/2963
3.   "   "   "
4. W/D (N.A.)   7th Queen's Regt.   WO95/2051
5. W/D (N.A.)   12th York & Lancaster Regt.   WO95/2365
6.   "   "   "
7. *Royal Cornwall Gazette*   July 1916
8.   "   "
9.   "   "
10. *History of the DCLI, 1914-18* (reprinted by The Naval & Military Press)
11. *Royal Cornwall Gazette*   August 1916
12.   "   "
13.   "   "
14.   "   "
15. *Wycliffe & The War*
16.   "
17.   "
18. *History of the DCLI, 1914-18* (reprinted by The Naval & Military Press)
19. *The Devonshire Regiment 1914-1918* (reprinted by The Naval & Military Press)

CHAPTER FIFTEEN — COMMEMORATION

1. Cornwall Studies Library, Redruth
2. Service Record (N.A.)   Lt E. Hampson   WO339/15217
3. S/R (N.A.)   2nd Lt C.T. Gill   WO339/45911
4. Inscription on a gravestone

CHAPTER SIXTEEN — CONCLUSION

1. Courtesy of Truro College Archives
2.   "
3.   "

Bibliography

The First Day On The Somme (Martin Middlebrook, Penguin Books)

The Imperial War Museum Book of The Somme (Malcolm Brown, Pan Books in association with the IWM)

The Somme Day By Day Account (Chris McCarthy, Brockhampton Press, London)

A Military Atlas of the First World War (Arthur Banks, Leo Cooper); *British Regiments 1914-18* (Brig. E.A. James, reprinted by The Naval & Military Press)

De Ruvigny's Roll of Honour (reprinted by The Naval & Military Press)

The History of The Duke of Cornwall's Light Infantry 1914 -1919 (reprinted by The Naval & Military Press)

The Devonshire Regiment 1914-1918 (reprinted by The Naval & Military Press)

Deeds That Thrill The Empire (reprinted by The Naval & Military Press)

Index

Names of Servicemen

Cornish Place Names